T0319873

INDUSTRIAL DEVELOPMENT IN
A FRONTIER ECONOMY

INDUSTRIAL DEVELOPMENT IN A FRONTIER ECONOMY

The Industrialization of Argentina, 1890–1930

YOVANNA PINEDA

STANFORD UNIVERSITY PRESS

Stanford, California

2009

Published with the assistance of Saint Michael's College

©2009 by Board of Trustees of the Leland Stanford Junior University. All rights reserved.

Parts of Chapter 5 were originally published in "Manufacturing Profits and Strategies in Argentine Industrial Development, 1904–1930," *Business History*, Taylor & Francis ©2007. Reprinted with permission. Parts of Chapter 4 were first published as "Sources of Finance and Reputation: Merchant Finance Groups in Argentine Industrialization, 1890–1930," by Yovanna Pineda, from the *Latin American Research Review*, 41:2, pp. 3–30. Copyright ©2006 by the University of Texas Press. All rights reserved.

No part of this book may be reproduced or transmitted in any form or by any means, electronic or mechanical, including photocopying and recording, or in any information storage or retrieval system without the prior written permission of Stanford University Press.

Printed in the United States of America on acid-free, archival-quality paper

Library of Congress Cataloging-in-Publication Data

Pineda, Yovanna.
  Industrial development in a frontier economy : the industrialization of Argentina, 1890–1930 / Yovanna Pineda.
     p. cm. — (Social science history)
  Includes bibliographical references and index.
  ISBN 978-0-8047-5983-0 (cloth : alk. paper)
  1. Industrialization—Argentina—History. 2. Industries—Argentina—History. 3. Argentina—Economic conditions—19th century. 4. Argentina—Economic conditions—20th century. I. Title. II. Series: Social science history.
HC175.P567 2009
338.098209'041—dc22

2008042354

Typeset at Stanford University Press in 10/14.5 Minion

For my parents, Alba & Marco

Para mi abuelita, María Mercedes Rivas Sarti (1916-2004)

CONTENTS

TABLES AND FIGURES

Tables

Figures

Generous grants from several institutions between 1996 and 2005 made it possible for me to research, write, and complete this book. I first wish to express my gratitude to the granting agencies that supported my early years of research in Argentina. In 1996, the UCLA International Studies and Overseas Program granted me my first grant to do preliminary research in Argentina. I am deeply grateful to the generous support, from 1998 to 2000, of the Fulbright Institute of International Education, National Science Foundation, National Security Education Program, UCLA Department of History, and UCLA Latin American Center for supporting stages of my research in Argentina. From 2002 to 2004, this project was supported from different agencies. I would like to thank the Committee on Research in Economic History for Arthur H. Cole Grants-in-Aid; Library Scholars Summer Grant for Research at the Latin American Library Collections at Harvard University, awarded by the David Rockefeller Center for Latin American Studies; Travel Grant for Buenos Aires, Argentina, from the U.S. Department of Education Title VI Grant; and finally Saint Michael's College for supporting certain stages of research in Argentina and the United States.

I am also indebted to the many archivists and librarians who kindly facilitated my research at the Biblioteca Tornquist, Biblioteca Nacional, Archivo General de la Nación in Buenos Aires; the Widener, Lamont, and Langdell Law Libraries at Harvard University; and the Science, Industry, and Business Library in New York City. I am particularly grateful to librarians Patricia León and Fabiana Salerno from the Biblioteca Tornquist for their professionalism, courtesy, and patience during my time in their library.

Many mentors, colleagues, and friends have helped shape and enhance this project over the years. My early understanding of industrialization and merchant financing is owed to Stephen Haber, Kenneth Sokoloff, Naomi Lamoreaux, and especially Bill Summerhill. Reading their works and listening to their lectures shaped my interest in late-industrializing countries. At the University of California Los Angeles, I am particularly indebted to

Bill Summerhill and Naomi Lamoreaux, who read and reread many early versions of this work and encouraged improvement of it for publication. I would also like to thank José Antonio Sánchez Román, Kristen McCleary, Moramay López Alonso, Ted Beatty, and my anonymous reader for reading sections, or the entire book, to provide thoughtful and essential comments needed to improve this book. At Saint Michael's College, I would like to thank my history colleagues who strongly encouraged and motivated me at each writing stage. Finally, I would like to thank Tom Finnegan for his detailed copyediting; my undergraduate assistant, Christal Marsh, who in the summer of 2003 helped photocopy and diligently input data for Chapter 3; and Gerald Feldman for kindly sharing the exchange rates of four foreign currencies from 1890 to 1930. It made converting foreign currencies to the British pound go much more smoothly.

I would like to thank the publishers of *Latin American Research Review* and *Business History* for extending permission to use parts of my earlier work. Parts of Chapter 4 were previously published in "Sources of Finance and Reputation: Merchant Finance Groups in Argentine Industrialization, 1890–1930," *Latin American Research Review*, June 2006, 41:2, 3–30. Parts of Chapter 5 appear in "Manufacturing Profits and Strategies in Argentine Industrial Development, 1904–1930," *Business History*, March 2007, 49:2, 186–210.

I am very thankful to Jon for challenging and always supporting me through the long book-writing process. His support helped me finish the book.

I owe my deepest gratitude to my parents who first introduced me to their factory jobs in downtown Los Angeles. At the age of three, my recollection of the textile factory was that it was a fun place to be; machines roared, the scent of freshly sewn cloth filled the air, and without daycare, all the workers' children gathered and played on the shop's shiny, slippery floor.

Journals

BOB	*Boletín oficial de la bolsa de comercio de Buenos Aires*
BORA	*Boletín oficial de la República Argentina*
BUIA	*Boletín de la Unión Industrial Argentina*
MSA	*Monitor de sociedades anónimas*
REA	*Revista de economía argentina*
RRP	*Review of River Plate*

Organizations and Company

ADOL	Argentine Department of Labor
CGF	Compañía General de Fósforos
UIA	Unión Industrial Argentina

Chapter 1

Argentine Industrialization: An Introduction

Industrialization began at a modest pace in nineteenth-century Argentina and accelerated after 1914, when the government intervened in the process. Before 1914, entrepreneurs—foreign and domestic—and newly arrived immigrants began investing in Argentina's manufacturing sector for different reasons: to diversify investments, substitute imports, or make a living. In the early years of industrialization, manufacturers came from all social classes and invested whatever capital they could afford into a manufacturing venture. By 1914, domestic industry was relatively small by international standards but was growing; it could be characterized by development of a few large-scale modern factories alongside many small-scale, family-owned shops. After the First World War, industrialization attracted political supporters partly because of the new postwar international economic conditions. Politicians, military officers, and intellectuals debated industrial policies to protect local manufacturers and create new incentives to invest in manufacturing. These discussions regarding the support of industry were not a novel phenomenon in Argentina. Policymakers, supporters of industry, and manufacturers had previously examined Europe for the historical blueprint of how to modernize a new nation, and industrialization was common among developed nations. Also, Argentina had its own history of heated industrial debate; in the 1870s National Deputy Carlos Pellegrini called industry the most fundamental base of a country's prosperity.[1] After 1914, bringing together the supporters of industry was their belief that the country was wholly capable of importing and adopting machinery, factory designs, and manufacturing methods from European nations to develop a successful industrial sector. Some supporters believed that industrial development started with imports from across the Atlantic: "to advance toward manufacturing . . . in three weeks we could see the arrival of skilled European labor, technical knowledge, capital, and obtain good prices [for supplies]."[2] As with most Latin American nations in this period, Argentine policymakers and the economic elite had an interest in progress. By 1930, industry had an impact on nearly all social groups and on the economy.

Between 1870 and 1912, European observers of Argentina's progress wrote that the country was becoming a first-rate developed nation. After national reunification in 1861, economic growth accelerated. Political stability and unity was achieved with ratification by Buenos Aires province of the 1853 Constitution of the Argentine Confederation. Before the turn of the twentieth century, Argentina quickly adopted European models of constitutional rights, developed urban centers, and imposed compulsory public education for all children (foreign and native-born). The goals of this new nation were to build political and economic institutions; develop the nation's infrastructure and communication, transport, and currency systems; and expand international commerce.[3] Argentina's relative political stability and nation-building processes succeeded in attracting foreign investors. By 1914, foreign investment represented about half of Argentina's total capital stock, and its value was two and a half times that of gross domestic product (GDP).[4] In 1917, foreign capital invested summed up to 4 billion gold pesos, half from British sources.[5] Much of this foreign capital flowed toward construction of infrastructure such as utilities, a subway system in Buenos Aires, ports, and railroads.

Much of Argentina's fast growth and development happened within a relatively short period of five decades, prompting entrepreneur Carlos Tornquist to write that Argentina's progress and "development in the last fifty years demonstrates that its soil, its race, its ideals, its social, political and economic organization will make it, within a few years, one of the most powerful nations of the Earth."[6] Indeed he would not have known any other way to describe his rapidly growing country. Between 1862 and 1912, Argentina was transformed from an underpopulated region of grasslands to a rich and densely populated urban nation. Argentina's vast grasslands, the pampas, became a bread basket for Europe. The export of agricultural goods, meat, and leather laid the foundation for economic growth. By 1900, Argentina was one of the top world exporters of grain, beef, wool, and leather,[7] and a leading economic power in South America. By 1921, its financial institutions held 73 percent of South America's gold. By 1926, the nation accounted for 50 percent of South America's foreign trade and 43 percent of its railroad track.[8] GDP per capita grew at an average annual rate of 3.9 percent between 1875 and 1912.[9] The growth of GDP per capita is particularly impressive given that the Argentine population was expanding rapidly; between 1869 and 1914, the average rate was 3.4 percent per year.[10]

Argentina's wealth attracted large-scale European immigration that rapidly fueled population and urban growth. A little over half of these immigrants settled permanently in Argentina (between 1857 and 1930, 53 percent remained[11]), helping the population grow from 1.8 million in the first census (1869) to more than 11 million by 1930.[12] Between 1880 and 1930, most of these immigrants arrived from Italy and Spain, were relatively young, and settled in the federal capital and cities of the littoral provinces. The immigrant population helped make Argentina by far one of the most urbanized Latin American countries. Buenos Aires became "the second largest city on the Atlantic seaboard (after New York City) and the largest south of the equator."[13] Between 1910 and 1914, the population living in major cities (defined here as having fifty thousand or more inhabitants) was 31.2 percent.[14] In comparison, 7.6 percent of the population in Mexico and 10.7 percent in Brazil lived in cities of fifty thousand inhabitants or more.[15] Before 1936, the municipality of greater Buenos Aires was consistently home to at least 20 percent of the national population.[16] Young urban immigrants accounted for the rising number of active wage earners and consumers of manufactured goods in the cities.[17] Argentina also had a relatively high fraction (39 percent) of children and elderly in the population, which increased the dependency rate and raised the country's "propensity to consume."[18] These new urban immigrants and the relatively high dependency rate helped push demand for manufactured goods.

Demand for consumer goods was met through imports and expansion of domestic production. Between 1890 and 1935, Argentina's trade data show a consistent rise in imports of basic consumer goods.[19] Domestic production also grew, and by 1913 the manufacturing sector had become a vital component of the domestic economy. That year, value-added manufacturing accounted for 16.6 percent of real GDP.[20] Overall, industrial production grew at an average of 7.5 percent annually between 1900 and 1914 and 4.2 percent annually between 1914 and 1934.[21]

Also, industrial census data record the growth of domestic industry. The number of industrial enterprises increased from 22,204 in 1895 to 48,799 by 1914. Census takers estimated that the number of enterprises in similar industrial activities[22] inched upward from 39,189 in 1914 to 40,613 by 1935. The capital stock of these enterprises rose substantially from $150 million real paper pesos in 1895 to more than $3 billion real paper pesos by 1935.[23] Value-added also increased;[24] it grew from $435 million real paper pesos in 1914 to more than $1 billion real paper pesos by 1935.[25] Much of this growth in the number and output of industries resulted from increased investment in new production methods in factories.

Despite the market potential and industrial growth over time, Argentina's manufacturing sector could not satisfy domestic demand. Also, domestic factories relied on imports of machinery, fuel, and raw materials. By 1930, Argentine manufacturing was much larger and more productive than it had been in the late nineteenth century, but it remained relatively underdeveloped, concentrated, and far from being able to sustain overall economic growth. A few dominant firms in each sector surrounded by thousands of small-scale, labor-intensive shops that produced nondurable consumer goods for internal markets characterized Argentine manufacturing. Agro-industries, largely food processing of flour, beef, dairy, and lamb, pushed the rate of industrial growth, but consumer goods such as soap, cotton textiles, and metallurgy remained underdeveloped. Bulmer-Thomas referred to Argentine industrialization as "a great disappointment" if one considered its immense wealth before 1914.[26] Compared with European countries having smaller populations and lower real income per capita yet with more developed consumer-goods sectors, Argentina's industrial development was particularly unimpressive.[27]

Early-twentieth-century Argentina seemingly had all the prerequisites to industrialize: a highly productive agricultural sector, the densest railroad network in Latin America, an integrated and growing urban consumer market, expanding capital markets, and legal institutions created to protect property rights and encourage investment. Yet it failed, like other Latin American nations, to enter the phase of "self-sustaining industrialization that took hold in England or the United States."[28] By 1930, substantial investment and government support of domestic industry helped it maintain a position as the second most important economic sector behind the agrarian. Interestingly, the agrarian sector received limited government support but was still productive.[29] Before 1930, both agrarian and industrial sectors encountered several obstacles, but industry relied on government support. Industry was also troubled by occasional input shortages of raw materials and fuel, and it suffered from capital shortages.

There is no one determinant that limited successful industrialization in any Latin American nation, including Argentina.[30] Instead a combination of factors and an absence of certain essential features "would certainly work against successful industrialization."[31] In Mexico, for instance, obstacles to economic and industrial growth included an inadequate transport system, inefficient economic organization, and the absence of a national market.[32]

Similarly, between 1890 and 1930 Argentina saw external and internal factors hinder successful industrial development. External factors were the nation's volatile economic cycles, banks' restrictive lending practices, and inefficient industrial legislation. First, Argentina's economic volatility resulted from being closely tied to international markets; in particular, its economy was linked to fluctuations in the Atlantic economies.[33] These cycles influenced investment in manufacturing not because industrialists were using money gained from agriculture to invest in manufacturing per se but rather because agro-export cycles were an indicator of economic health. Typically, whenever sales from agricultural exports went up, investment in manufacturing machinery also increased.

A second external factor influencing industrialization was the banking system. By 1910 Argentina's banking system was well developed, but banks had stringent credit practices, seldom offering long-term credit arrangements and limiting the amount that a company could borrow. The most common type of long-term loan was a mortgage, but factories also needed capital to invest in machinery, raw material inputs, and perhaps labor training. If companies wanted additional capital, they sometimes made ad hoc arrangements with banks or tried to find buyers to sell company bonds and shares. But not all companies had the ability to make such arrangements, leading most manufacturing companies to depend on self-financing or be capital-starved.

Finally, a third external factor inhibiting industrial development was inefficient industrial legislation. Although the intent behind tariff policy pointed toward some interest in developing manufacturing, the tariff rate failed to accelerate industrial development because political rather than economic interests drove the debate. Economic and political groups used the fight over tariff rates to negotiate favors and build alliances. Several bills for industry came up for debate in Congress, but policymakers largely focused on arguing over adjustment of the tariff rate. Beginning in 1881, the Argentine government raised tariff rates, and between 1881 and 1932 the Congress often modified the tariff schedule and rates. Until 1923, the rate was a 25 percent duty (ad valorem) on imports of most consumer goods.[34] Law 11281 of 1923 raised tariff levels for all finished consumer goods, varying between 35 and 50 percent. (Some products had specific duties permitting them to have a higher rate.[35])

In addition to these external factors, manufacturers were burdened with problems internal to the firms. Four such problems were low labor productivity; high costs because of reliance on imported inputs of machinery, raw materials, and fuel; problems with adaptation of new technology; and the inability to realize economies of scale. First, labor productivity was low for different reasons in the early and later periods of industrialization. In the early period (1880–1912), low labor productivity was partly due to an unskilled immigrant workforce. Human capital of the immigrant labor force rose over time, however, helping to increase labor productivity in some sectors. After 1912, low labor productivity was partly because several manufacturing activities remained largely labor-intensive activities. In these sectors, labor productivity failed to increase quickly in comparison to activities that adopted capital-intensive methods.

The next three obstacles internal to firms are intimately interconnected. In Argentina, dependence on imported machinery, raw materials, and fuel meant that start-up costs were high. Also, Argentine manufacturers needed to purchase the correct raw materials and fuel to operate the machines, and in some cases try to emulate factory conditions from the country of origin, such as keeping the environment cool so the machines did not overheat. But these conditions were difficult to accomplish. If there were input shortages or breakdowns, machines remained idle, making it impossible to realize economies of scale or take machinery to full capacity. Even if taken to full capacity, some manufacturers found that their machinery produced beyond domestic demand and then shut it off to control inventory. Ultimately, the internal problems raised the costs of production.

Manufacturers were aware of the obstacles to industrialization. In response to these problems, leading manufacturers sought to insulate their firms from exogenous shocks and endogenous dilemmas by focusing on strategies to reduce risk. They focused on short-term and inward-oriented strategies to best control their unpredictable and volatile environment. These strategies were intended to deal with unpredictable situations, but they also helped maintain a concentrated and underdeveloped manufacturing sector. Leading manufacturers had substantial influence in business and industry. They typically had their origin in trading and merchant activities, using existing information and social networks to ease into manufacturing, and in some cases to identify the most profitable manufactured goods to produce for domestic markets. Most successful manufacturers created networks to raise capital, find partners, and obtain information needed to efficiently operate their business. But these entrepreneurs also set up networks to control their environment and increase market share at the expense of other manufacturers. Leading Argentine entrepreneurs set the pace of business, selected which industries to promote, and lobbied for favorable industrial legislation.[36] These entrepreneurs were a risk-averse lot and were aware of their inability to control external factors. In large part, they made decisions in the hope of controlling resources and gaining bargaining power with the government.

In essence, this book is about the extent and weaknesses of early industry in Argentina from 1890 to 1930. It closely examines how a wealthy nation with sufficient resources failed to develop its manufacturing sector. Comparatively, Argentina was developing its industrial sector at the same time as other late-industrializing countries (Meiji Japan, Brazil, and Mexico) that also faced obstacles like those found in Argentina, such as the shortage of inputs and the high cost of entry. But in Argentina, industry was especially poorly developed, even failing to fill national demand despite the capacity to do so in some cases. (Typically, other late-industrializing nations could at a minimum fill internal demand.) In examining why industry was so poorly developed, this book asks, Did the government interfere too much in the industrial process? Did it enact the wrong policies? Were economic elites simply rent-seekers looking to increase company profits through higher tariffs? How did these elites influence industrial outcome?

In seeking answers, this work specifically analyzes how obstacles affected industrial productivity, investment, entrepreneurship, profits, and policies. Several scholars have analyzed Argentina's "incomplete industrialization,"[37] and each has contributed to expansion of our knowledge. *Industrial Development* digs deeper and explores Argentine industry through detailed yet wide-ranging analyses of fifty-nine manufacturing companies across ten consumer goods sectors from 1890 to 1930 (Table 1.1). It uses national, sector, and company-level sources to estimate profits, concentration levels, and investment. It also examines business strategies and entrepreneurial behavior. It creates four databases to analyze, gauge, and follow productivity, profits, investment, and networking over time to explain Argentina's poor industrial development before 1930. The failure of Argentina to successfully develop a self-sustaining industrial sector with forward and backward linkages cannot be attributed to a wrong course of action or even to a set of actions by the government or manufacturers. Instead this book discusses both what happened and what failed to happen during the course of industrialization.

Evolution of Argentine Industrial Development

Argentina's incomplete industrialization between 1890 and 1930 has long intrigued scholars of Latin American economic history. This interest is fueled by the assumption that Argentina's agricultural wealth, large-scale European immigration, strong ties to international markets, and growing capital

Table 1.1. Names of Fifty-Nine Companies and
Their Industrial Activities, 1890–1930

Company name	Industrial activity	Year of Incorporation	Year of bankruptcy, if applicable	Merger, if applicable
Cervecería Argentina Quilmes	Brewery	1889	–	–
Cervecería Argentina San Carlos	Brewery	1908	–	–
Cervecería Buenos Aires	Brewery	1898	–	–
Cervecería del Norte	Brewery	1913	–	–
Cervecería Palermo	Brewery	1897	–	–
Cervecería Rio Segundo	Brewery	1893	–	–
Cervecería Schlau	Brewery	1908	–	–
Bolsalona, Comercial e Industrial	Burlap sacks	1921	–	–
Del Sel, R. y N.	Burlap sacks	1921	–	–
Primitiva, Fábrica de Bolsas de Arpillera	Burlap sacks	1889	1936	–
Salinas Hermanos, Fábrica de Bolsas	Burlap sacks	1890	1931	–
Fábrica Argentina de Alpargatas	Canvas shoes	1885	–	–
Argentina de Cemento Pórtland	Cement	1915	–	–
Cemento Argentina	Cement	1909	1911	–
Compañía General de Envases	Glass	1903	–	–
Cristalerías Papini	Glass	1913	–	–
Cristalerías Rigolleau	Glass	1882	–	–
Compañía General de Fósforos Súdamericana	Matches	1888	–	–
Fosforera Argentina	Matches	1907	–	–
Unión, SA Cooperativa de Fósforos	Matches	1908	1910	–
Acero-Platense, Empresa Siderúrgica	Metallurgy	1905	1911	–
Anglo-Argentine Iron Company	Metallurgy	1909	1924	1924
Cantábrica, Talleres Metalúrgicos	Metallurgy	1902	–	–
El Eje, Fundición	Metallurgy	1903	–	–
Elaboración General del Plomo	Metallurgy	1904	–	–
Ferrum, Industria Argentina de Metales	Metallurgy	1911	–	–
Lametal, La Metalúrgica Argentina/Thyssen	Metallurgy	1922	–	1927
Talleres Metalúrgicos San Martín (TAMET)	Metallurgy	1908	–	1924
Unión Herradores	Metallurgy	1904	1910	–
Unión, Fundición y Talleres	Metallurgy	1907	–	–
Americana, Fábrica de Papel	Paper	1906	1908	–
Argentina, Fábrica de Papel (Zarate)	Paper	1888	–	1924
Buenos Aires, Fábrica de Papel y Cartones	Paper	1906	1908	1908
Fábrica de Papel (Casati) de San Nicolás	Paper	1910	1924	1926
Fenix, Fábrica de Papel	Paper	1913	1924	1924
Papelera Argentina	Paper	1925	–	1925
Compañía de Productos Conen	Soap	1903	–	–
Argentina de Tejidos	Textiles	1920	1924	–
Argentina de Tejidos de Punto	Textiles	1926	–	–
Baibiene y Antonini, Fabricacion de Tejidos	Textiles	1922	–	–
Campomar y Soulas	Textiles	1922	–	–
Compañía Nacional de Tejidos y Sombreros	Textiles	1900	1912	–

Company name	Industrial activity	Year of Incorporation	Year of bankruptcy, if applicable	Merger, if applicable
Compañía Textil Sud Americana	Textiles	1910	1921	—
Cotonoficio Dell'Acqua	Textiles	1917	1922	—
Dasso-Crotto, Hilandera Argentina de Sisal	Textiles	1922	—	—
Hilandera Argentina	Textiles	1918	—	1924
Hilanderías Argentinas de Algodón	Textiles	1905	1913	—
Manufactura Algodonera Argentina	Textiles	1925	—	—
Masllorens Hermanos	Textiles	1923	—	—
Sedalana, Fábrica de Tejidos y de Punto	Textiles	1925	—	—
Textil Argentina	Textiles	1918	1928	—
Argentine Tobacco Company	Tobacco	1912	1918	—
Ariza, J. M.	Tobacco	1915	1917	—
Compañía General de Tabacos	Tobacco	1906	1911	—
Defensa, Donato Didiego	Tobacco	1913	—	—
Introductora de Buenos Aires	Tobacco	1901	—	—
Nacional de Tabacos	Tobacco	1913	—	—
Piccardo Tabacos	Tobacco	1914	—	—
Tabacalera Argentina	Tobacco	1914	—	—

Source: Data from *Boletín oficial de la República Argentina, Boletín oficial de la Bolsa de Comercio de Buenos Aires,* and *Monitor de Sociedades Anónimas.*

institutions should have ensured a formidable industrial base. Despite these favorable attributes, however, the outcome of a strong and sustainable manufacturing sector was clearly not the case, and this paradox generates much discussion among scholars.

Examination of Argentina's manufacturing sector in the twentieth century has largely fallen into four schools of thought: (1) dependency studies, (2) entrepreneurship studies, (3) criticism of Argentina's landholding class for holding back industrial development, and (4) "old" and "new" economic histories. These works brought forth important questions and hypotheses on Argentine industry; they remain important as an initial step toward understanding the dynamic issues behind Argentina's early industrial phase, 1881–1930. I will briefly comment on these schools.

First, dependency theorists of the 1950s and 1960s argued that Argentine industry failed because the government did not actively promote industry before 1930. Dependency scholars endorsed state support of industry through import substitution industrialization (ISI) policies. ISI featured a strong state role in promoting industrial growth and closing the economy to imports of manufactured goods. One of the leading *dependistas,* Andrés Frank, argued that Latin America's strongest period of industrial growth coincided with "weakened links" between the international economy and the Latin American region during the First World War.[38] He recommended that Latin America sever its ties to international capitalism and that governments promote inward-oriented policies to develop industry. By the midtwentieth century, Argentina became one of the top Latin American countries to strongly support ISI policies.

Dependency theory influenced many thinkers and policymakers in Argentina. Several scholars used the tenets of dependency theory to explain Argentina's industrial underdevelopment. Two dependency thinkers in particular, Aldo Ferrer and Ricardo Ortíz, argued that an ISI program should have been implemented as early as 1914 for early industrial development.[39] They asserted that a strong industrial sector could have lowered Argentina's reliance on imported manufactured goods, eliminated trade deficits, and pushed overall economic growth. Dependency scholars drew from the theoretical work of the structuralist group associated with the United Nations Economic Commission for Latin America (ECLA). The structuralists, led by Raúl Prebisch, advocated state-sponsored industrialization.[40] They emphasized that development required creating the conditions necessary for economic efficiency and growth.[41] They mainly used macro data to support generalized assertions for most Latin American countries. These data did not permit analysis of specific conditions in each country during a particular period; in most cases, the data collected supported only a limited number of conclusions. Colin Lewis argued that the basis of the ECLA argument was an assumption that strong economies in Latin America would result from "benevolent state action to liberate [economies] from the constraint of unfair foreign competition in order to foster endogenous development driven by rapid industrialization headed by national capital."[42]

Two additional reasons dependency theory cannot explain industrial underdevelopment are its macro solution style and failure to take into account long-term data. First, the dependistas purported to offer a macro solution for economic development in all developing nations. They advocated similar theories to solve problems of poverty and underdevelopment across such broadly diverse regions as East Asia, the Middle East, South Asia, and Latin America. But their universal prescription of state-sponsored industrialization ignored unique national variables such as politics and culture. When this prescription failed, dependistas tended to blame the countries' entrepreneurs or governments rather than reexamining the utility of ISI and structuralism.

Second, long-term data indicate that strong ties to international markets actually helped industrial development in developing regions. By the 1970s, revisionist studies showed that industrial growth was greatest during periods of high trading activity between Latin America and international markets.[43] According to Carl Solberg, despite the assumption that Argentine manufacturing performed well during the import shortages and economic isolation caused by the First World War, "in fact, Argentina's industrial output fell during the early years of the war and did not recover to prewar levels until 1918."[44] Argentine scholars Ezequiel Gallo and Lucio Geller based their arguments on the staple theory of growth to show that Argentine industry benefited from international ties and development of its export sector.[45] Gallo asserted that exports of grain and livestock products set the pace for the economy before 1930.[46] He used basic economic indicators to show that a correlation existed between a rise in agro-exports and increased industrial activity between 1900 and 1930[47]; the correlation was particularly strong between 1918 and 1930.[48] His findings concluded that industry did well when international trading was strongest. He added that Argentina's final industrial boom was from 1925 to 1929, which coincided with the last climax in the export economy. These findings implied that the closing of markets in favor of ISI damaged the Argentine economy by limiting access to capital through international trade.

A second group of studies weaves in entrepreneurship patterns and behavior in its discussion of industrial underdevelopment in Latin America. The extant literature demonstrates a relatively diverse perspective on the role played by industrial entrepreneurs in Latin America and Argentina. Early works argued that local entrepreneurs were monopolists and rent seekers, contributing to the failure of state-sponsored industrialization. Marxists and dependistas, for instance, asserted that government-sponsored industry failed because local manufacturers squandered profits on conspicuous consumption rather than investing in innovative production methods.[49] Neoclassical writers emphasized that heavy government intervention stifled economic development and encouraged "self-interested persons to redistribute income toward themselves rather than working to raise efficiency and national income."[50] Authors across disciplines argued that ISI polices failed because they encouraged corruption, supported rent-seeking behavior, and weakened competition.[51] They faulted governments for sponsoring corrupt, inward-oriented policies that could not be sustained and led to weak industrial performance. For the most part, these studies pointed toward inept policymakers and self-interested entrepreneurs as the causes of underdevelopment.

These early entrepreneurship studies portrayed Latin American entrepreneurs as lacking an "entrepreneurial spirit," interested only in maximizing profit at the expense of others. Frits Wils contends that there was a tendency in the literature to compare the Latin American entrepreneur alongside descriptions posed by Joseph Schumpeter's innovative and creative entrepreneur or Alfred Chandler's teams of managers who efficiently coordinate and monitor numerous and diverse activities within a firm.[52] When compared, the Latin American entrepreneur fared rather poorly because his business strategies and business culture did not quite fit within a preconceived model of success.[53]

In recent historiography, business history scholars demonstrate that informal business groups or business families dominated in regions where property rights were not so well defined.[54] Argentine scholars argue that prior to 1980s the formation and culture of business groups in the country received scant attention in the literature.[55] In Latin America, managers adapted to the presence or absence of formal legal institutions and to uncertain economic conditions. In practice, business groups operated by developing wide networks of social contacts to obtain the information needed to be relatively efficient in business.

The final two schools of studies are specific to Argentina's industrial experience. The first school blames the landholding class for industrial underdevelopment. The standard historiography held that industry was underdeveloped because politically powerful and wealthy landowners masterfully inhibited implementation of industrial policies before 1914. Solberg stated that "nineteenth century Argentine governments, dominated by the rural elite, had kept tariffs low and had designed them to produce revenue rather than stimulate industrialization."[56] Adolfo Dorfman also claimed that industry was relegated to secondary importance because of the overwhelming political influence of agricultural interests.[57] The "landowner versus industrialist" theory was a long-standing feature of the historiography premised on a belief in the "feudal and regressive nature of large landowners."[58] Although this theory was largely accepted, it was often not based on empirical evidence. Roy Hora explains that landowners were blamed for industrial underdevelopment because they were the most influential group before 1930 and believed to be wholly self-interested; the "Argentine economy as a whole, and its economic elite in particular, depended (and benefited) from land and agrarian production to a degree unknown in other Latin American countries."[59] In his study of twenty-six wealthy and large-scale rural entrepreneurs, he found that although they favored agrarian investment there was no evidence of their using political and economic influence to deter industrialization.[60] Unlike other economic sectors, he posits, the agrarian sector was not looking for special favors from the government. This sector was largely concerned that the government act as the neutral enforcer of property rights and public order.[61]

Hora's central conclusion is that there is no clear evidence landowners organized against industrial interests.[62] Juan Korol and Hilda Sábato support these conclusions. They believe the scholars of Argentine industry "could not seem to find the answer to their concerns. These concerns were satisfied, in contrast, by preconceived notions" of that time about the relationship between agrarian and industrial interests.[63] Also, primary source evidence shows that after 1900 the government implemented policies promoting industry at the expense of other economic sectors. Hora explains how landowners initially expressed some concern about the government's promotion of industry but ultimately were not threatened by industry because the agro-export sector remained lucrative and dominant.[64] The industrial sector also failed to surpass the economic importance of the agro-export sector. For the most part, landowners focused on their agrarian ventures and left the government to support industry.

Finally, the last group of studies examining industrial underdevelopment in Argentina is a myriad of economic histories that can be divided between old and new. The early economic histories expanded our knowledge of the country's industrial history but were largely "centered on the historian's narrative tools of description."[65] Several of these studies concluded that Argentine industry was underdeveloped because of the lack of government involvement and the landowners' ability to block beneficial industrial legislation. Although these studies have been subject to revisionist critique, the narratives bring forth hypotheses and ask important questions about the underdevelopment of Argentine industry. They were limited in some cases because authors lacked quantitative evidence or the econometric skills to test or confirm hypotheses and reveal fuller understanding of Argentina's industrial dilemma.

Recent historiography on Argentine industry and economic development uses an array of statistical evidence and applies econometric approaches to examine economic development between 1870 and 1930. These studies rely on empirical evidence and use both macro- and micro-level data to examine specific characteristics of Argentina's businesses, investment groups, banks, labor, legal institutions, and credit markets to explain industrial underdevelopment.[66] These works have enhanced discussion of how Argentina could have gone from one of the ten richest nations to a relatively poor one within a few decades. These studies present new theories and evidence as to why the Argentine economy slowed down and why industry remained underdeveloped despite having the prerequisites of financial systems, growing internal markets, transport infrastructure, and government support. For instance, although goods produced by local industry were intended to replace import of consumer goods, María Barbero and Fernando Rocchi argue that the "substitution effects were limited."[67] The number of goods produced domestically increased, but so did imports of consumer goods, indicating that markets grew and local producers failed to meet domestic demand.[68]

As part of this new history, this book aims to revise some of the standard conventions about Argentina's manufacturers, industrial legislation, and obstacles to industry. It examines manufacturing productivity, investment, company profits, entrepreneurs' strategies, and industrial policies to assess the performance of Argentine industry. Macro- and company-level sources came from fifty-nine companies across ten manufacturing sectors[69]; most were leading domestic joint-stock companies in their respective activities.[70] All joint-stock companies under study were legally required to disclose detailed financial information, such as balance sheet and income statements and earnings and losses statements. The government also required joint-stock companies to release monthly and annual reports discussing operations and performance. These reports were rather detailed and discussed a range of issues, including but not limited to owners' death, labor strikes, profits, reserves, dissolution, bankruptcy, mergers, and the selling of debt or shares. This disclosure presents a wealth of data heretofore underexamined.[71]

Organization of the Book

Through use of these company-level sources, this work answers several foundational questions about the nature of industry to examine why it remained relatively underdeveloped between 1890 and 1930. Chapter 2 discusses the origins and productivity level of Argentina's modern manufacturing sector and asks: How productive and efficient were these manufacturing companies? How productive was labor? How concentrated was Argentine industry in 1895? Which were the leading companies in 1895, and why? This second chapter examines the structure of industrial production between 1895 and 1935. It estimates labor and total factor productivity and industrial concentration, first approximating labor productivity for twelve manufacturing activities using sector-level data from Argentina's published industrial censuses of 1895, 1914, and 1935. It then estimates concentration level, total factor productivity, and economies of scale for twelve manufacturing sectors using company-level data from the manuscript census of 1895. The results from these estimations suggest that there were several inconsistencies with production.

Chapter 3 assesses the volume and timing of machine investment. It asks: How much was invested in manufacturing machinery? Which factors influenced the timing of this investment? How was this technology adapted in Argentina's factories? The scholarly literature on Argentine industry commonly emphasizes growth of imports of machinery.[72] Discussion of imported machinery, however, has usually been limited to congressional debate on importation of duty-free machinery and fuel. Few works examine the actual values spent on machinery between 1890 and 1930. The findings from this chapter satisfy a need for estimates of investment in imported manufacturing machinery. It then analyzes the factors influencing this investment, arguing that economic cycles and industrial policies affected volume and timing. Lastly, it examines entrepreneurship and technological competencies to answer how, despite this investment, Argentina's manufacturing sector remained relatively underdeveloped.

The next series of questions, analyzed in Chapters 4 through 6, examine key issues about Argentine industrialization. Chapter 4 examines the sources of finance for the Argentine entrepreneurs who owned the fifty-nine manufacturing corporations under study. Who were the owners? What were their management strategies? How did they obtain finance capital, and how was it spent? The source of entrepreneurship is central to any discussion of industrialization; this chapter analyzes why and how these industrial financiers invested in the manufacturing sector before 1930. It focuses on five leading business groups that owned the country's largest manufacturing firms between 1890 and 1930. Study of these business groups illustrates how a few of them rose to prominence in their manufacturing activities. The advantage these five groups had over other groups or individual entrepreneurs was their cultivation of personal and business relationships that would ultimately aid their ability to obtain finance capital. Their relationships enabled them to attract outside capital from domestic and foreign investors. This capital was needed to sustain large-scale manufacturing. This chapter uses an original compilation of biographical information on 1,282 directors and shareholders who owned the fifty-nine companies under study between 1890 and 1930.

Chapter 5 asks: How profitable were manufacturers' companies? How were returns distributed? What were groups' management strategies? How did these strategies affect overall industrial performance? This chapter examines profits and discusses how Argentine groups' aversion to risk dominated in the strategies they created to protect their companies. Managers sought to overcome obstacles to industry by concentrating their sector. Qualitative data from domestic company reports and the representative industrial lobby, Unión Industrial Argentina (UIA), demonstrate that owner-managers perceived an unusually hostile economic and legal environment. They closely scrutinized the fluctuating macroeconomic climate and on-going tariff debate in Congress. Owners had significant power in internal decision making, but they felt vulnerable when changes outside their control affected the company's productivity or significantly raised its manufacturing costs.

They often blamed external factors for lower-than-expected company performance. In part, it was the strategies of leading groups to consolidate their respective sectors that helped maintain a concentrated manufacturing sector in Argentina before 1930.[73]

Finally, Chapter 6 examines industrial legislation and the politics of industry between 1890 and 1930. It asks: To what extent did the government protect industry? What were the short- and long-term effects of politically motivated industrial policies? For the most part, the failure of industrial legislation to promote successful industrialization stemmed from the absence of a well-defined plan. It analyzes how and why tariff protection became closely associated as a necessity for the development of industry. By 1917, the national rhetoric was that Argentina had seemingly passed its first phase of growth, and industrialization was a natural progression toward the next phase of economic growth. For most of the twentieth century, tariff rate increases were the outcome of political compromises among political players: political parties, regional interests (interior provinces), the industrial lobby, and manufacturers. Each group had its own agenda but expected to benefit, at least partially, from a compromise on tariff levels. In the end, modifications to the tariff rate demonstrated the ability of political groups to compromise on the tariff issue.

The Promise of Industrialization

This book takes an interdisciplinary approach to examine the multiple factors of industrialization, among them profit, policy, productivity, investment, and company strategy. Though these are inanimate things indeed, the human experience, initiative, and behavior contribute to the existence and formation of these aspects. Economic elite and policymakers played key roles in developing the industry that they imagined and hoped for. In the turn of the century, Argentina did not share the gross inequalities in income and class that other Latin American countries as Mexico and Brazil were plagued by. Before 1914, the country had its troubles associated with its fast growth, quick urbanization, and entry of millions of immigrants. But despite the problems, economic elite viewed themselves as responsible caretakers; they sought to support laws sustaining long-term growth and enhancing their own legacy. Those in favor of industry viewed their interests as aiding the future of the nation.

Was the government supportive of industry? A study of industrial policy suggests the government encouraged development of industry. Although the economic elite influenced, they did not control the making of policy that only favored their interests. Policymaking for industry was largely based on conciliation among political players and emulation of progressive laws coming from developed nations. If the government passed laws increasing industrial tariffs for instance, it was doing so as part of an agenda to bolster the economy through diversification (industrialization), and was not encouraging rent-seekers or trying to weaken the agrarian sector.

Why did the government support industrialization when clearly the agrarian sector was the most productive? Industrialization had potential; its promise was not in what it had achieved as in the agrarian sector but in what it could accomplish. Industrialization is an infinite process—one can always buy another machine, develop a new marketing technique, and make a new investment—rather than a clear progression toward one point in time. Though the well-developed literature of industrialization in England and the United States might sometimes make us believe the contrary, there is no steadfast plan that a developing country can easily learn and emulate. Industry progresses at different rates and develops unique outcomes in each region.

From 1890 to 1930, the literature coming from industrial advocates (the UIA, intellectuals, policymakers) suggests that they were well aware of the inherent contradictions in pushing industrialization in a country that owed its wealth to the export of agricultural goods. Different factions supporting industry seldom exalted Argentina's industrial performance; instead they devoted time to explaining why industry was failing: insufficient protection (or protection arriving too late[74]), inadequate credit markets, "the present policy (or lack of it),"[75] raw material and fuel shortages[76], and poor labor training. Many authors (including me) analyze these issues to seek reliable answers to the puzzling fact of underdeveloped industrialization. Nevertheless, part of the solution lies in understanding why policymakers, investors, and businessmen backed industry despite its lower-than-expected performance. They encouraged it in part because it connected Argentina with Western European and North American countries, most of which were at some stage of industrialization. Developing industry helped Argentina stay globally connected; the country bought foreign machinery and vehicles, adopted the foreign metric system[77] for industrial use, borrowed from international funds, and attracted foreign multinational companies and foreign investment. Indeed, industrialization invited global interconnectedness and it offered humans the opportunity to believe in its potential. By 1930, Argentina had an industrial base, imperfect and capital-starved, but a foundation indeed for the long twentieth century.

Chapter 2

Manufacturing Productivity and Concentration, 1895–1935

Since independence in 1810, manufacturing enterprises had been growing in number, but they were largely labor-intensive shops that produced for small and local markets. These shops' contribution to overall economic growth was considered small, as reflected in the first national census of 1869 failing to report statistics in industry. Such neglect of industry was not lost on policymakers; in the mid-1870s, they began debating the appropriate tariff rate to foment domestic industry. By 1889, the industrial census of the city of Buenos Aires prominently featured new industries using modern imported machinery.[1] It was expected that Argentine manufacturing would eventually absorb domestic demand and substitute imports of consumer goods. Indeed between 1890 and 1930, Argentina's industrial output and productivity expanded rapidly.[2]

But this fast industrial growth is also marred by numerous obstacles.[3] Few studies quantify these developments before 1930, and even fewer estimate industrial concentration and productivity using company-level data in the late nineteenth century. This has been a setback in understanding Argentina's initial phase of industrialization. This chapter examines the structure of industrial production to identify some obstacles blocking successful industrialization. It empirically examines Argentina's structure of industrial production between 1895 and 1935. Specifically, it estimates labor productivity, total factor productivity, economies of scale, and industrial concentration at the sector and company level. We first estimate labor productivity for twelve manufacturing activities using sector-level data from Argentina's published industrial censuses of 1895, 1914, and 1935.[4] Findings show that labor productivity grew for all sectors under study between 1895 and 1935 thanks to a switch to capital-intensive methods, growth in the number of skilled work-

18

ers, and increased government support over time. Between the censuses of 1914 and 1935, however, this growth slowed and decreased in four sectors (brewing, matches, burlap sacks, and tobacco) perhaps because of disrupted access to production inputs and major changes to labor laws. But overall labor productivity grew between 1895 and 1935.

Second, we estimate total factor productivity, industrial concentration, and economies of scale for twelve sectors using company-level data from the manuscript industrial census of 1895. Results from the estimates of economies of scale indicate that most industries were operating at a suboptimal size in 1895. Findings from the concentration ratios show that all industries except blacksmithing had high industrial concentration. Lastly, we examine how certain firms came to dominate their sector and why they failed to fill demand despite their relatively large market share.

Census Data Description

The census of 1895 recorded company-level information for all Argentine industries. This chapter has information for 1,011 companies in twelve manufacturing activities.[5] In addition, it uses information from three published national censuses and two industrial censuses of Buenos Aires province and city. It analyzes qualitative reports from the national and provincial governments and the Argentine Department of Labor (ADOL). In 1939, ADOL provided a detailed and insightful study of the textile industry between 1929 and 1938. These censuses and government sources offer a wealth of information on capital stock, value of output, material costs, machinery, and labor.[6] Other national industrial reports, annual company reports, and firm-level information published in business journals of the time were also employed in this chapter.

Estimates and Analyses of Labor Productivity

Estimates of Argentine labor productivity offer several insights about productivity and the structure of industrial production between 1895 and 1935. Over time, manufacturing firms adopted capital-intensive methods, explaining an increase in labor productivity in nearly all sectors under study. But labor productivity was slightly hampered by input shortages and perhaps also by managers' reliance on labor-intensive methods.

In the following measures, labor productivity is isolated to determine the specific effects of the number of workers on output. These estimates indicate whether labor contributed to greater output of finished goods with fixed in-

Table 2.1. Estimates of Labor Productivity, 1895–1935 (Twelve Activities, Real Pesos)

Sector	Census year	No. of observations[a]	(1) Real gross output/No. of workers	(2) Real value added/No. of workers	(3) Real gross output/No. of workers[b]	(4) Real value added/No. of workers[b]
(1) Beer	1895[c]	61	2,486.70	1,004.19	2,499.76	1,009.47
	1914	29	7,687.80	5,980.98	7,815.60	6,080.41
	1935	18	5,892.91	4,279.42	5,922.66	4,301.02
(2) Cement	1895[c]	4	375.49	262.31	381.97	266.83
	1914	29	2,630.45	1,410.80	2,710.16	1,453.55
	1935	72	5,342.24	3,849.93	5,358.83	3,861.89
(3) Glass	1895[c]	3	1,087.18	593.42	1,087.18	593.42
	1914	16	1,115.28	783.50	1,223.07	859.23
	1935	35	1,921.46	1,450.29	2,096.34	1,582.29
(4) Matches	1895[c]	5	1,593.12	593.44	1,891.71	704.67
	1914	16	2,534.66	1,892.10	3,396.38	2,535.36
	1935	18	2,297.65	865.71	2,933.01	1,105.10
(5) Iron and steel[d]	1895[c]	44	932.24	186.20	937.80	187.31
	1914	2,187	1,525.96	879.66	1,581.78	911.84
	1935	1,708	14,077.97	6,044.89	18,474.02	7,932.49
(6) Small-scale machine shops and blacksmiths	1895[c]	501	552.94	207.56	555.77	208.63
	1914	1,088	2,078.76	973.43	2,142.47	1,003.26
	1935	909	2,148.32	1,596.21	2,331.35	1,732.20
(7) Paper	1895[c]	1[e]	332.45	[f]	332.45	[f]
	1914	11	2,506.80	1,179.46	2,758.16	1,297.73
	1935	22	4,326.45	2,060.92	4,636.53	2,208.63
(8) Soap	1895[c]	78	2,716.14	256.23	2,756.57	260.05
	1914	294	5,746.61	1,753.11	5,879.41	1,793.62
	1935	239	8,577.20	1,968.04	9,035.17	2,073.12

(9) Tobacco	1895[c]	207	781.69	318.94	832.86	339.82
	1914	234	4,558.23	3,139.84	5,520.50	3,802.68
	1935	152	3,881.06	1,154.44	4,728.19	1,406.42
(10) Alpargatas	1895[c]	45	1,409.91	1,103.98	1,632.52	1,278.29
	1914	241	1,973.06	896.48	2,259.94	1,026.82
	1935	254	2,914.65	833.99	3,636.69	1,040.59
(11) Burlap sack	1895[c]	5[e]	785.56	777.89	787.28	779.60
	1914	24	11,806.69	1,793.39	14,472.20	2,198.28
	1935	22	12,815.78	990.39	15,539.13	1,200.85
(12) Textiles[g]	1895[c]	36[e]	1,470.46	564.96	1,671.16	642.07
	1914	2,458	1,448.45	638.72	1,748.44	771.01
	1935	4,727	4,598.42	1,504.34	5,514.00	1,803.87

Sources: Data from República Argentina, "Censo social e industrial, 1895," Manuscript (Buenos Aires: Archivo General de la Nación, 1895); for breweries only, Argentina, *Segundo Censo Nacional: Censo de las Industrias de 1895*, Vol. 3 (Buenos Aires: 1898); Argentina Ministerio de Hacienda, *Tercer Censo Nacional: Censo de las Industrias, 1914*, Vol. 7 (Buenos Aires: Talleres Gráficos de L. J. Rosso y Cía, 1917); Argentina Dirección General de Estadística de la Nación, *Censo Industrial y Estadística Industrial* (Buenos Aires: Ministerio de Hacienda, 1937).

Notes: Base year is 1920 = 100. Real pesos were determined by using the wholesale price index calculated by Leonard I. Nakamura and Carlos Zarazaga, "Economic Growth in Argentina in the Period 1900–1930: Some Evidence from Stock Returns, Table 9.1 Price Indexes," in John H. Coatsworth and Alan M. Taylor, eds. *Latin America and the World Economy Since 1800* (Cambridge: Harvard University Press, 1998), 254.

[a] The number of observations includes firms that reported value of output and costs.

[b] Adjusted for age and gender.

[c] Information comes from the manuscript industrial census of 1895. The 1895 published census failed to report value of output or costs except for breweries.

[d] This category includes all iron and steel foundries and lead processing manufacturers except blacksmith, forge, and machine shop.

[e] Number of observations differs from other tables because this table is considering only firms that reported value of output and costs.

[f] Costs were not reported and value added could not be determined.

[g] Textiles category includes cotton, linen, wool, elastics, other natural fibers, hats, and mixed knits. After 1930, this category also includes nylons, synthetic elastics, silks, and synthetic fibers.

puts of capital and labor. There are two measures of labor productivity: value added per worker and gross output per worker in real terms. Table 2.1 shows the results of labor productivity using real value of output and real value added divided by the equivalent number of workers.[7] The number of workers was used as a proxy for labor input.[8] Gross industrial output and costs were taken from the manuscript census of 1895 and the published censuses of 1914 and 1935.[9] The manuscript census of 1895 reported the number of workers for the first semester of 1895, and costs and value of output for the whole year of 1894.[10]

The first measure counted each worker, regardless of age or gender, as equal to one unit. It is simply:

Labor productivity = value of output / number of workers

Labor productivity = value added / number of workers

In the second measure, workers were adjusted for differences in age and gender. This method attempts to isolate the contribution of adult male, female, and child labor.[11] The second set of estimations values the labor input of one male worker at 1.00, the labor input of females at 0.75, and that of children at 0.50:

Labor productivity = value of output / ((male worker = 1) + (female worker = 0.75) + (child worker = 0.50))

Labor productivity = value added / ((male worker = 1) + (female worker = 0.75) + (child worker = 0.50))

It is particularly important to isolate for age and gender because external factors may have affected the productivity of female and child labor. The female and child labor laws of 1907 (no. 5291) and 1924 (no. 11317), for instance, could have lowered their productivity because these laws restricted working hours and increased the number of obligatory breaks. Also, women and children were more likely to perform labor-intensive tasks in the factory because of cultural perceptions limiting them from working with heavy machinery.

Findings in Table 2.1 show that labor productivity grew for all sectors under study between 1895 and 1935. Estimates indicate that real value of output per worker grew between 0.7 and 16.5 percent annually between 1895 and 1914 in the twelve industries under study (column 3). For the whole period between 1895 and 1935, real value of output per worker grew on average between 1.1 and 7.7 percent annually (column 3). Labor productivity declined in four industrial activities (beer, matches, burlap sacks, and tobacco) between 1914 and 1935, but overall there was significant labor productivity growth for all industries under study between 1895 and 1935.

Growth in labor productivity between 1895 and 1935 was largely for two reasons. First, some industries reduced their workforce to smaller groups to operate newly imported machinery. Use of machinery or capital equipment facilitated changes in production processes that increased the rate at which raw materials could be processed into finished goods with a given amount of labor. By 1914, for example, the soap and candles industry had changed its methods of production and organization, resulting in increased labor productivity. In the late nineteenth century, Argentina's soap production largely consisted of labor-intensive churning and boiling of animal fats inside copper kettles contained in brick bins in the ground.[12] Similarly, candle production required placement of a number of wicks on a wooden rod and hand dipping them in melted tallow repeatedly until the candles reached the desired size.[13] Thus before the twentieth century, candle and soap manufacturing in Argentina required little skilled labor and lengthy preparation methods.[14] After 1914, soap and candle production became mechanized in larger factories. The soap company Compañía de Productos Conen, for example, produced more soap and candles with a smaller but more skilled workforce after it imported modern machinery in the late 1900s.[15]

A limited number of manufacturers were able to afford imported machinery partly because of new tariff laws and their access to credit. The government raised tariffs on selected manufactured goods to protect domestic industry from competition of imported goods; it also lowered duties on machinery, raw materials, and fuel needed for the production processes. Manufacturers imported most machinery and raw material inputs with zero or low duty thanks to increased government intervention to promote manufacturing. The adjustment of tariff levels was the main way the government intended to help industry so it could meet domestic demand.[16] Also, some manufacturers had access to credit through their domestic and international networking system that allowed them to raise capital for manufacturing and other ventures.

A second reason for growth in labor productivity was that the quality of immigrant labor force improved over time. Between 1881 and 1930, Argentina received a net immigration of 3.8 million, with foreigners making up 35 percent of the total urban population in 1895 and 37 percent in 1914.[17] Sánchez-Alonso found that over time the quality of young immigrant labor improved and immigrants "were better able to match their skills with opportunities in the local labor market."[18] Most of these immigrants made up Argentina's urban labor force in commerce, industry, and general unskilled labor.[19]

Labor productivity grew significantly in foundries, textiles, and glass.

These three sectors experienced noteworthy changes in labor organization and production methods, and beginning in the 1920s two sectors (textiles and metallurgy) received significant government support. In the glass industry, by 1890 four glass bottle enterprises had an annual output of 12,000 kilograms of clear and colored glass bottles and containers; one company, Cristalerías Rigolleau, produced 8,000 kilograms.[20] By 1892, Cristalerías Rigolleau produced 66 percent of the national output of glass bottles.[21] Thanks to its access to a number of capital sources, the company expanded rapidly and imported up-to-date machinery to produce various types of glass products. It was a leader in imported glass technology, and the first to possess the technology to produce window glass before 1930. It was also pushing overall productivity in its sector.

Increases to labor productivity were particularly marked in the metallurgy and textiles sectors. Owners of large-scale metallurgy and textiles companies used their financial networks to raise capital to buy imported and modern machinery. Also, beginning in the 1920s, these two sectors received direct support from the government. Congress debated bills to purchase machinery and subsidize industrial and technical training schools for these two industries. For the metallurgy industry, the Argentine government eventually approved programs to recycle domestic scrap iron and remove custom duties from imported scrap iron.[22] The government also sponsored oil exploration in southern Argentina; the aim was to supply local industries, in particular the metallurgy industry, with heavily subsidized domestic petroleum.[23] The government also sought to improve labor productivity and efficiency in cotton textile production.[24] Beginning in 1929, the government furnished funds to purchase machinery from abroad and subsidize cotton production in the Argentine interior. The government office Junta Nacional del Algodón was developed specifically to "promote the development of cotton in Argentina" for textiles.[25] ADOL recorded the performance of the textile industry and reported increased labor productivity over time. It surmised that productivity was rising because men and machines were replacing women and child workers in textile manufacturing. The ADOL also reported that the number of spindles significantly increased from 20,232 in 1929 to 156,152 in 1938.[26]

Although there is overall growth in all sectors between 1895 and 1935, the estimates from Table 2.1 also illustrate that labor productivity declined in beer, matches, and tobacco sectors, and slowed in burlap sacks between 1914 and 1935 (columns 3 and 4). In this latter period, overall decline was nearly 32 percent in brewing, 16 percent in matches, and 17 percent in tobacco (column 3). Labor productivity slowed considerably in burlap sacks between 1914 and 1935, and did not grow as it did in the 1895 to 1914 period. The average annual growth and decline for all twelve industrial activities ranged between negative −1.4 and positive 12.4 percent between 1914 and 1935 (column 3); labor productivity declined in only three industries under study in this period.

Two possible reasons for the slight decrease or slowing in labor productivity in beer, matches, burlap sacks, and tobacco sectors were inconsistent access to production inputs and changes to labor laws. First, the economic slowdowns after 1914 and after 1930 temporarily affected the flow of fuel, raw materials, and machine inputs, slowing labor productivity. The brewing industry, for instance, depended on imported inputs of malts and hops to maintain production, and it could have been particularly vulnerable to economic changes that followed the First World War. During the Belle Époque period (1900–1914), Argentina experienced an unprecedented rate of GDP growth. In 1914, the crisis period began when the First World War brought on trade shortages and economic decline, which persisted through 1918.[27] By the late 1920s and early 1930s, brewers claimed that input shortages were then due to high international prices for raw materials coming from the North Atlantic economies.

Second, significant changes in labor laws in the 1920s and early 1930s that shortened the work day might have affected the labor-intensive and female-dominated industries of burlap sacks, matches, and tobacco (cigars and cigarettes). At the turn of the century, workers labored an average of nine hours per day including Sundays.[28] In the 1920s and 1930s, new labor legislation radically changed previous ways of labor organization and work intensity. New laws shortened work days, prohibited work on Sundays, lengthened rest periods during the work day, and prohibited night work. Law 11544 of 1929, for instance, limited the work day to eight hours and forty-eight hours per week. Law 11837 of 1934 mandated that all commercial and most industrial enterprises close by 8:00 p.m.

Also, gender based legislation[29] limited what women and minors could do in the factories, notably barring them from night work and from certain sectors. The aim of such legislation was to protect women's role as mothers, and it mandated that mothers take a rest every three hours to feed nursing children. Within the factory, women were limited to an eight-hour work day and forty-eight hours per week, and minors were limited to six hours per day and thirty-six per week.[30] Women were restricted from working in any area considered dangerous or toxic, and prohibited from operating heavy machinery.[31]

The burlap sack, match, and tobacco industries could have been vulnerable to these labor law changes because women made up more than 60 percent of the workforce in these three sectors (Table 2.2). There were more

Table 2.2. Female and Child Workers, 1895–1935 (Twelve Activities)

Sector	Census year	No. of firms	Female/All workers (percentage by sector)	Children workers[d]/All workers
(1) Beer	1895M[b]	61	2.1	[c]
	1914	29	0.2	3.2
	1935	18	0.6	0.7
(2) Cement	1895P[d]	159	4.3	[c]
	1895M	4	6.8	[c]
	1914	29	0.5	5.7
	1935	72	0.3	0.5
(3) Glass	1895M	3	0.0	[c]
	1914	16	2.4	16.4
	1935	35	11.9	10.7
(4) Matches	1895M	5	63.1	[c]
	1914	16	65.6	17.9
	1935	18	69.0	8.8
(5) Iron and steel foundries[e]	1895P	1,052	4.9	[c]
	1895M	44	2.4	[c]
	1914	2,187	3.5	5.3
	1935	1,708	31.6	31.8
(6) Small-scale machine shops and blacksmiths	1895P	2,111	4.3	[c]
	1895M	501	2.0	[c]
	1914	1,088	1.0	5.4
	1935	909	0.2	15.6
(7) Paper	1895	2	[c]	[c]
	1914	11	27.5	4.5
	1935	22	19.8	3.5
	1954	952	36.0	9.2
(8) Soap	1895P	152	6.9	[c]
	1895M	78	5.9	[c]
	1914	294	3.7	2.7
	1935	239	12.0	4.1
(9) Tobacco	1895P	584	33.2	[c]
	1895M	207	24.6	[c]
	1914	234	63.9	2.9
	1935	152	62.8	4.4
	1954	112	58.1	3.2
(10) Alpargatas	1895P	96	60.2	[c]
	1895M	45	54.5	[c]
	1914	241	36.5	7.2
	1935	254	50.4	14.5
(11) Burlap sack	1895P	15	74.1	[c]
	1914	24	60.0	6.9
	1935	22	69.7	0.2
(12) Textiles[f]	1895P	378	70.3	[c]
	1914	2,458	57.4	5.6
	1935	4,727	49.3	8.5
	1954	5,967	48.7	4.6

female workers in these sectors than in any other. The decline in female labor productivity over time could also indicate problems in managers' decisions on how to efficiently use female workers.

Labor laws, however, did not drastically lower women's productivity in all the female-dominated sectors. The most impressive increases in labor productivity were in a female-dominated activity, textiles, wherein productivity increased by nearly three times between 1895 and 1935 (recall Table 2.1). By the 1930s, manufacturers hired more women in their factories partly because they were said to be productive workers, but they were hired largely because women were not part of the male-dominated unions and could be paid lower wages. Consequently, women contributed to production in such traditionally male sectors as paper and metallurgy (iron and steel). By 1935, women represented 31.6 and 19.8 percent of the labor force in the metallurgy and paper industries respectively; they made up 36 percent of the paper manufacturing workforce by 1954. By 1935, women were 12 percent of the workforce in each of the male-dominated sectors of glass and soap (Table 2.2). By 1933, the glass company Cristalerías Papini noted success in favoring female over male workers in recent hiring. In the 1920s the company had suffered losses because of labor strikes, but in the 1930s it was documenting for a public relations photo shoot how they incorporated more female workers in the factory and were proud of women's work values.[32]

Over time, the absence of a severe decline in labor productivity in some female-dominated industries was perhaps due to increased work intensity while in the factory and longer hours by taking work home. Women were hired because most industries had a high number of labor-intensive tasks that were customarily given to women and children. Adult women and girls were considered ideal for unskilled jobs because of cultural norms regarding

---

Notes to Table 2.1

    Sources: República Argentina, "Censo social e industrial, 1895," Manuscript (Buenos Aires: Archivo General de la Nación, 1895); Argentina, *Segundo Censo Nacional: Censo de las Industrias 1895*, Vol. 3 (Buenos Aires: Ministerio de Hacienda, 1898); Argentina Ministerio de Hacienda, *Tercer Censo Nacional: Censo de las Industrias, 1914*, Vol. 7 (Buenos Aires: Talleres Gráficos de L. J. Rosso y Cía., 1917); Argentina Dirección General de Estadística de la Nación, Title varies, *Censo Industrial* and *Estadística Industrial* (Buenos Aires: Ministerio de Hacienda, 1937); República Argentina, Dirección Nacional de Estadística y Censos. *Censo industrial de 1954* (Buenos Aires, 1960).

    [a] This category includes all boys and girls under the age of 18.

    [b] "1895M" indicates that information comes from the manuscript industrial census of 1895. Manuscript data supplements information excluded from the final publication of the census of 1895 ("1895P").

    [c] The number of female and/or child workers was not reported.

    [d] Published data include vertical kilns and other cementlike processing centers. It was not possible to distinguish between modern cement factories and vertical kiln shops in the published report. All were listed under a category of asphalt and cement production.

    [e] Foundries, iron and steel manufacturing, lead processing. All iron, steel, and lead categories except blacksmith, forge, and machine shop.

    [f] Textiles category includes cotton, linen, wool, elastics, other natural fibers, hats, and mixed knits. After 1930 also includes nylons, synthetic elastics, silks, and synthetic fibers.

women as temporary workers who could be paid significantly lower wages than male workers.

Estimates from the Manuscript Census, 1895

Firm-level census data were available to estimate total factor productivity (TFP), economies of scale, and industrial concentration. Firm-level data came from the manuscript industrial census of 1895.[33] The results from these estimates permit clear assessment of efficiency on the part of capital or labor and reveal levels of concentration. Firm-level census data were unfortunately unavailable for later years. But the problems with the structure of production were present from the beginning of industry in the late nineteenth century and persisted into the early twentieth century.

TOTAL FACTOR PRODUCTIVITY

We estimated TFP and economies of scale using firm-level data from the manuscript census of 1985. A production function is used to show the dimensions of efficiency, and to obtain an equation specifically linking a company's output to its inputs of labor and physical capital. Typically, higher productivity comes from increased efficiency of both capital and labor. The Cobb-Douglas production function was used to indicate the relationship between output and inputs of capital and labor.[34] This production function satisfies the assumptions of the classical linear regression model. Also, adding the two output elasticities demonstrates increasing, constant, or decreasing returns to scale in Argentine manufacturing industries in 1895. In other words, the sum of ß2 and ß3 (ß2 + ß3) yield the coefficient of scale. If there are constant returns to scale, this would be represented by $\beta2 + \beta3 = 1$. A sum of ß2 and ß3 greater than 1 indicates increasing returns to scale such that doubling the inputs will more than double the output.[35]

The logarithms of each variable were taken to transform the relationship between inputs and output into linear form. The specification used:

$$LnQ = \beta0 + \beta2(lnK) + \beta3(lnL) + ui$$

where Q is the value of output, K is capital stock and equals the value of fixed assets (land and buildings) and machinery, and L is the labor input measured as number of workers. The natural log of output is the dependent variable and the explanatory variables are the natural log of capital and the natural log of labor.[36] This work applied the ordinary least-squares method to this form.

Table 2.3 shows the results using the Cobb-Douglas production function. The findings indicate that seven industries had significant coefficients and

Table 2.3.   Total Factor Productivity of Manufacturing Firms, 1894

Industry	No. of observations	Intercept	B2	B3	Sum of B2 + B3
(1) Alpargatas	33	5.35★	0.265★	0.91★	1.175
		se =0.657	0.112	0.253	
		t =8.13	2.38	3.60	
		R² =0.500	Adj R² =0.467		
		df =2, 30			
(2) Forge	430	4.545★	0.304★	0.839★	1.143
		se =0.238	0.035	0.074	
		t =19.07	8.68	11.35	
		R² =0.454	Adj R² =0.452		
		df =2, 427			
(3) Soap, fats, and glycerin	67	3.859★	0.560★	0.498★	1.058
		se =0.693	0.096	0.150	
		t =5.57	5.84	3.32	
		R² =0.732	Adj R² =0.723		
		df =2, 64			
(4) Wool and cotton textiles	35	2.3667★	0.572★	0.687★	1.259
		se =0.295	0.080	0.176	
		t =8.01	7.16	3.9	
		R² =0.914	Adj R² =0.909		
		df =2, 32			
(5) Brewery	44	3.718★	0.593★	-0.286★	0.307
		se =0.727	0.072	0.106	
		t =5.110	8.21	-2.7	
		R² =0.657	Adj R² =0.641		
		df =2, 41			
(6) Foundry	40	2.933★	0.63★	0.266	0.896
		se =1.435	0.180	0.229	
		t =2.040	3.50	1.16	
		R² =0.499	Adj R² =0.472		
		df =2, 37			
(7) Tobacco	120	5.167★	0.330★	0.573★	0.902
		se =0.567	0.078	0.119	
		t =9.12	4.24	4.83	
		R² =0.390	Adj R² =0.379		
		df =2, 117			

Source: "Censo social e industrial," Manuscript (Buenos Aires: AGN, 1895).
Notes: (Ln[value of output 1894] = intercept + B2★Ln[physical capital] + B3★Ln[number of workers]).
The industries with insignificant coefficients are not shown here: burlap sack, matches, glass, cement, and paper. There were too few observations to obtain adequate results. Also, several firms were dropped by the statistical program. There may be fewer observations in this table than in other tables.
★ Significant at 95% CI.
se = standard error; t = t-stat.

show which inputs most affected output. Not surprisingly, the estimates for labor-intensive industries—alpargatas,[37] forge, textiles, and tobacco—show that labor input led on average to more growth in output than capital alone. Three industries—foundry, brewery, and soap—were becoming increasingly mechanized by the late nineteenth century. Their significant coefficients show that capital input led on average to a greater increase in output than did labor alone. In the case of the brewing industry, labor input led on average to decreased output: a 1 percent increase in labor input yielded on average about a 0.27 percent decrease in output. The statistical coefficients for three other industrial activities—glass, burlap sack, and matches—were in the positive direction, indicating increasing returns to scale. But these statistical results were not significant because of the small number of observations in each activity.[38]

The statistical results in Table 2.3 (sum of two independent variables, B2 and B3) indicate that brewing, foundries, and tobacco manufacturing were operating inefficiently. The decreasing returns to scale indicate that there was a decline in efficiency for both capital and labor inputs in these industries in 1895. Perhaps the brewing and foundry industries were suboptimally large in terms of number of workers and machines.

Suboptimal performance could result from several factors, among them unproductive labor, technical inefficiencies, and disruption in the flow of raw materials and fuel. A way to determine labor productivity is to examine real wages. In two long-run studies on Argentine labor productivity, scholars showed that real wages were significantly low before 1930. Lower wages are partly a result of lower productivity. Alan Taylor argued that before 1914 immigrant workers "drove down real wages by about 25 percent."[39] Although manufacturing benefited from immigrant labor inflows, he argued, these workers lacked skills needed by the newly mechanizing industries of the late nineteenth century. In another study on Argentina's labor productivity, Galiani and Gerchunoff also found that labor productivity grew slower between 1900 and 1930 than in the remainder of the twentieth century. They attributed the slower growth in part to unskilled immigrant labor.[40] Also, technical inefficiencies could disrupt production and could have occurred because imported machinery was not being used efficiently. For instance, machinery could have been shut off to control inventory or not been well maintained. Disruption of trade in raw material and fuel inputs occurred from 1914 to 1918, but after that period interruptions in the flow of inputs were partly due to the higher costs of these materials. All three factors could adversely affect the operation of these three industries.

In 1895, labor-intensive industries such as alpargatas, forge, soap, and textiles had increasing returns to scale. Productivity increased in these four sectors in terms of both capital and number of workers. Although all four industries had started using capital-intensive methods, these industries still had positions for nonmechanical and unskilled jobs. It appears that labor-intensive industries were more efficient relative to their inputs of labor and capital than the capital-intensive industries of 1895. Such results indicate the greater flexibility with which companies could adjust their labor inputs through hiring and layoffs. It was more difficult, however, to adjust capital inputs once machinery was installed.

In 1895, increases to total factor productivity were typically driven by one dominant firm in each sector (except forge) that used labor-intensive methods and imported advanced capital-intensive methods. For example, within alpargatas, textiles, and soap, there were numerous labor-intensive small shops that worked alongside one dominant firm in each respective sector. Beginning in the 1890s, these few large-scale firms imported sophisticated machinery that quickly gave them production advantages over shop producers. These dominant firms had very little competition in sectors saturated with many price-taking[41] artisan shops. Owners of dominant firms purchased up-to-date machinery and patent licenses that gave their companies a technological advantage over small-scale competitors. Large-scale firms with modern machinery quickly dominated their respective sectors. For example, by 1892, the alpargatas company Fábrica Argentina de Alpargatas held 33 percent of the market because of its combination of capital and labor-intensive production methods.[42] Fábrica Argentina had imported modern machinery, giving it the advantage of economies of scale.[43] The company lowered its per unit costs and presumably offered lower prices. Its competitors were small-scale shop producers using traditional handicraft methods. These hand-produced alpargatas were more expensive to produce and sold for higher prices than those offered by Fábrica Argentina. In 1899, the journal *Boletín Industrial* attributed Fábrica Argentina's successful "capture of 30 percent of the alpargatas market to its lower prices."[44] By lowering per-unit production costs, this company offered lower prices than its small-scale competitors, and it still yielded a healthy 16 percent return on equity in 1899.[45]

ECONOMIES OF SCALE

All industries under study were tested for economies of scale using the manuscript census of 1895. Scholars have often hypothesized that Argentine firms were unable to realize economies of scale because domestic markets were too small to absorb the large output from imported machinery. María Inés Barbero, for instance, argued that manufacturing production was limited to internal consumption, which "caused difficulties in scale economies" because of low demand.[46] In 1895, Argentine markets were still developing, and demand was low relative to the available output capacity of imported machinery.

Economies of scale can be tested using this specification:

$$Q/L = \beta 0 + \beta 2 \ast (K/L) + \beta 3 \ast L + ui$$

Table 2.4.   Economies of Scale of Manufacturing Firms, 1894

Industry	No. of observations	Intercept	K/L	No. of workers
(1) Forge	502	702.096★	0.159★	40.196★
		se =71.91	0.03	15.98
		t =9.76	5.20	2.51
		R² =0.060	Adj R² =0.057	
		df =2, 499		
(2) Brewery	77	976.98★	0.380★	9.48
		se =374.64	0.08	5.89
		t =2.61	4.62	1.61
		R² =0.266	Adj R² =0.246	
		df=2, 74		
(3) Tobacco	208	987.350★	0.309★	0.829
		se =153.582	0.621	3.299
		t =6.430	4.990	0.25
		R² =0.109	Adj R² =0.099	
		df =2, 205		
(4) Soaps, fats, and glycerin	79	2048.276★	0.813★	49.72
		se =642.295	0.22	29.28
		t =3.190	3.77	1.70
		R² =0.183	Adj R² =0.162	
		df =2, 76		
(5) Textiles	36	−11.263	1.237★	26.012★
		se =44.122	0.100	1.469
		t =−0.26	12.310	17.70
		R² =0.954	Adj R² =0.951	
		df = 2, 33		

Source: "Censo social e industrial," Manuscript (Buenos Aires: AGN, 1895).

Notes: Y= value of output/worker.

★ Significant at 95% CI; se = standard error; t = t-stat.

Here Q is value of output divided by labor (L). Capital (K) in this estimation is defined as land and buildings excluding machinery and tools. Labor (L) is the number of workers.

The results in Table 2.4 show that only forge production had all significant coefficients, demonstrating that it operated to scale. Most firms in other industries were not functioning at equilibrium in 1895 either because the technology was not operating optimally or labor was not highly productive. Labor's lower productivity could have been because of a high number of unskilled immigrant workers, or because managers were not efficiently using their labor sources. In Table 2.4, the partially significant results for the other four industries may have been because there were too many workers given the value of output or the level of capital investment.

In sum, the estimated results from the Cobb-Douglas function and economies of scale indicate that forge production was the only activity with increasing returns to scale and operating to scale. Forge technology improved through better anvils, sharpening tools, and forge-welding techniques. In 1894, the costs to enter this industry were relatively low, and many artisans undertook blacksmithing. Most forges were family-owned traditional shops with fewer than five workers. These shops focused on small-scale production of such items as horseshoes, nails, bolts, and rivets for a circumscribed local region.

INDUSTRIAL CONCENTRATION

Estimates of concentration indicate the level of competitiveness in an industry. A higher level of concentration indicates less competition and the ability of one or a few firms to influence prices. Concentration is measured using the four-firm ratio (CR4) and the Herfindahl-Hirschman index (HHI). CR4 determines the market share of the four largest firms in the industry. Market share is the proportion of total market sales accounted for by one firm. CR4 calculates the total market share of just the four largest firms. HHI is a measure of industrial market concentration.[47] The values of HHI and CR4 equal 1 when there is a single firm in the industry and tend toward 1 when there are few firms and a greater degree of inequality in market shares.

Table 2.5 shows that all twelve industries under study except blacksmithing had high industrial concentration in 1895. For blacksmithing, the four-firm ratio (CR4) indicates that its top four firms held 18 percent (value of output) and 20 percent (value added). HHI was 0.02 in terms of both value

Table 2.5. Indices of Industrial Concentration, 1894

Industry	No. of firms	Value of output		Value added	
		CR4	HHI	CR4	HHI
(1) Alpargatas	45	0.89	0.42	0.95	0.65
(2) Breweries	72	0.82	0.31	0.82	0.38
(3) Burlap sack	5	1.00	0.72	1.00	0.74
(4) Cement	4	1.00	0.37	1.00	0.55
(5) Glass	3	1.00	0.71	1.00	0.61
(6) Matches	5	1.00	0.40	1.00	0.36
(7) Metallurgy shops (forge)	501	0.18	0.02	0.20	0.02
(8) Foundries: iron, steel, and lead	44	0.33	0.13	0.64	0.29
(9) Paper	1	1.00	1.00	1.00	1.00
(10) Soap	78	0.57	0.13	0.49	0.11
(11) Tobacco	207	0.55	0.15	0.66	0.14
(12) Cotton, wool and mixed knits	36	0.99	0.43	0.99	0.31

Source: "Censo social e industrial, 1895" Manuscript (Buenos Aires: AGN, 1895).

of output and value added. These CR4 and HHI results were lower in black-smithing relative to other industries because this was a relatively competitive activity and the costs to entry were low.

Industrial concentration for all other industries demonstrates that a few firms produced the greatest output in their industries. They produced heavily because they used imported machinery with large productive capacity and hired the largest number of workers. Also, most dominant firms established in 1895 maintained control in their sector through 1935.

In 1895, large-scale firms dominated their sectors because they were the largest among a pool of mostly labor-intensive and small-scale enterprises. The manuscript census of 1895 indicates that the majority of manufacturing enterprises were family-owned artisan shops that used traditional hand-production methods. The average number of workers per artisan shop in all industries was typically fewer than five. The amount of capital stock invested was on average less than 1,000 paper pesos per shop. By contrast, in 1895 the average number of workers in one of the dominant firms numbered in the hundreds,[48] and the average amount invested in capital stock ranged between 100,000 and 1.5 million paper pesos.[49] In 1895, a large-scale firm would quickly dominate its respective sector.

Table 2.5 illustrates the results from the concentration ratios. In 1895, five industrial sectors—alpargatas, burlap sack, cement, paper, and glass—had HHI estimates above 50 percent (value-added). The brewing and match industry estimates were above 30 percent. The Argentine wool and cotton textile industry was similarly concentrated, with an HHI level of 0.31 (value added) in 1894. By comparison, the Mexican and U.S. cotton and wool textile industries had HHI estimates in 1893 of 0.022 and 0.077 respectively.[50]

The four-firm ratio (CR4) measures how much output was produced by the top four firms in each industry. Some industries were newly emerging, so perhaps it is not surprising that concentration was high in those sectors. The estimates from CR4 in Table 2.5 indicate that the top four firms in eight industries (paper, alpargatas, brewing, burlap sack, cement, glass, matches, and cotton and wool textiles) controlled between 80 and 100 percent of market share in 1894. Each industry had one firm that either produced or exceeded 50 percent of output. In the Argentine wool textile industry, for instance, CR4 indicated that one firm, the Campomar textiles company held 46 percent of national market share (value added).[51] The Felipe de la Hoz Woolen Textiles mill had the second largest market share in textiles; it held 16 percent of national market share (value added).[52] (Using value of output, CR4 indicated that Campomar held 62 percent of national market share and Felipe de la Hoz held 8 percent). The paper industry consisted of only one operating firm, Argentina Fábrica de Papel, which had 100 percent of market share; the cement, glass, and match industries had fewer than five firms each. Between 1890 and 1930, Cristalerías Rigolleau dominated in glass production and Compañía General de Fósforos was the largest firm in the match industry. There were only four firms in the cement industry; its top producer was Marset Bialet, which held 48 percent of market share (value of output).[53]

In textiles, soap, tobacco, and iron foundries, there were numerous small shops operating within each industry with one or a few large firms capturing most of the market share. CR4 analysis shows that the canvas shoe (alpargatas) company Fábrica Argentina de Alpargatas held 62 percent of national market share (value of output).[54] Similarly in the burlap sack industry, CR4 shows that the company Primitiva held 84 percent of national market share in 1894 (value of output).[55] Among foundries, the leading four firms held 64 percent of market share (value added). In the soap and candle industry, the top four firms held 49 percent of market share. CR4 analysis also indicates high concentration in the tobacco industry, where the leading four tobacco firms had a market share of 66 percent in 1894 (value of output).

Similarly, in the brewing industry leading producers held a substantial market share. Bieckert, a British-owned brewery, held 59 percent of national market share (value added).[56] Three other domestic breweries also held significant market shares: Quilmes, 16 percent; Río Segundo, 4 percent; and Schlau, 2 percent (value added).[57] In terms of gross output measured in hectoliters,[58] these top four producers accounted for 82 percent of beer output. The productive capacity of these four brewers filled nearly all national demand; Quilmes produced 49 percent of all beer consumed in Argentina while Bieckert produced 27 percent, Río Segundo 4 percent, and Schlau 2 percent.[59] Quilmes manufactured 92–95 percent of all beer (measured in hectoliters) produced in Buenos Aires province between 1894 and 1896.[60]

The larger companies' output helped maintain a concentrated structure because it was difficult for new entrants of equal size to compete in the same market. For example, within the brewing industry concentration increased between 1890 and 1935. In 1895, there were seventy-two breweries in Argentina, but by 1915 there were thirty-one and by 1935 only eighteen remained in business.[61] This trend toward concentration was partly because of improved brewing and refrigeration methods, permitting fewer firms to produce and transport beer across Argentina. In 1916, the brewing industry attributed this drop in the number of firms to declining demand and increasing costs. Between 1900 and 1914, brewers alleged they were losing customers to wine consumption. (They suspected that the large number of immigrants from Spain and Italy preferred wine to beer.) The brewing industry reported that annual beer consumption per inhabitant declined from 13.97 liters in 1913 to only 9.39 in 1915, while annual wine consumption per inhabitant increased from 50.31 liters in 1913 to 59.92 by 1915.[62] On account of this decline in beer consumption, the brewing industry cut its prices and decreased production by more than 1.7 million liters.[63] The productive capacity of twenty-five breweries in Argentina in 1916 was 1.78 million hectoliters, but production was only 771,000 hectoliters, or 43 percent of capacity.[64] Some brewers liquidated or merged with other brewers because the costs of production exceeded sales.

Similarly, Compañía General de Fósforos (CGF) had the annual capacity to produce 180 million wax matches and 20 million wood matches.[65] By 1907, CGF was producing more than 21.5 million boxes of wood and wax matches, only a fraction of its actual capacity.[66] But the large output contributed to the small number of new entrants in the match industry. Even though wax matches were protected with a 60 percent duty above the price of imported goods,[67] there were few new entrants. CGF depended on selling its output to the domestic market and could potentially glut the market. Consequently, the number of match firms grew slowly: five companies in 1895, fifteen in 1915, and only eighteen by 1935.[68]

Some of the dominant companies of 1895 controlled their industries through 1930. They dominated because new entrants were constrained by the high cost of entry and the absence of long-term credit. Ideally, new entrants could help reduce high industrial concentration. But between 1890 and 1930, the absence of new entrants with equal productive capacity resulted in limited competition or none within certain industrial activities.

A Noncompetitive Industrial Sector

The costs of entry into modern manufacturing were high, and a noncompetitive industrial structure developed because only a few manufacturing groups could afford the expense of importing modern machinery, hiring foreign engineers, and training labor to work on imported machines. Additional expenses included routine maintenance of machinery and imported inputs. The owners of dominant firms were groups of investors using their financial and business networks to raise capital for the start-up, operation, and maintenance costs of large-scale manufacturing.

How did firms come to dominate their sectors? Beginning in the late nineteenth century, the wealthier partners, finance groups, or investors merged, created, or acquired companies. A merger was a quick way to consolidate assets, equity, and investor capital. This process helped investors gain greater market share for their manufacturing companies. There are several examples illustrating horizontal mergers[69] among Argentine companies. Three key company mergers were the soap company Compañía de Productos Conen, the paper company Argentina Fábrica de Papel, and the match company Compañía General de Fósforos. These companies first merged in the late nineteenth century and dominated their respective sectors through 1930.

Mergers typically began with acquisition of small firms and partnerships. In 1896, for example, José Conen and José Berisso first created the sociedad en comandita[70] (partnership with limited liability rights) José Conen y Compañía. Later in 1901, this company obtained additional finance partners (Tornquist group) to expand its production. It also legally incorporated and became Compañía de Productos Conen, dominating its sector through 1930. Similarly, in 1888 the two paper sociedades en comanditas, Maupas Compañía and Estrada, Escalada y Compañía, formed the corporation Argentina Fábrica de Papel, creating the largest paper factory in Argentina. Before 1900, it controlled 100 percent market share. Lastly, in 1889 CGF was also the result of a merger of three medium-scale match companies, Ambrosio Dellacha y Hermanos, Francisco Lavaggi e hijo, and Bolondo y Lavigne.[71] By the early 1890s, CGF held significant national market share; CR4 indicated it as 35 percent (value added).

Given their significant contribution to national production, did these dominant companies influence prices? Despite high concentration, the three large-scale manufacturers complained they could not influence prices the way they had hoped because imports of manufactured goods competed with their products. They claimed that competition from imports saddled them with excess inventories thanks to insufficient domestic demand. Industries came up with their own reasons for not being able to control prices, but in most cases they blamed input shortages, competition from imports, and low demand.

Manufacturers claimed that low demand and competitive forces were to blame for their underuse of machinery because they were forced to reduce production to prevent high inventories. For instance, in 1899, the kitchenware firm Oscar Schnaith y Compañía (renamed Ferrum in 1911) imported machines with the capacity to produce thirty-six hundred kitchen pieces daily[72]; however, the company used only a third of that capacity and reported that this output satisfied domestic demand.[73] Similarly, in 1899 the soap and candle company Compañía de Productos Conen purchased imported machinery with the productive capacity to manufacture 180,000 candles every ten hours and 24,000 kilograms of detergent soap in twenty-four hours.

The company never ran its machinery anywhere near full capacity; Conen reported manufacturing 120,000 candles every twenty-four hours, or 28 percent of its productive capacity, and only 6,849 kilograms of detergent soap per day, or 29 percent of its soap-making capacity.[74] The soap company reported that these amounts satisfied demand and kept prices above cost.[75]

Although domestic manufacturers complained that insufficient demand resulted in underuse of machinery, the amount of imported manufactured products grew during the same period. For the most part, imports of manufactured consumer goods filled 20–75 percent of demand between 1890 and 1930, despite the dominant firms' potential to fill most domestic demand.[76] For some products, such as cotton textiles and newsprint, imports filled nearly all demand. Between 1923 and 1930, for instance, domestic production of cotton textiles satisfied only 5–10 percent of national demand despite the industry tripling in size in this period.[77] Part of the problem was that the local textile industry suffered from shortages of the cotton appropriate for imported machinery. In some cases, raw cotton was imported because it was cheaper and of better quality; only a few regions in Argentina grew cotton.

Demand for imported products increased over time, but local producers were not able to fill local demand. Idle capacity of machinery should have diminished as markets expanded and manufacturers discovered new methods for efficient use of machinery and labor, or tried new factory organization. But for the most part, by the 1910s Argentine manufacturers' correspondence revealed how they focused on short-term and immediate problems such as competition from imports (internal competition in some cases) and the absence of policies granting local producers exclusive access to domestic markets. It could be added that they underestimated local demand because they lacked a good information system to adequately measure it. But most important, Argentine manufacturers were perhaps not directly interested in tackling large-scale internal obstacles to industry. Such tactics would be fruitful if manufacturers were willing to change their long-term practices of how they ran their companies. Most large-scale manufacturers had their origins in trading and financing and viewed manufacturing as another long-term investment venture with the potential to control national markets. If the government intervened, manufacturers stood a chance to gain substantial market share.

The estimates from labor productivity, total factor productivity, economies of scale, and concentration ratios reveal that there were problems with Argentina's structure of industrial production. Argentine industry was technically inefficient from the beginning, and it seems that over time it relied on government intervention to remain profitable. A major problem for most dominant firms was their inability to fill domestic demand because of input shortages and other technical inefficiencies. Although production grew over time, it failed to truly substitute for imports of consumer goods. Imports continued to enter the country because of increasing consumer demand for such manufactured goods. The inability to supply this demand suggests input shortages of raw materials and fuel as well as technical inefficiencies, and perhaps it also demonstrates local producers' limited knowledge about how to efficiently substitute imports and satisfy domestic demand.

Chapter 3

Argentina's Investment in
Imported Machinery, 1890–1930

The process of becoming a modern nation included democracy, social aware-ness, commitment to new technologies, and the use of science to adopt and adapt these technologies in Argentina. Diverse works from seminal academic studies such as Di Tella and Zymelman, *Las etapas del desarrollo económico argentino*; Díaz Alejandro, *Essays on the Economic History of the Argentine Republic*; nonfiction works such as Sarlo, *La imaginación técnica*; and even fiction such as Robert Arlt's *The Seven Madmen* refer to the economic and cultural significance of interest in new technologies and invention, and increasing investment in imported machinery between 1890 and 1930.[1] But there is little scholarly work specifically examining the long-term outcome of these investments and their relation to Argentine politics and economic cycles.

Argentina's transition from labor-intensive to capital-intensive produc-tion methods in the late nineteenth century contributed to an average an-nual industrial growth rate of 6.2 percent between 1890 and 1930.[2] In-vestment in capital-intensive production methods—specifically, machinery imported from Europe and the United States—was motivated by several factors, among them improved economic conditions and expansion of the export of agricultural and pastoral products. Other issues prompting invest-ment were the transition to more favorable industrial policy and the wish on the part of domestic financiers to diversify portfolios by investing in manu-facturing. They planned to offer domestic substitutes for imported manufac-tured consumer goods.

Several scholars have discussed the economic significance of increasing in-vestment in imported machinery from 1890 to 1930, but they have not mea-sured the actual amounts imported.[3] Di Tella and Zymelman, for instance, reported an upward swing in imports of machinery and raw materials beginning in 1920 and attributed investment in innovative capital-intensive methods as helping to push economic growth during the 1920s.[4] Recent scholarship also discusses how increased investment pushed economic growth in the 1920s.[5] In terms of comparative GDP for the Latin American region, "in the mid-1920s Argentina had the biggest weight" partly because of investment in capital-intensive methods.[6] But despite scholarly attention to the topic of investment in imported machinery in Argentina, few works have estimated the actual amount spent between 1890 and 1930.[7] Even fewer works have analyzed the reasons for the troughs and peaks of investment in machinery or examined which sectors received the most up-to-date imported machinery.

This chapter fills the gap with needed estimates of investment in imported machinery between 1890 and 1930. In addition, it examines investment cycles and explains manufacturers' reasons for investing in imported machinery. It then discusses the benefits and limits to investing in and relying on imported manufacturing machinery. Despite a considerable amount invested in machinery, the manufacturing sector remained relatively underdeveloped.

Data and Methods

Findings come from a newly created dataset on Argentine investment in imported machinery, machine parts and accessories, and fuel. In Argentina, there are no serial publications listing values invested in machinery between 1890 and 1930. Argentina's trade statistics were recorded in the *Anuario de la Dirección General de Estadística* (1892–1914) and the *Anuario del comercio exterior de la república Argentina* (1915–1931). Prices of imported machinery, however, are not reported in these series. Instead, valores de tarifa or official tariff values and ad valorem custom duties are reported.[8] These values were based on valuations (avalúos) instead of actual prices on the world market. The sources report quantities of imported machinery and their country of origin, offering information about where imports of machinery came from. Nearly all machinery, fuel, and replacement parts were imported from Great Britain, the United States, Germany, and France. Argentina also imported agricultural machinery from Belgium, Canada, and other countries, but in smaller quantities.

Such information makes it possible to obtain an approximate value of machine investment by examining the exports of machinery from four countries to Argentina: Germany, United States, United Kingdom, and France. This method was used by Wilson Suzigan in *Indústria Brasileira* (1986) to determine machine investment in Brazil.[9] Data for the United States and

United Kingdom trade series came from the serial publications *Annual State-ment of the Trade of the United Kingdom with Commonwealth Countries* and *The Foreign Commerce and Navigation of the United States*.[10] Data from the German government trade series *Statistik des Deutschen Reichs*, 1890–1929, and the French trade series *Tableau general du commerce et navigation*, 1890–1928, are available at Harvard and Columbia Universities. All data values were con-verted to nominal British pounds and then into real pounds using a capital goods price index for plant and machinery (1890–1930).[11]

Investment Cycles of Machinery

How did Argentine entrepreneurs set the investment agenda? Factors such as national ideology, favorable legislation, and government support as well as practical matters such as costs, access to ports, and markets motivated the entrepreneurs' investment agenda and decisions to invest in specific sectors. Investment decisions also evolved over time with the changing political and economic climate of Argentina. For example, the Tornquist group owned several metallurgy companies and sugar mills. It seems they invested more in their metallurgy firms because these companies were located in urban areas near ports and markets. Being near ports allowed easier access to imported machinery and fuel, but there was also more competition near urban mar-kets, and they sought to stay up-to-date with the latest technology. They in-vested less in machinery for their sugar mills because domestic sugar produc-tion was protected through high tariffs, permitting nearly exclusive access to internal markets. Also, a practical issue was that the mills were located in the interior of Argentina, and it was more expensive to ship and transport sugar machinery to the interior.[12]

Although business groups were willing to take on some risk and use fi-nance sources to invest in up-to-date manufacturing machinery, they were largely a risk-averse lot. Typically, investment went toward areas that were known or expected to provide a high return. Between 1890 and 1930, Ar-gentina spent well over 180 million real British pounds on machinery. But machine investment went toward two specific sectors: 38 percent for agri-cultural machinery, implements, and their components and 34.3 percent for unspecified industrial machinery (Table 3.1). These results coincide with findings in the literature that agriculture was the most important sector in the economy, and industry was second. The general category of industrial machinery limits our knowledge of which specific machines were imported, but we know from company reports that investment went to machines that produced popular imported products. Business groups did not typically introduce entirely new products into Argentine markets. Their conception of industrialization was to replace imports and produce for internal markets. They did not intend to break into new product markets because doing so was viewed as too risky.

Table 3.1 shows estimates of Argentine investment in machinery between 1890 and 1930. It reports the amount invested annually in twelve machine categories. Figure 3.1 graphs the troughs and peaks of this overall growth over time. The linear trend in the figure shows that machine investment grew consistently between 1890 and 1930. Manufacturers purchased and imported a mix of used and new machinery, equipment, replacement parts, and belts. Table 3.2 shows the percentage increases in investment in physical capital per worker for most industries under study. During this period, the average rate of growth in overall machine investment was 4.3 percent per year and the average growth rate per capita was 4.2 percent. In the same period, investment in industrial machinery grew on average 3.8 percent per year and the average growth of investment in agricultural machinery was 7.8 percent annually.

Between 1890 and 1930, economic cycles largely influenced the timing and volume of investment in machinery. Other factors such as availability of finance capital, industrial policy, and internal consumption played a role in the timing of investment in machinery, but economic cycles seem to best explain the volatility of this investment. Figure 3.1 shows that the annual amount spent on imported machinery largely correlates with Argentina's cycles and subcycles, which have been well examined in the extant literature. Sanz-Villaroya confirms that "exports and investment were the explanatory variables behind all the cycles before 1932, given that they show the highest levels of correlation with GDP."[13] Exports were highly correlated with GDP from 1881 to 1918, and investment "establishes relevance during the next cycle, 1919–1932."[14]

Observation of short-term subcycles is useful for determining reasons for investment. The low point of investment in imported machinery was during the 1890s, largely because Argentina was in a recessive phase from 1893 to 1902; average annual growth rate was 2.72 percent, compared with 5.68 percent in the previous decade, 1881–1892.[15] There was a 23 percent decrease in machine investment between 1890 and 1899. Very little was invested in 1891 and 1892, followed by slow and volatile recovery of machine investment between 1893 and 1899. From 1892 to 1902, the country was recovering from its banking crisis of 1891, and focusing resources on exports of agricultural and pastoral products to help economic growth. It was also reestablishing investor confidence by creating new commercial, tariff, and banking laws to

Table 3.1.   Argentine Investment in Machinery, 1890–1930 (Real British Pounds, 1913)

Industry	1890	1891	1892
Industrial machinery, not specified	406,468	29,539	42,363
Agricultural machinery, implements, and their components	197,431	35,882	135,253
Steam engines and machinery (except for locomotives)	677,439	2,357	958
Electrical machinery for industry	–	–	–
Metal making and metal working	–	343	290
Wood-working machinery	28,871	11,529	13,544
Textiles machinery	12,275	4,380	3,960
Paper-making machinery	–	–	–
Sugar machinery	–	–	–
Brewery machinery	–	–	–
Cement-making machinery	–	–	–
Implements, tools, belts, replacement and spare parts	–	–	–
TOTAL for all machinery and parts	1,322,484	84,031	196,368
Fuel: cinder, coal, coke, petroleum, (gasoline after 1924)	–	–	–

Industry	1900	1901	1902
Industrial machinery, not specified	474,501	486,284	384,960
Agricultural machinery, implements, and their components	373,035	275,220	353,913
Steam engines and machinery (except for locomotives)	227,491	287,018	221,627
Electrical machinery for industry	50,312	44,441	39,270
Metal making and metal working	–	–	–
Wood-working machinery	61,720	50,386	49,727
Textiles machinery	37,110	36,756	23,229
Paper-making machinery	996	5,554	215
Sugar machinery	–	–	–
Brewery machinery	759	5,012	475
Cement-making machinery	–	–	–
Implements, tools, belts, replacement and spare parts	56,901	57,052	55,421
TOTAL for all machinery and parts	1,282,824	1,247,723	1,128,837
Fuel: cinder, coal, coke, petroleum, (gasoline after 1924)	742,030	727,076	673,357

Industry	1910	1911	1912
Industrial machinery, not specified	2,187,603	2,010,634	2,591,657
Agricultural machinery, implements, and their components	1,165,775	1,435,880	1,440,591
Steam engines and machinery (except for locomotives)	104,605	235,707	289,733
Electrical machinery for industry	47,705	53,665	57,778
Metal making and metal working	88,176	85,504	85,347
Wood-working machinery	210,593	186,337	209,400
Textiles machinery	116,648	125,469	169,996
Paper-making machinery	3,230	7,572	20,891
Sugar machinery	53,036	15,279	17,323
Brewery machinery	15,845	6,130	12,112
Cement-making machinery	–	–	–
Implements, tools, belts, replacement and spare parts	176,389	173,292	203,688
TOTAL for all machinery and parts	4,169,605	4,335,470	5,098,517
Fuel: cinder, coal, coke, petroleum, (gasoline after 1924)	1,995,774	2,299,917	2,718,577

1893	1894	1895	1896	1897	1898	1899
290,648	261,025	217,212	165,250	347,740	274,738	353,880
224,602	246,516	163,147	139,207	69,511	63,984	307,562
236,125	237,773	148,756	134,138	133,009	153,905	204,037
–	–	–	–	–	36,965	21,017
3,036	779	427	429	1,442	323	6,551
28,799	20,712	22,957	31,358	38,218	25,107	42,604
11,217	11,642	8,689	16,816	33,746	13,099	26,359
–	–	–	–	–	–	–
–	–	–	–	–	–	–
–	–	–	–	–	–	–
–	–	–	–	–	–	–
62,198	36,436	30,429	40,316	31,863	34,201	55,325
856,626	814,884	591,620	527,515	655,530	602,321	1,017,334
353,240	408,873	440,274	400,871	404,372	446,144	594,925

1903	1904	1905	1906	1907	1908	1909
650,375	1,208,759	1,856,597	2,998,694	3,032,603	2,180,210	2,264,010
505,366	711,081	893,619	1,105,248	734,761	797,211	915,772
263,816	56,999	20,475	37,272	71,749	81,888	117,416
39,853	42,395	30,488	73,817	30,092	53,186	40,994
–	–	–	–	68,806	57,442	74,494
52,644	73,023	103,659	134,737	168,454	154,333	164,991
29,518	52,477	90,183	134,819	114,148	88,267	115,587
3,172	1,481	–	1,832	3,825	4,503	1,135
–	–	–	–	12,690	21,159	22,880
296	2,582	–	3,315	19,620	13,552	6,288
–	–	–	–	–	–	–
70,634	97,750	105,419	153,190	136,707	142,488	169,811
1,615,674	2,246,545	3,100,441	4,642,923	4,393,456	3,594,239	3,893,379
736,484	921,135	1,083,518	1,501,170	1,661,231	1,815,069	1,592,772

1913	1914	1915	1916	1917	1918	1919
2,551,218	1,532,173	1,070,733	986,518	694,232	869,891	2,336,849
1,364,901	857,740	445,826	1,041,102	1,009,608	1,944,210	2,561,114
210,481	112,787	31,732	91,721	167,978	401,241	784,292
129,986	75,658	58,187	148,255	348,894	326,709	946,558
107,071	21,222	6,567	43,452	60,602	55,321	241,085
24,020	3,504	1,345	2,377	16,452	2,035	27,498
200,262	187,909	34,752	92,881	106,999	134,894	335,710
726	–	1,747	51	3,926	971	45,677
17,468	4,001	1,541	10,831	14,056	18,027	210,813
56,139	34,807	52,899	40,044	34,160	127,450	243,399
–	–	–	–	–	5,383	26,498
223,269	87,351	85,206	154,836	115,657	241,046	600,207
,885,541	2,917,152	1,790,533	2,612,069	2,572,564	4,127,178	8,359,701
,233,931	2,431,095	1,984,667	1,331,904	767,219	1,006,840	4,286,972

Table 3.1—*continued*

Industry	1920	1921	1922
Industrial machinery, not specified	3,960,148	3,180,482	807,218
Agricultural machinery, implements, and their components	4,172,564	3,483,078	1,380,696
Steam engines and machinery (except for locomotives)	1,635,090	843,494	752,966
Electrical machinery for industry	1,393,138	1,032,137	145,695
Metal making and metal working	365,548	155,831	46,157
Wood-working machinery	63,633	25,337	9,134
Textiles machinery	667,839	281,273	293,140
Paper-making machinery	44,028	4,130	1,907
Sugar machinery	643,057	127,449	8,333
Brewery machinery	108,204	71,172	26,178
Cement-making machinery	33,396	9,668	6,171
Implements, tools, belts, replacement and spare parts	1,029,485	510,794	220,453
TOTAL for all machinery and parts	14,116,130	9,724,845	3,698,048
Fuel: cinder, coal, coke, petroleum, (gasoline after 1924)	2,865,860	2,758,337	3,264,407

Industry	1930	Total by sector	Percent of investment
Industrial machinery, not specified	1,812,616	62,015,943	34.30
Agricultural machinery, implements, and their components	3,995,596	68,639,703	37.97
Steam engines and machinery (except for locomotives)	124,729	12,545,574	6.94
Electrical machinery for industry	790,925	11,938,586	6.60
Metal making and metal working	73,187	3,941,781	2.18
Wood-working machinery	3,984	2,198,929	1.22
Textiles machinery	108,370	6,957,606	3.85
Paper-making machinery	332	254,957	0.14
Sugar machinery	24,466	1,439,984	0.80
Brewery machinery	74,231	1,488,340	0.82
Cement-making machinery	118,637	1,633,250	0.90
Implements, tools, belts, replacement and spare parts	180,238	7,739,763	4.28
TOTAL for all machinery and parts	7,307,311	180,794,416	100.00
Fuel: cinder, coal, coke, petroleum, (gasoline after 1924)	3,084,727	88,760,420	

prevent another such economic crisis, gain credibility among investors, and encourage foreign investment. By 1899, the economy was well on its way to recovery. That year, the government created the conversion office (Caja de Conversión) to stabilize the country's currency. The Caja regulated banks and the national gold supplies to control Argentina's international exchange rate.[16]

By 1900, the economy recovered and investment in machinery increased annually between 1900 and 1912. The largest growth happened during this period, a 297 percent increase. From 1900 to 1912, the average annual growth rate of overall machine investment was 12.1 percent, 8.2 percent per capita. Investment in industrial and agricultural machinery swelled during this period; investment in industrial machinery grew on average 14.9 percent

1923	1924	1925	1926	1927	1928	1929
879,420	1,177,039	2,338,701	2,909,310	3,339,043	4,526,246	2,328,353
3,258,449	4,308,555	4,205,121	4,102,523	3,958,318	5,155,373	9,104,362
372,022	634,852	773,782	114,523	458,714	746,594	344,283
269,250	328,951	652,334	875,181	1,295,922	1,294,333	1,164,493
54,686	60,676	369,416	269,378	314,318	599,303	624,572
5,529	14,138	11,872	–	–	–	104,366
221,409	265,025	568,749	446,965	625,805	677,034	432,198
4,709	–	–	–	–	–	92,349
7,364	27,795	24,354	17,318	11,582	–	129,161
26,221	61,752	54,729	90,312	114,274	36,920	149,462
24,294	141,414	90,948	168,939	262,539	279,961	465,402
255,809	255,442	286,770	279,494	455,542	494,703	373,950
5,379,161	7,275,639	9,376,777	9,273,944	10,836,057	13,810,467	15,312,951
4,238,567	7,262,326	5,953,814	4,277,207	6,140,428	5,692,004	6,663,309

Source: Data from various sources. Deutschland, Kaiserliches Statistisches Amte (after 1919, Statistischen Reichs-amte), *Statistik des Deutschen Reichs, Auswartinger Handel des Deutschen* (Berlin: Verlag des Königlich Preussichen Statistischen Bureaus, 1890–1904, 1906–1913, 1923–1929). In Germany, export trade statistics were not separated by country between 1914 and 1922, and 1930. République Français. Direction Générale des Douanes, *Tableau Général du Commerce et de la Navigation: Commerce de la France Avec ses Colonies et les Puissances Etrangères, Vol. 1* (Paris : Imprimerie Nationale, 1897–1905, 1907–1914, 1921–22, 1926–1928). U.S. Department of Commerce, Bureau of Foreign and Domestic Commerce, *The Foreign Commerce and Navigation of the United States* (Washington: Government Printing Office, 1890–1930). United Kingdom, *Annual Statement of the Trade of the United Kingdom with Foreign Countries and British Colonies* (London: H.M.S.O., 1893–1930). *The Economist:* "Monthly Trade Supplement, Accounts Relating to Trade and Navigation in the United Kingdom of 1890" (Jan. 10, 1891), p. 27. Capital goods price index (plant and machinery) for British pound from C. H. Feinstein, *Statistical Tables of National Income, Expenditure, and Output of the U.K., 1855–1965* (Cambridge, 1972), pp. T136–T138.

Note: See chapter section "Data and Methods" for explanation of data.

annually while investment in agricultural machinery increased an average of 11.9 percent per year. Investment in agricultural machinery was largely due to strong international demand and farmers' desire to increase production through mechanized methods imported from abroad.[17] In manufacturing, by 1909 the industrial lobby group Unión Industrial Argentina applauded the fast growth of investment in industrial machinery. It sought to nurture this growth by requesting higher tariffs to further protect infant industries. The UIA wanted to promote domestic industry by reducing "harmful competition from imported goods."[18]

Investment in machinery expanded partly because of a growing economy. The period from 1900 to the First World War has been well recorded in the primary and secondary literature as Argentina's Belle Époque and described as showing the fastest economic growth. Immigrants flocked to the city of Buenos Aires because of the promise of high wages and an improved standard of living compared to their own countries.[19] Foreign investment was also substantial and helped develop the country's transport sector, drainage and

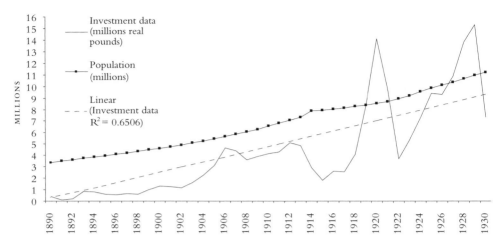

Figure 3.1. Argentine Investment in Manufacturing Machinery, Population, and Linear Investment Trends, 1890–1930. (Real British Pound, 1913). *Sources:* For Germany: Deutschland, Kaiserliches Statistisches Amte (after 1919, Statistischen Reichsamte), *Statistik des Deutschen Reichs, Auswartinger Handel des Deutschen* (Berlin:Verlag des Königlich Preussichen Statistischen Bureaus, 1890–1904, 1906–1913, 1923–1929). Export trade statistics were not separated by country between 1914 and 1922, and 1930. For France: République Français. Direction Générale des Douanes, *Tableau Général du Commerce et de la Navigation: Commerce de la France Avec ses Colonies et les Puissances Etrangères*, Vol. 1 (Paris : Imprimerie Nationale, 1897–1905, 1907–1914, 1921–22, 1926–1928). For United States: U.S. Department of Commerce, Bureau of Foreign and Domestic Commerce, *The Foreign Commerce and Navigation of the United States* (Washington: Gov't. Printing Office, 1890–1930). For United Kingdom: *Annual Statement of the Trade of the United Kingdom with Foreign Countries and British Colonies* (London: H.M.S.O., 1893–1930). *The Economist*, "Monthly Trade Supplement, Accounts Relating to Trade and Navigation in the United Kingdom of 1890" (Jan. 10, 1891), p. 27. Capital goods price index (plant and machinery) for British pound from C. H. Feinstein, *Statistical Tables of National Income, Expenditure, and Output of the U.K., 1855–1965* (Cambridge, 1972), T136–T138.

waterworks systems, and general infrastructure.[20] Similarly, Suzigan finds that the peak of machine investment in Brazil was also during its expansive phase of growth just before the First World War, from 1902 to 1914.[21] Generally, this was a period of fast growth for the southern cone region.[22]

    In addition to the fast economic growth of the Belle Époque, Argentine investment in machinery expanded rapidly for three other reasons. First, in 1900 many domestic manufacturing entrepreneurs were merchant import-

Table 3.2. Percentage Changes Within Census Years, Estimates of Capital, Labor, and Value Added, 1895, 1914, 1935

Sector	Years compared	Real physical capital/No. of workers (%)	Real value added/No. of workers (%)
(1) Beer	1895/1914	41.8	495.6
	1914/1935	64.8	(28.4)
	1895/1935	133.8	326.2
(2) Cement	1895/1914	3,364.5	437.8
	1914/1935	160.0	172.9
	1895/1935	8,907.9	1,367.7
(3) Glass	1895/1914	46.8	32.0
	1914/1935	22.8	85.1
	1895/1935	80.3	144.4
(4) Matches	1895/1914	(52.5)	218.8
	1914/1935	522.4	(54.2)
	1895/1935	195.7	45.9
(5) Iron and steel	1895/1914	163.5	372.4
	1914/1935	208.2	587.2
	1895/1935	712.1	3,146.4
(6) Small-scale machine shops and blacksmiths	1895/1914	298.7	369.0
	1914/1935	(6.8)	64.0
	1895/1935	271.5	669.0
(7) Paper	1895/1914	(64.6)	254.8
	1914/1935	40.4	74.7
	1895/1935	(50.3)	519.9
(8) Soap	1895/1914	98.7	584.2
	1914/1935	56.0	12.3
	1895/1935	209.9	668.1
(9) Tobacco	1895/1914	231.0	884.5
	1914/1935	(48.2)	(63.2)
	1895/1935	71.6	262.0
(10) Alpargatas	1895/1914	(24.3)	(18.8)
	1914/1935	(14.4)	(7.0)
	1895/1935	(35.2)	(24.5)
(11) Burlap sack	1895/1914	130.4	130.5
	1914/1935	(90.2)	(44.8)
	1895/1935	(77.5)	27.3
(12) Textiles	1895/1914	64.3	13.1
	1914/1935	134.4	135.5
	1895/1935	285.1	166.3

Source: see Table 2.1.

ers of manufactured goods and therefore among the first to observe growing consumer demand. A high birth rate and massive immigration during this period swelled population, which more than doubled between 1890 and 1914. Figure 3.1 shows that population grew at a rate consistently above that of machine investment. Annual imports of consumer goods increased during this period, and domestic merchants saw the potential for substituting the import of these manufactured consumer goods. In the 1900s, they began expanding and diversifying their investment portfolios to include manufacturing activities. The Argentine market was also highly urbanized and concentrated in the federal capital of Buenos Aires and the littoral provinces. Many of these merchant entrepreneurs established factories near ports and markets, reasonably believing their products could replace imports of consumer goods.

Second, in 1900 Argentina adopted the gold standard to stabilize the exchange rate between the peso and British pound.[23] The Argentine government used its currency reserves to maintain a favorable rate between the British pound and gold peso. A stable domestic currency had two effects. First, it became less expensive to import and install machinery from abroad (in this period, most of it came from Britain and the United States). Local domestic capital and a few foreign financiers began investing in the manufacturing sector, particularly through importation of foreign machinery. Second, a stable currency helped rise investor confidence and foreign investment increased, allowing domestic investors to invest in domestic manufacturing while foreign investors (from the United Kingdom, United States, France, Belgium, Germany, and other countries) invested in Argentina's infrastructure (merchant shipping, railroads, hotels, roads, public transportation, utilities, and construction). British investment in particular was devoted to building an extensive rail network.[24] Such railways helped connect outlying areas to Buenos Aires and began the process of building a national market for domestic goods.

A final reason for the surge in machine investment between 1900 and 1912 is that entrepreneurs who invested in manufacturing also preferred to import foreign machinery to quickly establish factories in the country. Local manufacturers were typically not inventors or machine makers. Several had an engineering education, but they were not involved in developing machinery. Of the best known manufacturers with an engineering background, most did not apply their knowledge in the factory. If they did, they learned how to operate, adjust, and maintain imported manufacturing technology rather than use their knowledge to design new and original machinery. Even after 1930, Torcuato Di Tella, a well-known manufacturer with an engineering background, used his knowledge to understand imported machinery and at times made small adaptations to it.[25] For the most part, manufacturers who studied engineering did so as part of their general education and not as a vocation. (Most were likely to be directors of other companies or hold politically appointed government positions outside the factory. For instance, the prestigious industrial family Bemberg sent a grandson, Otto Eduardo, to study engineering in France and Germany. Afterward he became a director of several firms in his career.[26]) For most companies, it was less expensive to import all the needed machinery for manufacturing than develop indigenous technology. According to the match manufacturer CGF, it was relatively less expensive to buy new machinery or replace machine parts every few years than to develop new machinery.[27]

After the Belle Époque, investment in imported machinery began to slow in 1913 and declined in 1914. The period from 1914 to 1918 was characterized by a considerable decline and slow recovery in machine investment as a result of the First World War, which limited foreign capital and disrupted international trade. Companies decreased their investment generally, and established firms suffered input shortages of fuel, machine parts, and raw materials during this period. Estimates in Table 3.1 show that investment would not exceed the 1913 level until 1919; there was a 63 percent decrease in machine investment from 1913 to 1915, followed by slow recovery.

This period of decline and recovery (1913–1918), however, was followed by Argentina's second period of substantial growth in machine investment. There was an 83 percent increase from 1919 to 1929. The average annual growth rate in machine investment was 6.2 percent, and average rate of growth per capita was 3.5 percent. Although this average percentage growth was not as high as from 1900 to 1912, the absolute amount spent on imported machinery was much greater than in any other period under study. Table 3.1 shows that manufacturers spent more than £107.2 million (real pounds) on imported machinery between 1919 and 1929, compared to the real £66 million spent between 1890 and 1918. In the 1919–1930 period, the average growth rate of investment in industrial machinery was 4.4 percent annually, while the average growth in investment for agricultural machinery was an impressive 10.1 percent per year, leading all other categories (Table 3.1).

The reasons for this substantial increase in the 1920s are markedly different from the situation in the Belle Époque. During this latter period, export receipts and foreign investment helped to push economic growth and local investment. In the 1920s, circumstances differed considerably. Argentina went off the gold standard and floated its domestic currency, and in general the economy did not grow as fast as it did from 1900 to 1912.[28] Neighboring countries also had economic difficulties in this period; Brazil had two short recessions in 1922–23 and 1926–1928.[29] In both Brazil and Argentina, however, investment in foreign machinery expanded despite fluctuating economic conditions. Perhaps increased investment was due to greater government intervention in industry.[30]

In Argentina, there are four reasons for the expansion in machine investment in the 1920s. First, this period of increased investment coincided with introduction of more favorable legislation for industry. Beginning in 1919, Congress debated a major increase in tariff levels across the board; protection for selected domestic manufactured products; duty-free imports of machinery, raw material, and fuel inputs; and other bills intended to protect and promote the growth of domestic industry. For instance, Congress debated whether to award monetary prizes to metallurgy firms that could process 100 tons of iron daily and whether to allow duty-free imports of all machinery for metallurgy firms.[31] A second bill proposed compelling the national mortgage bank, Banco Hipotecario Nacional, to offer mortgage loans on favorable terms to manufacturers seeking to expand production.[32] Such debates helped create a sense that the government was trying to create a friendlier environment for industry. Manufacturers increased their investment in machinery expecting these bills to pass into law.

The government had always played a role in the economy,[33] but it enhanced its intervention role beginning in the 1920s. Berensztein and Spector explain how it was a "critical turning point during the 1920s and 1930s as a series of institutional changes established the foundations of a state-centered economic and political system."[34] It was not that the government eagerly sought to take on this role, but after 1914 pressures from powerful interest groups from industry, the agricultural sector, and the interior provinces forced it to pursue a more active role in the economy. The debate to increase industrial tariffs gained momentum after the First World War brought on material shortages and economic uncertainty. Supporters of industry underscored the need for economic diversification by developing the industrial sector. They argued that protective tariffs were the means to protect and develop domestic industry.

By 1923, the government had passed several laws intended to foment local manufacturing. It increased tariffs on most imports of manufactured goods from 25 to 50 percent;[35] that year, Congress declared it was increasing tariffs to provide real protection to local industries. The new customs law also permitted duty-free import of capital goods, fuel, and raw materials. The government began to refine petroleum in southern Argentina to produce domestic fuel at a reduced rate for domestic industry.[36] This relatively favorable climate motivated industrialists to invest in up-to-date machinery as they expected to fill domestic demand.

A second explanation for the expansion of machine investment in the 1920s was that the unfavorable exchange rate between the peso and foreign currency made imports of manufactured goods costlier. In 1922, the government floated the peso. The new exchange rate and higher tariffs made imported manufactured consumer goods more expensive to Argentine consumers. Although the exchange rate would have made foreign machinery more expensive too, manufacturers counted on the higher tariff and prohibitive exchange rates to create favorable price conditions for import substitution. The peso began to appreciate after 1922, however, making machinery less expensive to import.

Third, in the 1920s manufacturers found various exporters selling similar and competing products, helping to reduce international prices for machinery. U.S. machine manufacturers, for instance, were interested in replacing British firms as suppliers to Argentine companies. These U.S. manufacturers offered such inducements as long-term financing (up to ten years), free shipping, and free repairs. During the First World War, the U.S. Department of Commerce sent agents on fact-finding trade missions to Argentina.[37] Once U.S. trading agents established that a market for American machinery existed in Argentina, producers began offering generous credit lines to Argentine manufacturers. U.S. machine makers and their distributors targeted key Argentine industrialists. In 1924, Lockwood, Greene, and Company from Boston quickly responded to the industrialist Carlos Alfredo Tornquist regarding his interest in U.S. cotton manufacturing machinery.[38] U.S. machine makers were apparently successful; in 1920, one British trading agent lamented that the United States had replaced the British in furnishing paper machinery to the Argentines. He noted that the United States had taken advantage of the situation during the First World War "when deliveries from Great Britain and Germany became scarce and irregular and the United States had a clear field" to "[branch] out into the paper business in Buenos Aires."[39] Although this British agent lamented a bygone era, U. S. agents started investing in Argentina before the First World War but enhanced and became major investors in Argentina during and after the War.[40] In the 1920s, U.S. manufacturers were also entering the Argentine market at a time when there was substantial merger activity there. Newly formed firms such as the paper company Papelera Argentina wanted to buy the latest technology to replace outdated machines. Some firms had not updated machinery since 1914.

A final factor leading to increased machine investment was that international shipping costs declined in the 1920s, making duty-free machinery even less expensive to import. Machines from the United States were also lighter and smaller, for easier handling and shipping to Argentina.

Between 1890 and 1930, economic cycles, industrial policies, and new international business conditions affected the timing and level of investment in machinery. Investment was low in the 1890s, but it expanded rapidly during the Belle Époque. The trade disruptions caused by the First World War decreased investment. As of 1919, however, investment increased steadily for a decade partly because of the emergence of favorable industrial legislation and new trading partners. Legislation, in particular, offered incentives to manufacturers who sought to produce in a protected environment. The world economic depression of 1930 interrupted this period by precipitating a dramatic drop in Argentine machine investment that year.

Entrepreneurship, Technology, and Industrial Development

LATE INDUSTRIALIZING COUNTRIES

Did imported machinery advance industrial development in Argentina? Machinery certainly helped advance several industrial sectors. Productivity grew substantially in all sectors under study except in burlap sacks and alpargatas (Table 3.2). Productivity fell slightly in the production of burlap sacks and alpargatas perhaps because of reasons discussed in Chapter 2: technical inefficiencies, unproductive labor, or inadequate management of female labor.

In theory, Argentina and other late industrializers had certain advantages in developing the manufacturing sector. Early studies by Alexander Gerschenkron and Albert Hirschman contended that developing economies could grow faster if they imported machinery from advanced countries.[41] Gerschenkron held that late-developing nations such as Germany and Russia imported the very newest technologies from already industrialized countries to catch up, sometimes surpassing the industrial development of established nations. In the case of Germany, it went from importer of manufacturing machinery to major exporter within a few decades. Floud argued that by the midnineteenth century German machine tool technology had already surpassed that of Great Britain.[42] Russia also experienced a fast rate of aggregate industrial growth that was due to importation of advanced technologies from industrialized economies.[43] Gerschenkron implied that the industrial processes of Germany and Russia could be analyzed as potential models for other late-industrializing countries. Similarly, Hirschman argued that imported machinery and equipment could advance industrial activity and spawn additional industries through backward and forward linkages. He claimed that late industrializers had the advantage of forming interdependent industries or linkages between industrial sectors. He defines linkages as backward and forward connections between industries that determine the structure of industry and become the "drivers of economic growth."[44]

The problem of Argentine manufacturing, however, lay not in its ability to raise productivity through the import of machinery but in its inability to sustain productivity without depending on imports. The manufacturing that developed in Argentina was rarely competitive and innovative.

For the most part, the manufacturing sector of late-industrializing Latin American countries remained relatively underdeveloped by international standards. Scholars have outlined four reasons for industry failing to sustain productivity and become a main driver of economic growth in Latin American countries. First, importer countries such as Argentina, Mexico, and Brazil had higher setup costs because of the need to import machines from the United States and Europe. Imported machinery entailed the additional costs of shipping, handling, and hiring engineers to set up the machinery.[45] Second, the high costs of establishing an industrial factory served as a barrier to entry, limiting the number of industrial entrepreneurs.[46]

Third, labor was not as productive in Latin America as in Europe and the United States. In Argentina, skilled and highly productive labor for large-scale and modern manufacturing was scarce. Before 1912 in Argentina, labor was described as a transitory immigrant labor force. Most immigrant labor, for instance, had little interest in developing skills or making any long-term commitments tying them to Argentina.[47] Most unskilled immigrant workers simply wanted to make money, perhaps through tenant farming, and then return to their home country.[48] Skilled immigrant laborers who remained in Argentina preferred to become shop proprietors rather than work for someone else.[49] The censuses of 1895 and 1914 show that immigrants established thousands of manufacturing shops; they were strongly represented in industry and helped shape the structure of industry.[50]

Lastly, despite growing legislation aimed at protecting and guiding industrial development, these laws failed to create a competitive and sustainable industrial sector.[51] Tariff policies in particular were short-sighted and largely enabled established companies to gain greater control over their industrial sector. Although after 1930 there were numerous new entrants, most were small-scale and inefficient producers that relied on the government's industrial programs for their survival.[52] These new entrants failed to threaten the established structure of industry.

The scholarly literature contributes to our understanding of late-industrializing Latin American countries, but perhaps we should also closely examine technological inefficiencies to understand industrial underdevelopment. Argentina's manufacturing sector operated at a suboptimal level and suffered from technological inefficiencies. There is no simple linear progression to achieve technological efficiency in industrialization, but entrepreneurs should actively accumulate technological knowledge for their firm and strive toward developing a "technologically mature firm."[53]

The heart of Argentine entrepreneurship was the industrialists' ability to develop broad and diverse networks. The function of networking was to seek information about technological innovations and raise capital for this technology. Once acquired, machinery was expected to function as it did in the home country. Becoming technologically efficient, however, requires a company to "build technological capabilities through learning processes"[54] rather than simply expecting the machinery to perform efficiently despite being under a wholly different set of conditions.

TECHNOLOGICAL UNDERDEVELOPMENT

In this section, we define technological capability and discuss why Argentine manufacturers failed to develop the technological capabilities needed to sustain industrialization. Linsu Kim defines technological capability as the "ability to make effective use of technological knowledge in efforts to assimilate, use, adapt, and change existing technologies."[55] There are three elements of technological capability: production, investment, and innovation.[56] A crucial component of building technological capability is industrial innovation: "a pioneering activity, rooted primarily in a firm's internal competencies."[57] Dutrénit adds that latecomer firms must develop core technological competencies. The concept of "core competency" denotes that firms remain active in many technical fields "outside what would appear to be their core areas."[58]

Technical capability differs from technical strategy. The purpose of the latter is to obtain machinery to start, update, or advance a specific sector. This is what most Argentine and Latin American firms did to substitute imported consumer goods. But a key characteristic in sustaining industrial progress and development is having an ongoing agenda of innovation and accumulation of technological knowledge.[59] In Argentina, most manufacturers developed a knowledge base that relied on learning through experience in handling and operating imported machinery. But they were not leaders in advancing technological capabilities. Chandler and Daems observed that in small markets protected by tariffs and containing only a few competitors, the emergence of the sophisticated and modern firm was much slower to develop (or not at all).[60] Argentina had a similar industrial environment: limited international competition and a small number of domestic competitors.

The skill to develop a complicated web of technological core competencies needed for innovation processes required a specific business culture. A business leader's skill stems from the fact that he "engineer[s] a culture specifically adapted to the industry and social environment in which his firm operates."[61] Establishing the skill to develop networks for expansion of technological knowledge would have been difficult in Argentina partly because it took a long time to establish and maintain informal networks.[62] A leading entrepreneur's technological strategy was to develop and use his extant network for information and finance of machinery. Members of his group most likely preferred that he spend his time establishing networks of finance rather than ones of technological knowledge.

This business climate had some effect on formation of technological capability, but three other factors stifled this development in most Argentine firms before 1930: reliance on imported machinery, tariff policy, and legal institutions. First, Argentine manufacturers relied heavily on imported machinery, placing them in a vulnerable position if the machinery failed to fit local conditions. An indicator that imported machinery failed to function "as is" is the rising number of patented modifications to machinery. Manufacturers realized that modifications were necessary, and they were able to patent these adjustments to imported machinery. Similar to investment in machinery, grants for invention patents increased significantly beginning in the 1920s. Part of the reason for an increase in patents was that policymakers revised patent law to encourage technology transfer and ease the transaction for foreigners to patent their inventions in Argentina; they reduced fees and simplified the paperwork process for taking out a patent. Between 1900 and 1940, more than forty-eight thousand patents were filed in Argentina. The number of filed patents increased nearly three times from an average from 663 per year between 1890 and 1921 to an average of 1,794 patents filed per year between 1921 and 1940. In the mid-1920s, on average about a fifth of patents (between 18 and 22 percent) were filed in machine and mechanical equipment categories.[63]

Patents are not necessarily an indicator of original innovation and inventiveness; innovation requires active participation in accumulating technological knowledge for its own sake and building heavily on existing ideas.[64] Instead debate on patent reform shows that policymakers' intention was not so much to promote domestic innovation but rather to encourage technology transfer. A consistent pattern in the numerous versions of the patent bill was that policymakers intended to make incentives for foreigners to bring their inventions to Argentina. Edward Beatty argues that it is more common for late-industrializing nations dependent on imported technologies to ease patent regulation for foreigners.[65] By the 1920s, legislators further increased incentives for foreigners and Argentines to patent, such as sponsoring contests for "new" inventions introduced in Argentina. (It is not clear, but it seems that even if the patent had been initially introduced in another country, the patent would be treated as "new" in Argentina.)

Tariff policy was a second factor hindering the development of technological capability. In the 1920s and 1930s, the government raised tariff rates to protect local industries from foreign competition. High tariffs created a protected environment with a small number of domestic competitors and limited international competition. Tariff policy affected industry in two ways. First, foreign producers started to establish factories within Argentina because tariffs were perhaps keeping out their exports, and they stood to benefit by producing internally for a protected market.[66] Foreign manufacturers patented their machinery and factory designs, which restricted domestic producers from using such patents and helped them gain a technical advantage over domestic producers. Second, high tariffs decreased domestic companies' incentive to pursue projects to expand technological knowledge. Large-scale and domestic companies were the best equipped and funded to expand technological capabilities. But in a highly protected environment, over time company owners could earn profits regardless of whether or not they were investing in expensive research and development projects.

Finally, another difficulty in developing technological capability was legal institutions. Several scholars contend that for companies to coordinate and monitor effectively, legal institutions must be fairly in place.[67] In Argentina, the government was in the process of creating and revising tariff, commercial, patent, labor, and finance laws during the early phase of industrialization.[68] For instance, it was difficult to predict how new legislation might affect productivity, profits, or machine output. According to manufacturers, new labor laws disrupted factory routine and production. In 1924, gender-based labor legislation severely curtailed women's ability to work on machines or do night work in factories. Gender-specific legislation was intended to protect the family, restrict women's mobility, and ensure that men predominated in the workforce.[69] The protective code lessened women's ability to effectively compete with male workers, and it may partly explain why alpargatas, textiles, and burlap sacks (female-dominated industrial activities) failed to grow as fast as they did in comparison with other Latin American regions.[70] For instance, although growing, Argentina's cotton textiles industry accounted for only 40 percent of total consumption by 1938.[71] In contrast, domestic cotton textiles production in Brazil and Mexico filled demand in domestic markets.[72]

Although labor legislation was long overdue and benefited laborers, to the manufacturer these sudden changes disrupted the workday and in some cases may have left work undone or machines unattended. In 1924, the UIA argued against laws that shortened the workday and limited female activities in the factory. In the case of gender-based laws, they argued that the increased number of mandatory breaks (for nursing and tending to small children) disrupted the "order and routine" of the factory schedule.[73] Some machines or activities needed to run consistently to function properly; a shortened workday increased the chances that some machines might be ruined or work would be undone. Within this labor law environment, perhaps managers had a difficult time making decisions about how to coordinate labor, machine use, and machine training.

Before 1930, laws to monitor accounting reporting practices were also in transition. Most firms had individual and unique accounting practices before 1923. They focused on profits and sales as the primary indicators of company performance; they had not yet developed an appropriate monitoring system for machinery. In 1923, the Argentine Ministry of Justice and Legal Practices standardized corporate accounting practices and forms; profit and sales remained as the primary indicators of performance. The ministry categorized machinery and new technological acquisitions as simply capital investment.

The structure of accounting reporting practices was inadequate for monitoring and understanding the function of machinery within a factory. Most firms did not have a separate system to monitor why a machine might or might not improve the performance of a factory. Keith Pavitt asserts that "mechanisms of coordination and control" are essential in understanding the technology.[74] It is important to note that some Argentine firms failed to observe higher profits as expected after installing machinery, and some simply shut off machinery to reduce inventory when profits were lower than expected.

The investment level in manufacturing machinery was impressive but not complemented with advances in new industries, original innovation, or dramatic risk taking. These three would have helped to sustain productivity and growth in industry. Argentine entrepreneurs were willing to take on risk and invest in manufacturing, but they preferred to do so with tariff protection or some expected guarantee that the investment would do well. Also, although patent data show a rise in the number of machine patents, patent data are not necessarily an indicator of inventiveness. Many patents were machine adaptations or foreigners taking out patents on their machinery and cannot be defined as technological innovation for sustained industrialization.

Chapter 4

Merchant Finance Groups
in Argentine Industrialization

A key issue in the historiography of Argentina's industrial underdevelopment has been the absence of long-term credit for manufacturing. After the bank panic of 1890–91, Argentine banks adopted conservative lending policies that limited extension of credit through the 1920s.[1] The problem was not a lack of capital because the nation had banks that performed well, had a high level of deposits, and often lent across activities. Indeed, credit shortages were due to Argentina's weak financial system before 1930.[2] Investment in manufacturing required access to finance capital through a relatively efficient finance system. Such a system is a "network of banks, brokers, and exchanges" with the ultimate responsibility to turn "illiquid physical assets into liquid contracts," making them "easy to value and exchange" between anonymous parties.[3]

Argentina's financial system was inefficient in several ways. First, the nation's leading banks maintained high reserves that remained immobile and deprived economic sectors of this additional capital.[4] Banks held onto reserves for two reasons: to protect themselves in case of another savings withdrawal crisis like that of 1890–91 and to cover potential bad debts. Second, Argentina had no discounting agency that would have helped companies to sell or transfer debt.[5] Third, most loans had a short-term maturity of three to six months. Although most loans could be renewed, and often were, the absence of long-term contracts was another obstacle in this financial system because the lender controlled whether or not to renew a loan. Fourth, capital was concentrated in only a few large-scale banks; they held the majority of the nation's savings. Finally, the stock market was underdeveloped and not a potent source of capital for manufacturing because most new companies did not incorporate or sell their shares on the Buenos Aires stock exchange.

Under these circumstances, investment for large-scale manufacturing came chiefly from domestic merchant finance groups.[6] In Latin America, these groups were stable but often informal associations of individuals. They accumulated wealth through their trading businesses and partnered with other merchants and investors to raise and pool capital to invest across activities in the absence of strong and well-developed banks and equity markets.[7] Members found that belonging to a group offered a faster and more secure source of capital than individual entrepreneurship. They invested in various sectors of the economy such as banking, retail, manufacturing, real estate, and agriculture. Investments were diverse to reduce risk from failure in any one activity.

In Argentina, leading groups obtained capital through their own finance houses and banks, but more important they raised capital from outside sources by creating informal alliances and networks with many other entrepreneurs, merchants, foreign businessmen, political leaders, and banks.[8] Groups also strived to develop a reputation as prudent and profit-making businessmen. Reputation played a key role in both solidifying ties among members and attracting outside capital. Group reputation had an explicit purpose in Latin American business transactions; in Mexico, for example, reputation served as a "form of intangible collateral to creditors" in the absence of secure property rights before 1930.[9]

Without an effective financial system that allowed easy value and exchange of capital between anonymous parties, a group's reputation served as a signal to outsiders. It indicated to outsiders that members behaved in a manner expected to promote a company's stability and profitability. Reputation could be used to attract outside capital to invest in company bonds and shares and in maintaining investor confidence during an economic downturn. Because economic volatility and company failures were relatively common before 1930 in Argentina, access to capital from outside sources was vital to long-term company success. Outsiders seeking profitable but relatively safe manufacturing investments viewed a reputable group's ventures as stable and profitable (outside investors were those who had neither business nor personal relationships with a company's senior management or board of directors). Depending on the company, these outsiders could be Argentines or foreigners investing through an investment broker, foreign or domestic banks, or other merchant finance groups. They felt confident in investing and buying company shares or bonds because they relied on the group's reputation. In turn, the group worked to fulfill its promises to outside investors because it gained a significant advantage in having access to alternative and outside sources of capital.

This chapter examines five leading merchant finance groups. They invested in a diverse array of activities: agriculture, banking, hotels, entertainment, real estate, fishing industry, and manufacturing. By 1930, these five groups owned Argentina's largest and most dominant manufacturing firms in their sectors. I have chosen to identify four groups—Tornquist, Bemberg, Devoto, and Soulas—by the leading director's family name;[10] the fifth ("Paper") group is so named because of the substantial stake its members held in the Argentine paper industry.[11] Although other and perhaps more important groups existed, we examine these five groups specifically because of their investment and involvement in Argentina's manufacturing sector. They demonstrate investment patterns common among most groups invested in large-scale manufacturing.[12]

Argentina's weak financial system helped create a manufacturing sector in which a few merchant finance groups exercised most of the control. These five groups succeeded in adapting to an environment without efficient credit markets by raising capital through their own banks and finance houses, and using their reputation to obtain additional money. It was typical for early banks to lend to affiliated companies, and to have a direct or indirect connection to a lender. The lack of anonymity between financial parties was common in other countries too, even in the United States. The difference, however, lay in manufacturers' ability to access credit. Early-nineteenth-century New England, for example, had a kinship-based banking system that lent largely to insiders.[13] But nearly all who needed industrial credit obtained it because the region's "financial system was shaped by a policy that allowed virtually free entry into banking."[14] The number of state-chartered banks grew in response to the region's need for credit from 1784 to 1860, helping to mobilize capital for industrial development.[15]

In Argentina, nearly all groups who incorporated their companies had a bank affiliation. Smaller groups, however, were affiliated with smaller banks that sometimes failed to efficiently raise capital through increasing deposits. Indeed, smaller and less-known groups had a limited number of ventures. They relied on self-financing, and as a result their companies remained relatively small-scale and unable to effectively compete with large-scale and established companies. By contrast, the five dominant groups had sufficient funds from multiple sources to increase the size and number of their ventures. The lack of competition within manufacturing only reinforced the fact that these five groups dominated their manufacturing sectors.

In the following section, we discuss the data and methods used in identifying and analyzing merchant groups. The third section examines the historical formation and financial capacities of merchant finance groups in Argentina between 1890 and 1930. The fourth section analyzes the specific characteristics of the five groups under study. In section 5, we explore why nondominant companies and groups were generally less successful in obtaining additional sources of capital than the dominant five groups.

Data and Methods

The evidence for this chapter comes from a newly created dataset of 1,282 company directors and prominent shareholders from fifty-nine companies across ten manufacturing sectors between 1890 and 1930.[16] These ten sectors were textiles, metallurgy, paper, matches, cement, glass, brewing, tobacco, soap and candles, and burlap sacks. This dataset traces directors' affiliations to banks, government institutions, insurers, manufacturing companies, and mercantile firms. It also identifies directors' membership in the Chamber of the Buenos Aires Stock Exchange, the Jockey Club, Sociedad Rural Argentina, British Chamber of Commerce in Argentina, and Unión Industrial Argentina.[17] The annual *Quien es Quien* also furnished additional information on social club and business memberships.[18]

By identifying which clubs and organizations company directors belonged to, we gain a picture of who was in their network circles. Directors relied on their networks to obtain capital, expand wealth, and increase influence in business and industry. These networks reveal a high level of corporate interlocking and consequently make up a short list of the key Argentine businessmen of the time. They were some of the most reputable and influential businessmen in Argentina.

Two criteria were used to identify the leading finance groups whose firms dominated their manufacturing sectors. The first criterion is that all group members must be corporate directors who collectively own the majority of ordinary stock (voting shares) in at least eight companies. Holding a directorial seat and being a major shareholder indicated that a member had considerable control over a company's affairs. By the same token, collective ownership of eight or more ventures showed that these members invested together repeatedly; it served as a measure of a group's cohesion. The second criterion is that members must be directors of at least two banks or finance houses. As a bank director, a member potentially had access to capital sources for initial setup of a manufacturing firm. Table 4.1 lists these five finance groups and some of their investments.

Individual manufacturers and other more loosely organized and small groups of merchant financiers were studied too. They failed to dominate any manufacturing sector. In the case of small groups, at least two characteristics

Table 4.1. Finance Groups and Their Investments and Companies

GROUP 1: Bemberg
Otto Bemberg, founder of the group
Frederico Otto Bemberg, Mario Dané, Ricardo Hofer, Guillermo Jaccard, Carlos Sepp

Banking: Caja de Crédito Hipotecario; Crédito Industrial y Comercial
Brewery: Cervecería Argentina Quilmes[a]; Cervecería del Norte[a]; Cervecería Palermo[a]; Cervecería Schlau[a]; Maltería y Cervecería de los Andes[b]; Cervecería Buenos Aires[a, b]
Glass: Cristalerías Rigolleau[b]
Textiles: Manufactura Algodonera Argentina[c]
Tobacco: Tabacalera Argentina[b]
Tramways: Compañía de Tramways de Buenos Aires y Quilmes

GROUP 2: Devoto
José Devoto, founder of the group
Antonio Alemanni, Antonio Devoto, Tomás Devoto, Guillermo Franchini, Honorio Stoppani, Pedro Vaccari, Victor Valdani

Devoto Cervellera[b]
Banking: Banco de Italia y Río de la Plata; Banco el Hogar Argentina
Brewery: Cervecería del Norte[a, b]
Cotton plantation: Algodonera en Resistencia, Chaco
Glycerin: Compañía de Estearina, La Plata
Electricity: Compañía Italo Argentina de Electricidad
Insurance: La Inmobiliaria, Compañía Argentina de Seguros Generales
Matches: Compañía General de Fósforos[a, d]
Metallurgy: Cantábrica[a, b]
Paper: Fábrica de Papel en Bernal[f]; Papelera Argentina[a, g]
Publishing: Compañía de Imprenta y Litografía
Refrigeration: Frigorífico Argentino[b]
Textiles: Compañía Fabril Financiera; Compañía Nacional de Tejidos y Sombreros[a, e]

GROUP 3: Paper[h]
Angel Estrada, Tomás Estrada, founders
Enrique Becquerel, Orlando S. Casati, Pablo Denti, Ernesto Maupas, Henry Py

Banking: Banco Comercial Argentino[b]; Banco de la Nación Argentina; Banco Francés del Río de la Plata
Glass: Cristalerías Rigolleau[a, b]
Paper: Argentina, Fábrica de Papel[a]; Celulosa Argentina; Fenix[a]; Papelera Argentina[a]; Casati, Fabrica de Papel[a, b]
Refrigeration: Frigorífico Argentino

GROUP 4: Soulas
Pedro Soulas, Santiago Soulas, founders
Carlos Campomar, Miguel Campomar, Lino Landajo

Banking: Banco de Avellaneda; Eduardo Soulas, Financiera y Comercial
Furniture, wood: Grumbaum-Soulas, Curtiembres, La Argentina
Woolen textiles: Campomar y Soulas[a], Lanera Argentina, Masllorens Hermanos[a]
Wool washing: J. Soulas et fils, Curtiembres y Lavaderos de Lana
Shoes: Compañía General de Calzado, S.A.

GROUP 5: Tornquist
Ernesto Tornquist, founder; Carlos Alfredo Tornquist leads group after 1908
Cristián Altgelt, Guillermo Altgelt, Enrique Berduc, Rodolfo Datwiler, Gustavo A. Frederking, Máximo Hageman, Jacobo Kade, Emilio J. Korkus, Ernesto Pasman, Guillermo C. Pasman, Miles A. Pasman, Eduardo Tornquist, Martín Tornquist

Banking, mortgages, and credit houses: Crédito Ferrocarrilero Argentino; Crédito Territorial Argentino; Ernesto Tornquist y Compañía, Casa Financiera y Comercial; Industrial y Pastoril Belga Sudamericana de Amberes

Financial consultants (under Carlos Tornquist): Banco de Prestamos Territoriales; Banque Union Financiere D'Anvers; Crédito Ferroviario e Inmobiliario, S.A.

Brewery: Cervecería Palermo[a, b]

Furniture company, surveying, produce, and wood: Plantadora Islena

Glass: Cristalerías Rigolleau[a, i]

Hotel: Briston Hotel del Mar del Plata

Insurance: Buenos Aires Seguros

Land surveying: Estancias y Colonias Tornquist; Estancias y Colonias La Verde; Estancias y Colonias Curamalan

Lumber: Quebracho, S.A.; Quebrachales Tintina

Metallurgy: Ferrum[a], Talleres Metalúrgicos San Martín[a, j]

Mortgage loans: Alianza Amberesa

Railroad and tramways: Compañía Belga Argentina de Ferrocarriles; Compañía Nacional de Transportes, "Expreso Villalunga"

Refrigeration: Compañía Sansinena de Carnes Congeladas

Soap, candles, and glycerin: Compañía de Productos Conen[d]

Sugar: Compañía Azucarera Tucumana; Refinería Argentina (Sugar Refining)

Tobacco and salt: Introductora de Buenos Aires[d]; Piccardo Tabacos[a, i]; Compañía de Productos Kemmerich

Whale fishing: Compañía Argentina de Pesca

Sources: Data gathered from 1885–1930, *MSA*, *BOB*, and *BORA*. See also Jorge Gilbert, "El Grupo Tornquist, 1906–1930," unpublished work (Universidad de Buenos Aires, Conference XIV Jornadas de Historia Económica, Fall 1998); J. Gilbert, "Los negocios del holding Tornquist," in José Villarruel (ed.), *Prosperidad y miseria. Contribuciones a la historia económica argentina*, Chapter 4 (Buenos Aires: Editorial Al Margen, 2004); *Ernesto Tornquist y Cía., Ltda y sus Compañías afiliadas, Manuscript* (1932), BTQ; *Quien es quien en la Argentina: Biografías contemporáneas* (Buenos Aires: Guillermo Kraft, 1939).

Notes:

[a] Company is one of fifty-nine corporations under study.

[b] Company was not founded by the group, but one or more members sat on the director's board and were major shareholders in the company.

[c] Some Bemberg members began investing in the late 1920s. The company was acquired around 1934–1936.

[d] Factories were located in Buenos Aires province and Montevideo, Uruguay.

[e] Filed for bankruptcy in 1912.

[f] Sold to Papelera Argentina in 1926.

[g] Compañía General de Fósforos received a large number of Papelera shares as payment when it sold the Bernal Paper Factory to Papelera Argentina.

[h] This group is also known as the French group because of investment through its affiliated bank, Banco Francés y Río de la Plata. Andrés M. Regalsky, "La evolución de la banca privada nacional en Argentina (1880–1914): Una introducción a su estudio." In Pedro Tedde and Carlos Marichal (eds.), *La formación de los bancos centrales en España y América Latina. Vol. 2: Suramérica y el Caribe.* (Madrid: Banco de España, 1994), 35–59.

[i] Tornquist group were invested, but not the majority shareholders with voting power. The Rigolleau and Piccardo families obtained substantial financing from the Tornquist group, but they maintained voting power over their companies.

[j] Talleres Metalúrgicos San Martín was the merger of six metallurgy firms in 1926. It was initially Rezzónico y Ottonello from 1902–1909, then incorporated in 1909, and became Talleres Metalúrgicos from 1909 to 1925.

distinguished these nondominant groups from the five leading ones. First, these nondominant groups were not so cohesive, as evidenced by the smaller number of shared ventures. Perhaps they invested in fewer ventures together because they had little interest in strengthening group ties, had limited access to capital, or both. Second, these groups invested less in physical capital, unlike the dominant finance groups. Consequently, their firms failed to grow rapidly and remained relatively small or medium in scale. In most cases, these groups depended on self-financing, which curtailed company size.

Formation of Merchant Finance Groups

The extant literature demonstrates a relatively diverse perspective on the role played by immigrant entrepreneurs and merchant finance groups in Argentina's industrial growth. In the 1960s, scholars focused on the role of immigrant manufacturers and tried explaining how these foreign entrepreneurs failed to successfully expand industry before 1930.[19] They argued that manufacturers of the late nineteenth century were largely of immigrant status, lacking sufficient political power or modern entrepreneurial skills to develop a modern industrial sector.[20]

Recent historiography, however, centers on how immigrant origins and merchant status helped a manufacturer's ability to raise capital and build networks to support industrialization.[21] Beginning in the late nineteenth century, merchants and persons of similar backgrounds developed informal groups. They were "linked together not by a formalised management structure but by networks of family and quasi-kin relationships."[22] In Argentina, a group had stability that went beyond financial concerns; it also had administrative, legal, and technological advantages that helped to lower transaction costs.[23] Also, if a group intended to incorporate their company, developing a group satisfied the legal requirement that at least ten members constitute the initial stockholders of a joint-stock company.[24] Culture also determined appropriate business behavior and practices for raising investment capital.[25] It was important to have networks and in some cases patron-client relationships in order to diversify sources of capital and expand the number and size of industrial companies.[26]

By the late nineteenth century, merchant groups had two incentives to invest in manufacturing. First, they could take advantage of a fast-growing and concentrated urban market to sell their wares. The market was concentrated in Buenos Aires city and expanded rapidly from the influx of European immigration. The population grew from 1.6 million in the first census of 1869 to more than 10 million by 1925[27]; nearly 20 percent of the population lived in or near Buenos Aires city. A second incentive was to take advantage of tariff protection to supply internal markets. (Beginning in 1875, the government raised tariffs on most imported consumer goods to promote and protect domestic industry). By the early 1890s, some merchants established firms in Buenos Aires to become manufacturers. For example, the mercantile firm of Masllorens Hermanos imported finished wool textiles from Spain.[28] By 1898, they had established their own woolen mill in Buenos Aires to replace the import of finished merino wool and cashmere products.[29] Masllorens established its woolen textiles mill under a tariff rate of 30 percent for woolen textiles.[30]

A mercantile background aided entry into manufacturing in at least three ways. First, merchant financiers developed lending and credit systems through their affiliated banks and wholesale suppliers. This was a significant advantage given the considerable start-up capital needed to begin large-scale manufacturing. Some merchant financiers borrowed from their affiliated financial institutions. For example, the four leading directors of Argentina Fábrica de Papel held directors' seats in two of Argentina's largest banks, Banco de la Nación and Banco de la Provincia de Buenos Aires.[31] Two directors, Angel and Tomás Estrada, borrowed from Banco de la Nación for the paper company's first mortgage loan.[32] Altogether, the directors of Argentina Fábrica de Papel borrowed 122,019 paper pesos (nominal) from the Banco de la Nación between 1892 and 1896 and 1.38 million paper pesos (nominal) from Banco de la Provincia de Buenos Aires between 1906 and 1916.[33] This paper company was also a major client of Banco Francés del Río de la Plata. Three of the paper firm's board members also sat on the board of Banco Francés. Among these directors, Henry Py was both president and director of Banco Francés from 1892 to 1914 and was a major decision maker in how bank funds were lent.[34] Two other directors, Ernesto and Jean Maupas, also sat on the boards of both Argentina Fábrica and Banco Francés. For the most part, Argentina Fábrica had access to numerous sources of finance thanks to the connections of its directorial board. As a result, the company was able to borrow a relatively large amount for the period, permitting owners to establish Argentina's largest paper manufacturing firm. This firm nearly monopolized the nation's paper industry.

In addition, merchant financiers established credit arrangements with retail and wholesale suppliers. In turn-of-the-century Argentina, merchants used their established credit arrangements with European suppliers to purchase and import manufacturing machinery. For a long time, European suppliers had been extending credit to Argentine merchants, permitting them to purchase finished consumer goods.[35] The customary payment term extended by European cotton mills to Argentine importers was six months.[36] Merchants obtained similar credit terms for imported manufacturing machines and raw materials. Masllorens Hermanos, for instance, imported textile machinery from Spain, as well as high-quality cashmere and merino wool yarn from Spanish distributors.[37]

A second advantage that eased merchant financiers' entry into manufacturing was the fact that only a few senior men on the directorial board exercised control over a company. These senior directors could make policy decisions without lengthy or divisive discussion with their fellow directors. They often had some management experience and were relatively wealthy; they were expected to purchase the majority of the company's voting shares.[38]

Voting control over the company through ownership of its stock gave these leading directors the ability to make company decisions quickly, such as choosing management personnel, selling real estate, and negotiating contracts. Directors also decided on how to distribute financial reserves and whether to acquire another company to enhance market power.[39] Given the importance of voting shares, directors effectively limited their sale to close business associates or relatives. The board often consisted of the firm's president, some of his relatives, managers, and a few trusted friends. It was common for board members to share social or familial relationships independent of business affairs. They were careful to prevent outsiders from acquiring shares with voting rights. Nearly all of the directors of the wool textile firm Baibiene y Antonini, for instance, were related.[40] Similarly, in the 1890s Bemberg's partners in Quilmes brewery were relatives and trusted business associates.[41]

A key to the success of leading merchant groups was having leaders with the ability to quickly execute decisions. These leaders were keen on protecting their status within the company, controlling voting shares, and insulating the company from external disruptions or interference. In one litigation case against Quilmes Brewery, for instance, the Bemberg Group sought to maintain control of the company's voting shares. In this case, Juan Baenninger, a director of the breweries Schlau and Quilmes, had died in December 1919. In his will, he left his estate, including his Quilmes and Schlau shares, to his wife, three children, and a sister.[42] Baenninger was an engineer and director-manager for Schlau brewery when the Bemberg Group purchased it. In lieu of cash payment, he received voting shares, a directorial seat on both Quilmes and Schlau, and a 3 percent annual dividend from Schlau's profits. After he passed away, the family sought release of a portion of the shares for sale at market value and payment of the annual dividend of 3 percent. The Quilmes board of directors, however, refused to release his voting shares or make special dividend payments as requested by the inheritors. Initially, Quilmes's lawyers argued to dismiss the case because the family had not "proven their legitimate status as rightful heirs of Juan Baenninger."[43] Then the lawyers argued that Quilmes's bylaws clearly indicated shares were not transferable. The legal question posed by the lawsuit was whether such bylaws could trump application of Argentina's inheritance laws. But the case also shows that it was difficult for outsiders, in this case the rightful family heirs, to obtain voting shares. During the mediation, the directors offered to buy the family out by paying them the nominal value of his Quilmes stocks. The court eventually ruled in favor of Quilmes because the firm's bylaws clearly stated that voting shares were not transferable without the consent of the directorial board. In the end, the Baenninger family seems to have been paid only the nominal value of Quilmes stock.[44]

A third advantage easing merchants' entry into manufacturing was their established practice of selling goods on consignment or receiving partial payment until goods were sold. Merchant groups entered consignment and partial payment contracts with trusted distributors and retailers. The advantage was that their goods were placed on retailer shelves before those of their competitors, who were bound by traditional purchase arrangements. In practice, the sale of goods could take several months. Some merchant groups could wait for payment because they had other sources of income and did not rely on the income of one company. It was common for these manufacturing companies to report that up to 50 percent of the assets on the balance sheet were accounts receivable. In such a case, half of a firm's accounting value was anticipated income from consignment and partial payment contracts.

In sum, most merchant groups shared several characteristics as to how they initially formed and operated on first entering manufacturing. The main reason for investing in manufacturing was the promise of substituting their products for imported goods. Groups had at least three advantages that eased entry into large-scale manufacturing; as merchants they had a successful track record in obtaining finance capital and credit, securing corporate governance and control, and selling products on consignment.

Five Leading Finance Groups

The five leading finance groups were successful in attracting capital through their established and informal alliances to foreign and domestic bankers, merchants, businessmen, politicians, and companies. These alliances helped them expand the reach of influence and acquire a good reputation among outside investors. By the early twentieth century, these groups were known for their diverse investments as well as their concentration in specific industries (Table 4.1). The Bemberg group, for instance, was known as a promoter of the brewery industry. The Tornquist group was dominant in the metallurgy sector, and the Soulas Group was prominent in woolen textiles. The Devoto group was known for its stake in Compañía General de Fósforos, the Banco de Italia y Río de la Plata, and the Compañía Fabril Financiera. The Paper group promoted the growth of the paper industry; by 1926, it owned the largest such corporation, Papelera Argentina.

The founders of each group established networks and investments early in their careers. Although in most cases these were not traditional family firms, they contained certain features resembling them, such as succession handed down to a close male relative.[45] The case of Otto Bemberg (1827–1895) demonstrates how a leading member might begin his network and investments. Otto arrived in South America in the 1850s and married into a wealthy porteño family.[46] Once settled, he exported Argentine grains and imported manufactured goods.[47] Within a relatively short time, he established a network of trusted clients and financiers. In the 1860s, he and his wife moved to Paris.[48] In Paris, Bemberg continued his trading business and developed another network of trusted partners in France. By 1886, Bemberg and his French and Argentine partners had pooled capital to start a distillery in Argentina. After its initial success, Bemberg, his partners, and his son, Otto Sebastián (1858–1932), started the large-scale brewery Argentina Quilmes in 1887.[49] It was built primarily with French finance capital and supplied with French machinery.[50] By 1889, Quilmes was Argentina's largest brewery. After Bemberg Senior passed away, Otto Sebastián took over the business. His intention was likely to pass Quilmes onto his sons because he sent them to study brewery engineering in Europe.[51] Otto Sebastián maintained business with his father's partners and established new networks to continue to share information and expand investments.

Members were loyal to their groups; they trusted each other as a result of their business ties, consistent interaction in social clubs, and close geographic proximity[52] to each other (working and living in or near Buenos Aires city). Also, as members continued to invest together, they developed complicated webs of interlocks that kept members in close contact with each other and helped reduce the cost of monitoring one another. Company bylaws typically required that directors have a residence near the financial and corporate headquarters—in most cases, Buenos Aires city. The close proximity reduced the costs involved in setting up a time to meet, providing office space, and arranging correspondence. Such informal and relatively inexpensive networks allowed corporate members to quickly convene and make company decisions.[53] Although most company bylaws required one board meeting per year, the directors (particularly senior leaders) met more often to finalize decisions. Finance houses furnished the physical space where members could regularly meet and discuss investment projects. Generally, finance houses had multiple duties: lending capital to the groups' ventures, lending to known agents, serving as a retail center, participating in the import and export of merchandise, and functioning as a meeting center. Tornquist members, organized under the corporation Ernesto Tornquist y Compañía, for example, and held their meetings at their finance house to discuss their current and future investments.[54] Between 1874 and 1908, Don Ernesto Tornquist (1842–1908) and his trusted partners expanded their finance house's credit and trading services, increased business connections, and invested in a variety of activities.[55] On Ernesto's death in 1908, his partners and sons continued to meet at the finance house to discuss group operations and spread its investments.

Members had certain advantages in protecting their position as insiders, such as being privy to information about potential investments and other company news. But they were expected to be loyal to the group. Take the case of the Devoto group, which owned the match firm CGF, and the cotton textile Compañía Nacional de Tejidos y Sombreros.[56] In 1906, this textile company promised to become Argentina's largest hat and cotton manufacturer. But it began to fail around 1908. According to the company, the increasing costs of cotton and fuel, and the inability to raise prices thanks to the import of competing products, were reasons for failure.[57] The leading directors did not sell their individual interests and attempted to save the company. In 1910, the company curtailed its operations to reduce costs by producing only hats. Other group members followed the directors and did not withdraw their investment. Indeed, all group members remained invested until the company's official bankruptcy in 1912. Jorge Sábato argued that typically Argentine investors moved their capital very quickly among firms.[58] The Devoto group, however, could have been atypical in that members had more to gain in the form of an insider relationship and wealth if they remained loyal to the company and group. These insiders may have also feared being excluded from future investments if they pulled out of the failing textile company. They likely did not want to be perceived as disloyal and lose their privileged position within the Devoto group.

In less cohesive groups, members would liquidate a company if it failed to perform well for a few years. In this case, there was little or no incentive to stay in a slow or poor investment; instead the rewards were potentially great for moving capital elsewhere. In 1913, for instance, Hilario H. Leng, associate of the finance house Roberts, Leng y Compañía, was a major investor and president of two paper companies, Fenix and Fábrica Casati de San Nicolás.[59] His paper companies did well financially and even had double-digit profits between 1911 and 1921.[60] Beginning in 1922, however, both companies began to have losses. Rather than keep his investments, Leng elected to sell his Casati shares in 1924 and his Fenix shares in 1926 to the new giant paper corporation Papelera Argentina.[61] In lieu of cash payment, Leng received shares and a coveted seat on the board of directors of Papelera Argentina.[62] Leng's finance house acted as an agent for British investors, but he was free to choose independent investments. Hence Leng felt free to withdraw from the failing paper companies.

Over time, the reputation of the five groups under study increased as they invested in a larger number of companies and became associated with successful businesses. They made these reputations through a combination of talent, wealth, cooperation, discipline, and experience garnered from past behavior and decisions.[63] An example of such reputation building was Ernesto Tornquist, who married into a wealthy merchant family and took over its well-reputed international trading house in 1874. He increased the success of this trading house by expanding his international and domestic networks. His trading house became a finance house extending commercial credit and investing widely across activities. Part of his success also came from his connections to European financiers, which he initially established through networking broadly.[64] Before his death in 1908, he was an active member in business and social clubs, participated in politics, and held diverse investments that he managed through his finance house. His group's investments were in agriculture, beef, sugar, metallurgy, real estate, and various other manufacturing activities, which they managed through the finance house.[65] Ernesto also played a small role in helping to build Argentina's financial credit system.[66] He was described by his peers as a "man of vision and action"[67]; this was a reputation that continued even after his death and passed onto his sons. By 1906, Ernesto Tornquist y Compañía became a legal corporate entity whose board of directors consisted of Ernesto's close business associates and his two sons, Carlos Alfredo and Eduardo. After Ernesto's death in 1908, the group continued operating under the name of Ernesto Tornquist y Compañía and his associates continued to expand the number of businesses they owned and managed. Carlos substantially increased the group's investments over the course of his lifetime. The group obtained a substantial amount of outside capital partly because of the reputation Ernesto had built for the company.[68]

Once a favorable business reputation was established, members sought to protect and enhance it. A good reputation reduced the problems that resulted from poor communication between company insiders and outsiders. Dominant groups typically published reports, albums, and company histories in a number of languages for domestic and international investors. The company histories would trace the humble beginnings of the company directors or original founders[69]; these publications portrayed the directors as innovative entrepreneurs who helped build industry in Argentina. Such publications helped maintain the directors' image as successful businessmen and industrialists. Members also used their connections with journalists and editors to publish articles on a firm's excellent performance. In most cases, these articles embellished a company's role in the economy. A reporter from *La Nación*, for example, commended Quilmes brewery for being the leader in the brewery industry and importing modern machinery and techniques.[70] He failed to mention, however, that Quilmes was experiencing excess productive capacity and labor problems.[71]

Companies controlled by the five groups also appeared far more frequently than those of other firms in such international business journals as the *Review of the River Plate* and the *South American Journal* and *River Plate Mail*. These journals were targeted at foreign businessmen seeking relatively safe and profitable investments. Readers of such journals would frequently encounter the names Bemberg, Tornquist, and others. The *Review of the River Plate* even followed the social events of Carlos Alfredo Tornquist. For the most part, Carlos was well known among the international business community. He was even invited to be Argentina's delegate at the international finance conference sponsored by the League of Nations.[72] The Tornquist Group also started a magazine, *Revista TAMET*, that discussed all occurrences at their large-scale metallurgy firm TAMET. Also, Carlos Alfredo helped publish and write the annual introduction to the journal *Business Conditions in Argentina*. This English-language journal began in the early twentieth century to give international investors (particularly from Britain and the United States) relevant information about Argentina's economic conditions. These publications introduced outside investors to the leading manufacturing companies.

Most reputable members were invited to sit on other manufacturing companies' boards. New or less prestigious firms benefited by having reputable members sit on their board of directors; it signaled to potential investors that it was a legitimate enterprise and worthy of support. In some cases, members invited onto a board eventually took over the company. Palermo Brewery, for example, was performing badly after 1919 owing to high material costs, labor problems, and relatively low demand.[73] In 1922, members from the Bemberg group appeared on Palermo's board of directors. The owners of Palermo likely invited members of the prestigious Bemberg group to help restructure the firm. By 1923, Bemberg members became the major shareholders and bought director equity shares,[74] which gave Bemberg members substantial control over Palermo's operations.

SOURCES OF FINANCE

Dominant groups initially used funds from their own banks or finance houses to establish manufacturing firms. In the late nineteenth century, their banks were set up with funds from the groups' mercantile activities and were a good source to finance mortgages and buy imported machinery. The Demarchi family, for instance, established the Banco de Italia y Río de la Plata, and the Devoto family founded the Banco de Italia.[75] These families merged their banks and then used funds from the combined Banco de Italia y Río de la Plata to finance the merger and reorganization of three match companies. The three firms were then reorganized to become the large-scale match firm Compañía General de Fósforos in 1888.[76] Similarly, in 1903 Eduardo Soulas used his capital sources to refinance and reorganize the woolen textile firm Campomar.[77] Soulas became a major shareholder and the company was renamed Campomar and Soulas. In 1919, the Soulas group acquired another woolen textile company, Masllorens Hermanos. In both cases, the group used funds from their finance house, Eduardo Soulas Financiera y Comercial, and their affiliated bank, Banco de Avellaneda, to acquire and reorganize their acquisitions.[78]

Some of the groups' affiliated banks were relatively large.[79] The Devoto group's Banco de Italia y Río de la Plata represented 23–29 percent of all Argentine banks' paid-in capital (gold pesos) between 1902 and 1917 and 21–25 percent from 1918 to 1929.[80] Members of the Paper group sat on the boards of several banks: Banco Francés del Río de la Plata, Banco de la Nación, and Banco de la Provincia de Buenos Aires. The latter two were Argentina's largest, holding a substantial amount of all banks' paid-in capital. The Banco de la Nación, for instance, consistently held more than 40 percent of all paid-in capital between 1903 and 1914. Argentina's well-established banks typically held a substantial amount of reserves that did not mobilize in the economy and were used as a contingent liability fund.

One advantage in borrowing from an affiliated institution was that groups could negotiate debt and create special ad hoc terms for their companies. For example, in 1914, the glass company Cristalerías Rigolleau borrowed a mortgage loan of 850,000 gold pesos from the finance house, Ernesto Tornquist Comercial, Industrial y Financiera.[81] Between 1914 and 1917, Argentina suffered a sharp economic decline because of foreign capital shortages and interruption of trade during the First World War. During this period, Rigolleau began selling below cost and profits declined.[82] In 1919, the directors reorganized the company including rewriting bylaws and renewing the mortgage with Tornquist's finance house. Although the Rigolleau family maintained management control, Rigolleau needed its financiers. Carlos Tornquist and Otto Bemberg, for instance, held one thousand preferred shares each and helped finance the company.[83] President of the company Gastón Rigolleau negotiated a favorable loan discounting settlement with Tornquist's finance house. (Both Carlos Alfredo and Martin E. Tornquist sat on Rigolleau's board of directors.) The new negotiated terms would have reduced the loan to 700,000 gold pesos by 1919.[84] The contract stipulated that by the early 1920s, the original mortgage would be reduced to less than 400,000 gold pesos as a result of annual discounting and amortization.[85] In the original contract, the Tornquist finance house would have lost some of the loan value, but it likely benefited by gaining greater control of Rigolleau's operations. By March 1921, the loan was once again renegotiated and renewed for 750,000 gold pesos and the debt was sold as mortgage bonds (debentures).[86] In this instance, Rigolleau expanded its operations relatively quickly because of its connection to a finance house, which was willing to renew and negotiate flexible loan terms. Few companies under study enjoyed such a privileged relationship with a creditor.

Although the finance capital from the groups' banks and finance houses were important sources of capital for their manufacturing projects, companies expanded quickly once they had access to outside capital by selling long-term bonds (debentures) and nonvoting shares (preferred series A shares) to outsiders. These two issues had lower risk than ordinary shares and guaranteed an annual dividend but gave the stock or bondholder no voting rights.[87] The directors wanted investors' capital but did not wish to disrupt the balance of voting power over their company. Outside capital played a key role in ensuring long-term growth and stability. A group's reputation as successful owner-managers of manufacturing firms aided in attracting outside capital and maintaining investor confidence.

Successful directors raised significant amounts of equity capital by issuing preferred shares and bonds with a guaranteed interest rate. Cristalerías Rigolleau and Piccardo Tabacos, for example, offered a fixed annual return of 7.5 percent on preferred shares to attract investors. Groups paid dividends annually, even when profits were low or companies incurred losses. They used reserves to make dividend payments, or they paid out a slightly lower dividend.[88] They paid dividends to maintain investor confidence and promote their reputation as stable performers and successful owner-managers. In some cases, directors raised more than one million pesos by selling preferred shares and bonds. For instance, the Devoto group's CGF issued stock (ordinary and preferred) every few years so that paid-in capital increased over time. CGF increased its paid-in equity from 3 million in 1904 to more than 29 million by 1930.[89] Similarly, the tobacco firm Piccardo increased its paid-in capital from 7.5 million in 1914 to 45.5 million by 1920.[90] These companies also sold ordinary stock to insiders, but the sale of stock and bonds to outsiders helped the company expand rapidly.

These outside sources of capital were particularly important in times of crisis. In 1921, for instance, Talleres Metalúrgicos had a large loss and depleted its reserves to cover that year's setback of more than 570,000 Argentine paper pesos. The company also drew on paid-in equity capital to pay off debt. Thereafter, the directors planned to strengthen its financial position by first requesting that their wealthy shareholders buy a new issuance of equity shares.[91] The company then offered nonvoting preferred shares and bonds with a guaranteed fixed annual interest rate to attract outside investors.[92] Talleres Metalúrgicos's directors based their appeal for investors on their personal reputation as sound businessmen to weather this temporary setback. In this manner, the firm increased equity capital during its crisis, raising equity from 2.9 million paper pesos in 1920 to 6.6 million paper pesos by the end of 1921.[93] By 1924, Talleres Metalúrgicos was performing well, expanding operations, and negotiating a merger with six other metallurgy firms.[94]

Directors used their capital in at least two ways: to build a high level of initial paid-in equity and to invest in physical capital. First, directors preferred to keep paid-in equity high because it afforded the company stability. Although the Argentine Commercial Code of 1889 did not impose minimum capital requirements for incorporation, most successful firms under study had initial paid-in equity ranging from 100,000 to well over 1 million Argentine paper pesos.[95] Aggregate census data made it clear that only a few manufacturing firms actually incorporated because this entailed additional transaction costs such as legal expenses, taxes, and greater government scrutiny. Initial paid-in equity depended on what the first group of directors and shareholders could contribute. Having more than one million pesos in initial paid-in equity signaled that the company claimed a substantial number of wealthy directors and perhaps outside capital support.

Dominant groups sought to maintain such high equity as a source of stability and long-term survival through the often volatile Argentine business cycles of the early twentieth century. In a financial downturn, company losses could range from 50,000 to one million pesos.[96] If a firm had little equity relative to debt, such a loss could easily result in insolvency; one or two bad years could lead to losses amounting to nearly half of existing paid-in equity and reserves. Although losses amounting to less than half of the subscribed capital did not obligate owners to declare bankruptcy, most liquidated and sold company assets to pay creditors.[97] Others were compelled to do so because they had no financial reserves or other resources to weather the downturn. In 1909, the small match company Unión Fósforos, for instance, had a loss amounting to 16 percent of owners' equity in its first year of operations. It failed to recover from this first loss, and the debt-to-equity ratio increased from 0.873:1 in 1909 to 1.852:1 in 1910. The company directors borrowed additional short-term funds from some of their own, but in 1911 they decided to shut down operations because they feared greater losses if they failed to liquidate the company.[98]

The second way in which the directors used finance capital was to invest in their physical plant and expand physical operations. Directors invested in machinery and factory installations because it gave their company an advantage in economies of scale. They justified this expense on the expectation that they could produce more output and drive competitors out of internal markets. Buying up-to-date machinery or entering a new market helped reinforce their status as businessmen seeking additional profitable opportunities. In one case, the Bemberg group established the brewery Del Norte in the northwest Andes region of Argentina. The group paid substantial sums to acquire and transport machinery and technicians from Europe to the interior of Tucumán province. Del Norte was the only brewery in the region, but it failed to profit during its first decade of operation, 1913–1922.[99] Nevertheless, the Bemberg group did not liquidate the company or sell its interest. If it had done so, the group would have recouped only a fraction of the investment. Also, it would have been difficult for Bemberg to sell Del Norte because no other group had sufficient interest in purchasing the firm. Under such conditions, it was better for Bemberg investors, including both members of the group and outsiders, to continue their investment in Del Norte. Directors' reports during this period urged outside investors to be patient; profits were in Del Norte's future.[100] The reports also implied that the Bemberg group would ensure profitability by monopolizing the beer market in northwest Argentina. Indeed, there were no other competitors with similar production capabilities in the region that could effectively compete with Del Norte.[101] The group also began massive advertising to attract consumers.[102] By 1923, Del Norte began making profits.

These five dominant groups had the ability to raise capital despite a fluctuating business environment and an underdeveloped financial system. They had access to diverse capital resources to protect the company from failure. They could rely on reputation to raise capital from outside sources and maintain investor confidence. This was particularly important during a national crisis or business downturn, when it was difficult to obtain any type of credit.

Nondominant Groups and Their Sources of Finance

By contrast, nondominant groups relied less on outside sources of finance and loans and depended more on directors' funds and self-financing. As a result, these groups' investments were fewer in number and their companies remained small to medium-scale. In most cases, the groups had bank affiliations and some even had ties to foreign investors. But they were affiliated with smaller financial institutions that had less equity capital because they reached fewer clients. For example, the Banco Argentino Uruguayo and Banco de Galicia y Buenos Aires were two well-known banks in Buenos Aires city, but they had paid-in equity capital that represented only 3 percent of all banks' paid-in capital (in paper pesos) in 1929.[103] Companies remained relatively small to medium-scale for three reasons: there were insufficient funds in these banks to expand investment, groups did not want to take on debt, or they failed to efficiently use debt to develop.

Smaller groups were fortunate if they could develop links to external sources of capital. There were relatively good investment opportunities in Argentina, as in railroads, infrastructure, government and bank bonds, and bonds of well-established manufacturing firms. Most large-scale investment came from Europe, which turned problematic after 1914 when these European investors reduced investment abroad.[104] A few medium-scale companies, however, managed to obtain capital from foreign sources, particularly if they gave this source some control of company operations. For instance, owners of the lead manufacturing firm Elaboración General del Plomo had ties with a Spanish lead mining company, G. A. Figueroa, from 1916 to 1929.[105] In 1924, after the Figueroa company obtained additional shares in Elaboración, Figueroa financed the aluminum division in Elaboración's factory.[106]

For the most part, smaller groups tended to self-finance and borrow from directors to start and expand projects. Companies such as Unión Herradores (metallurgy), Elaboración General del Plomo (lead), and Baibiene y Antonini (wool textiles) listed directors' and owners' names on the liability side of the balance sheet. Why did smaller joint-stock companies rely on directors and profits rather than on loans or outside investment for their capital needs? Fernando Rocchi contends that small companies' reliance on self-financing had less to do with being denied for bank credit and more to do with the manufacturing culture of the small owner who wanted to build a large firm "through hard work, obsessive saving, and a driving passion for success."[107]

Such self-financing, however, often hampered growth and long-term survival. For example, the directors of Unión Fósforos noted the limitations of relying on directors' resources and self-financing to raise capital.[108] In 1906, they borrowed money from their directors and from a local bank to finance purchase of secondhand machinery, factory installation, engineers, and skilled workmen. They used the factory and their directors' personal property as collateral for the bank loan. Unión Fósforos directors also rented sections of their factory to bring in additional income. Though the directors believed they had adequately financed Unión Fósforos, the company slumped in 1909 when match prices dropped. Unión Fósforos reported it was selling below cost and needed higher revenues to cover costs and remain in business. Between 1908 and 1910, the company had a nominal average of 4.5 percent return on physical capital and 10.6 percent return on equity.[109] Although it was earning income, these profits were insufficient because the company was indebted to the directors and the bank. In 1911, the company declared bankruptcy after only three years in business.

For nearly all companies, the early years of operation were usually the least profitable, with losses common. In most cases, even successful firms had to endure volatile profitability. Companies that failed typically did so within the first decade. They often failed because they did not have consistent access to capital resources in the form of long-term loans, stock subscriptions, or outside capital. Their dependence on reserve funds rendered them at risk of failure once those funds were depleted. The directors of Unión Fósforos, for instance, discussed how all income in their first three years of operation barely covered the costs of production.[110] As a result, the company failed to build additional reserves, could not weather a downturn, and eventually liquidated.

Self-financing companies were particularly vulnerable during a downturn and could not raise additional equity. Between 1925 and 1930 the losses of the woolen textile firm Baibiene y Antonini compelled owners to try selling their stock. In the panic, the stock value collapsed and there were no new investors. The company's paid-in equity decreased from more than one million pesos in 1925 to 752,000 pesos by 1930.[111] The directors acknowledged the company's losses and financial problems but suggested the company would recover at some future date.[112] Owners of small or medium-scale firms could not rely on a new infusion of outside capital during a crisis. In most cases, small-scale firms simply curtailed operations and hoped their company could survive the downturn.

What was the source of smaller companies' instability or poor performance? According to most directors' reports, excess domestic and foreign competition rather than a need for capital was a major reason for their problems. For example, in 1926 directors of Fosforera Argentina attributed poor performance to competitive forces from its large-scale rival, CGF. Fosforera monitored its output carefully in order not to start any price wars with its larger rival.[113]

Other sources, however, indicate that nondominant firms were indeed capital-starved. Court cases of the time show a large number of family-owned, small or medium-scale companies suing customers and distributors for payment for goods purchased on credit. In most cases, the amounts involved were relatively small, often less than 500 pesos.[114] Litigation over such small amounts demonstrated that these firms were exceedingly dependent on collecting all capital owed to them. In one case, Baibiene and Antonini sued a customer for a mere 86 paper pesos in 1912.[115] By contrast, dominant groups wrote off such small amounts and simply used their reserves to cover such incidental losses.[116] Nondominant groups also seemed to have a difficult time enforcing collection of small debts even when the arbitration ruled in their favor. In the late 1890s, the metallurgy company Chientelassa Hermanos sued a client for failing to pay for machinery sold on credit.[117] The judge in the case ruled that the client had to pay Chientelassa Hermanos (the client, however, lived in the province of Tucumán and the Buenos Aires court could not enforce its judgment there).[118] In general it was difficult for small companies without connections in a region to collect payments due to them.

In Argentina, inefficient capital markets did not prevent the start of manufacturing but did limit the size and competitiveness of the manufacturing sector. Smaller and nondominant groups relied on self-financing, which limited the size of their ventures. These companies could not effectively compete with well-established and large-scale companies that tapped into diverse sources of capital. These small companies also remained relatively capital-starved because they had limited access to outside sources of finance. They posed little competition to the companies owned by the five business groups.

The leading five groups obtained capital through several sources. They developed and nurtured alliances with bankers, company directors, merchants, and other entrepreneurs to help them maintain these capital sources. Members' repeated transactions and contact helped increase their trust for each other and encouraged additional investment. Over time, these groups' reputation developed and became a source that was used to obtain alternative and additional sources of finance capital. Although most groups had access to capital through their affiliation with banks and finance houses, they needed additional capital to expand. Leading members obtained outside investment in part through the sale of company bonds and nonvoting shares.

Chapter 5

Manufacturing Profits and Strategies, 1904–1930

Leading finance groups developed strategies to cope with distress in the business environment. Among the five leading groups under study one finds methods such as diversification, self-financing, merging, and political lobbying to control the environment. The overall intent of these strategies was to protect the investment by concentrating their sector. For most groups, it was "in their ultimate interest to secure autonomy and an unchallenged control over crucial sectors of the economy."[1] Before 1930, Argentine regulation did not make it illegal to concentrate a sector. Although an Anti-Monopoly Law was passed in 1923, it was difficult to establish a violation; it largely functioned as a warning and did not lead to the arrest of anyone before 1930.[2] Hence leading directors publicly reported that merging with rivals and lobbying for protection were good ways to obtain greater market share.

Argentine groups' aversion to risk dominated in the strategies they created to protect their companies. Qualitative data from domestic company reports and the representative industrial lobby, Unión Industrial Argentina (UIA), demonstrate that corporate owner-managers perceived an unusually hostile economic and legal environment. They closely scrutinized the fluctuating macroeconomic climate and ongoing tariff debate in Congress. Owners had significant power in internal decision making but felt vulnerable when changes outside their control affected company productivity or significantly raised manufacturing costs. They often blamed external factors for lower-than-expected company performance. Although there were obstacles to industry, managers may have exaggerated and sought to overcome them by concentrating their sector. In part, it was the leading groups' strategy to consolidate their sector that helped create a concentrated manufacturing sector in Argentina prior to 1930.

The principal sources in this chapter come from two original datasets. The first set gathers information from 795 balance sheets and income statements of fifty-nine manufacturing companies between 1904 and 1930.[3] Financial statements are particularly valuable thanks to their extensive collection of information on company operations.[4] Profits are estimated from these financial statements. I used two cost-accounting methods to calculate profits. The first estimate is return on stockholder's equity, which is net income divided by stockholder's equity. The second calculation is return on physical capital, which is net income divided by physical capital. The methods in this chapter are preceded by works using firm-level financial statements and profitability to assess a company's performance.[5] The second original dataset was also used in Chapter 4 and is a compilation of information about the 1,282 company directors and prominent shareholders that owned fifty-nine companies.[6]

Qualitative data comes from company historical records, annual stockholder's meeting minutes, and annual directors' reports between 1900 and 1930.[7] Annual reports provided information on a company's performance, end-of-the-year profits, sales, and expected earnings and show how directors kept in front of Argentina's macroeconomic conditions. Synopses of annual stockholder meeting minutes were published in the *Monitor de sociedades anónimas* beginning in 1904. These synopses provided the results of directorial elections and discussed the distribution of profits. This information made it possible to follow how directors reinvested profits. It should be noted that directors' reports can be self-serving as well as dishonest regarding a company's financial situation. Therefore, using a variety of both qualitative and quantitative data can complement and yield additional information.

The following section of this chapter examines how economic cycles and tariff legislation affected company profit rates from 1904 to 1930. This section uses the profit data of fifty-nine companies to measure profit and volatility (manufacturers' main assessment of performance was profit and sales growth data). The third section analyses group strategies. Finally, the shortcomings and limitations of their efforts and strategies to achieve economic independence and concentrate sectors are assessed.

Profits, Business Cycles, and Tariffs

Argentina's fluctuating business cycles between 1890 and 1930 have been well documented in the primary and secondary literature.[8] The Bank of London and South America described Argentina's business climate as one where an investor could make a "fortune" or "lose their shirt" from one day to the next.[9] Although conditions were likely not so severe, indeed Argentina had significant growth, but it oscillated and was characterized by spurts as well as periods of recession and recovery.[10] Most scholars argue that Argentina's dependence on international markets for its agro-exports made it "vulnerable to instability in the world economy."[11] In actuality, the nation's downturns were precipitated by myriad conditions: changes in international prices, international war, bad harvests, annual precipitation, domestic disturbances, labor problems, and so on. These growth patterns resembled short-run macroeconomic variations.[12] Fluctuations, however, are relatively common in all countries, particularly in small and fast-growing new economies.

OBSERVATIONS IN THE PROFIT DATA

How were manufacturing profits affected by fluctuations in the economy? Manufacturers under study often complained that macroeconomic instability hurt their profitability.[13] Nevertheless, estimates of average profits showed that all industrial sectors under study except textiles and paper enjoyed double-digit profit rates from 1904 to 1930 (Tables 5.1 and 5.2). The average profit rate for other manufacturing companies producing finished consumer goods such as butter, shoes, and alcoholic beverages also exceeded 10 percent during this period.[14] Manufacturing industries generally had returns higher than those of government and bank bonds during this period; government bonds yielded on average 4.5–6 percent from 1900 to 1930,[15] and domestic bank bonds yielded between 2 and 8.5 percent from 1914 to 1929.[16]

Table 5.1.   Average Annual Rates of Return by Industrial Sector, 1904–1930 (Ten Activities, Fifty-Nine Firms, Nominal Values, Percentages)

Sector	(N)	Average return on physical capital (%)	Average return on stockholder's equity (%)
Brewery	7	15.2	13.9
Burlap sack	4	49.0	10.0
Cement	2	1.6	11.4
Glass	3	15.8	13.0
Match	3	18.0	13.2
Metallurgy	10	23.3	16.8
Paper	6	2.4	3.8
Soap	1	9.2	9.2
Textiles	15	1.0	1.6
Tobacco	8	43.4[a]	10.2

Source: Calculations by this author, financial statements dataset (March 2003). Data from balance sheets and income statements (795 financial statements recovered from fifty-nine companies, 1906–1930) in *MSA, BOB, BORA*.

[a] Tobacco companies typically reported low amounts invested in physical capital.

Table 5.2.   Average Annual Returns and Standard Deviation of Profit Rates,
Fifty-Nine Firms, 1904–1930 (Organized by Industry and Company)

Company name, years[a]	Yield on capital stock		Yield on stockholders' equity	
	Average	Standard deviation	Average	Standard deviation
BREWERY				
Argentina Quilmes, 1909–1915, 1924–1930	18.8%	8.9	29.1%	29.1
Argentina San Carlos, 1914–1930	11.0%	6.3	9.9%	5.2
Buenos Aires, 1906–1930	14.1%	9.4	10.4%	5.0
Del Norte, 1913–1930	4.2%	10.6	3.1%	11.1
Palermo, 1904–1930	14.1%	14.1	10.8%	6.6
Río Segundo, 1906–1930	12.1%	4.5	10.7%	4.1
Schlau, 1909–1930	32.4%	24.9	23.0%	11.9
BURLAP SACK				
Bolsalona, 1921–1930	11.1%	6.5	8.6%	5.0
Del Sel, 1921–1930	−5.4%	27.2	−5.2%	15.2
Primitiva, 1905–1930	80.1%	155.5	19.2%	23.3
Salinas, 1910–1930	110.3%	216.9	17.5%	40.4
CEMENT				
Argentina Cemento Pórtland, 1916–1930	17.4%	17.8	23.8%	24.7
Cemento Argentina, 1910–1911	−14.3%	42.0	−1.0%	9.6
GLASS				
Papini, 1913–1930	11.7%	11.4	11.6%	11.1
Rigolleau, 1907–1930	4.4%	5.2	6.3%	7.2
Compañía General de Envases, 1910–1930	31.3%	30.9	21.2%	19.0
MATCHES				
Compañía General de Fósforos, 1904–1930	35.7%	23.4	18.7%	8.7
Fosforera Argentina, 1909–1930	13.8%	23.3	10.2%	17.9
Union Fósforos, 1909–1910	4.5%	13.9	10.6%	35.0
METALLURGY				
Acero-Platense, 1905–1911	7.8%	7.4	8.6%	8.3
Anglo-Argentine Iron and Steel Company, 1925–1930	33.7%	20.1	42.6%	39.2
Cantábrica, 1905–1930	33.5%	43.1	14.4%	15.5
El Eje, 1905–1930	45.9%	30.4	17.5%	10.1
Elaboración General del Plomo, 1909–1930	14.4%	6.9	15.7%	6.8
Ferrum, 1911–1930	38.0%	27.8	23.7%	14.0
LaMetal/Thyssen-LaMetal, 1922–1930	36.4%	39.7	21.6%	26.9
Talleres Metalúrgicos/ TAMET, 1909–1930	6.3%	6.3	5.8%	4.7
Unión Fundición y Talleres, 1907–1930	11.8%	4.2	13.1%	4.7
Unión Herradores, 1910–1913	5.0%	11.5	5.3%	9.6
PAPER				
Americana, 1906–1908	4.8%	2.1	7.5%	2.4
Argentina, 1906–1924	11.2%	6.3	11.4%	6.3
Buenos Aires, Fábrica de Papel, 1906–1909	−22.0%	43.3	−16.1%	31.8
Casati, 1911–1925	5.8%	12.1	6.0%	12.6
Fenix, 1915–1924	2.6%	10.1	3.9%	12.9
Papelera Argentina, 1925–1930	12.2%	4.6	10.3%	3.8
SOAP				
Compañía de Productos Conen, 1910–1930	9.2%	14.1	9.2%	12.1

Company name, years[a]	Yield on capital stock		Yield on stockholders' equity	
	Average	Standard deviation	Average	Standard deviation
TEXTILES				
Argentina de Tejidos, 1921–1924	−26.7%	24.4	−11.8%	9.8
Argentina de Tejidos de Punto, 1926–1930	14.6%	17.8	4.6%	3.7
Baibiene y Antonini, 1923–1930	−3.7%	27.3	−0.9%	20.9
Campomar y Soulas, 1922–1930	25.7%	18.0	16.2%	9.8
Compañía Nacional de Tejidos y Sombreros, 1904–1910	7.2%	8.3	3.8%	3.9
Cotonificio Dell'Acqua, 1914–1920	8.6%	13.5	9.4%	17.8
Dasso-Crotto, Hilandera Argentina de Sisal, 1923–1929	−27.7%	13.1	−26.2%	12.4
Fábrica Argentina de Alpargatas, 1908–1930	21.7%	10.7	17.3%	8.2
Hilandera Argentina, 1919–1925	5.5%	5.9	8.1%	8.1
Hilanderías Argentina de Algodón, 1906–1912	−25.2%	27.4	−15.0%	16.4
Manufactura Algodonera Argentina, 1925–1929	6.4%	3.0	5.7%	2.5
Masllorens, 1924–1930	13.8%	8.6	10.6%	6.2
Sedalana, 1925–1930	20.3%	14.0	11.7%	5.7
Textil Argentina, 1919–1927	−17.3%	62.6	−4.7%	17.8
Textil SudAmericana, 1911–1921	−8.1%	11.5	−4.1%	6.6
TOBACCO				
Argentine Tobacco Company, 1912–1918	28.4%	22.8	4.6%	3.4
Ariza, 1915–1917	2.2%	16.6	2.5%	7.2
Defensa, 1921–1930	91.3%	153.8	7.8%	9.8
General de Tabacos, 1909–1911	19.0%	9.1	21.1%	6.5
Introductora de Buenos Aires (Cigars), 1904–1930	87.8%	131.7	14.9%	8.7
Nacional de Tabacos, 1913–1930	9.2%	39.5	0.7%	12.8
Piccardo, 1914–1930	66.1%	19.6	14.5%	7.0
Tabacalera Argentina, 1914–1930	[b]	[b]	15.5%	9.1

Source: Calculations by this author, financial statements data set (March 2003). Data from 795 companies' balance sheets and income statements, 1906–1930, *MSA, BOB, BORA.*

[a] Years that balance sheets and income statements were available.

[b] Company reported zero value for physical capital.

These double-digit averages are relatively high, but insufficient to determine yearly profit volatility. Because most owners reported volatile cycles as potentially damaging, it is necessary to determine annual profit fluctuations for each company. One way to reasonably determine profit volatility is to estimate the standard deviation of annual profit data for each company. The mean of the profit rate is a good indicator of how a firm performed on average over the period from 1904 to 1930. But it cannot show the degree to which profits fluctuate from the mean from year to year. The standard deviation is a statistic indicating the spread of the data around the mean. In this context, the standard deviation expresses the fluctuation of annual profits for each company. Simply put, a small number of standard deviation indicates there is little fluctuation in the annual

Table 5.3. Company Average Profit Rates and Standard Deviation, 1904–1930
(Organized by Ownership Group Category): Yield on Capital Stock

Ownership code	Company name, years[a]	Avg. profit rate (%)	Standard deviation
	GROUP 1[b]		
1	Americana, 1906–1908	4.8	2.1
1	Manufactura Algodonera Argentina, 1925–1929	6.4	3.0
1	Papelera Argentina, 1925–1930	12.2	4.6
1	Cristalerías Rigolleau, 1907–1930	4.4	5.2
1	Hilandera Argentina, 1919–1925	5.5	5.9
1	Talleres Metalúrgicos/ TAMET, 1909–1930	6.3	6.3
1	Argentina Papel, 1906–1924	11.2	6.3
1	Compañía Nacional de Tejidos y Sombreros, 1904–1910	7.2	8.3
1	Masllorens, 1924–1930	13.8	8.6
1	Cervecería Argentina Quilmes, 1909–1915; 1924–1930	18.8	8.9
1	Cervecería Buenos Aires, 1906–1930	14.1	9.4
1	Fenix Papel, 1915–1924	2.6	10.1
1	Cervecería Del Norte, 1913–1930	4.2	10.6
1	Casati, Fábrica de Papel, 1911–1925	5.8	12.1
1	Compañía de Productos Conen, 1910–1930	9.2	14.1
1	Cervecería Palermo, 1904–1930	14.1	14.1
1	Campomar y Soulas, 1922–1930	25.7	18.0
1	Piccardo Tabacos, 1914–1930	66.1	19.6
1	Anglo-Argentine Iron and Steel Company, 1925–1930	33.7	20.1
1	Compañía General de Fósforos, 1904–1930	35.7	23.4
1	Cervecería Schlau, 1909–1930	32.4	24.9
1	Ferrum, 1911–1930	38.0	27.8
1	Introductora de Buenos Aires (cigars), 1904–1930	87.8	131.7
1	Tabacalera Argentina, 1914–1930	*c*	*c*
	GROUP 2[d]		
2	Unión Fundición y Talleres, 1907–1930 (British)	11.8	4.2
2	Cervecería Río Segundo, 1906–1930 (British)	12.1	4.5
2	Bolsalona, 1921–1930 (Bunge y Born)	11.1	6.5
2	Elaboración General del Plomo, 1909–1930 (Spanish)	14.4	6.9
2	Fábrica Argentina de Alpargatas, 1908–1930 (British)	21.7	10.7
2	Cotonificio Dell'Acqua, 1914–1920 (Italian)	8.6	13.5
2	Sedalana, 1925–1930 (domestic banking group)	20.3	14.0
2	Argentina Cemento Pórtland, 1916–1930 (U.S.)	17.4	17.8
2	Argentine Tobacco Company, 1912–1918 (British)	28.4	22.8
2	Fosforera Argentina, 1909–1930	13.8	23.3
2	Hilanderías Argentina de Algodón, 1906–1912 (British)	−25.2	27.4
2	LaMetal/Thyssen-LaMetal, 1922–1930	36.4	39.7
2	Cantábrica, 1905–1930 (Spanish)	33.5	43.1
	GROUP 3[e]		
3	Cervecería Argentina San Carlos, 1914–1930	11.0	6.3
3	Acero-Platense, 1905–1911	7.8	7.4
3	General de Tabacos, 1909–1911	19.0	9.1
3	Cristalerías Papini, 1913–1930	11.7	11.4
3	Textil SudAmericana, 1911–1921	−8.1	11.5
3	Unión Herradores, 1910–1913	5.0	11.5

Ownership code	Company name, years[a]	Avg. profit rate (%)	Standard deviation
3	Dasso-Crotto, Hilandera Argentina de Sisal, 1923–1929	−27.7	13.1
3	Union Fósforos, 1909–1910	4.5	13.9
3	Ariza Tabacos, 1915–1917	2.2	16.6
3	Argentina de Tejidos de Punto, 1926–1930	14.6	17.8
3	Argentina de Tejidos, 1921–1924	−26.7	24.4
3	Del Sel, 1921–1930	−5.4	27.2
3	Baibiene y Antonini, 1923–1930	−3.7	27.3
3	El Eje, 1905–1930	45.9	30.4
3	Compañía General de Envases, 1910–1930	31.3	30.9
3	Nacional de Tabacos, 1913–1930	9.2	39.5
3	Cemento Argentina, 1910–11	−14.3	42.0
3	Buenos Aires, Fábrica de Papel, 1906–1909	−22.0	43.3
3	Textil Argentina, 1919–1927	−17.3	62.6
3	Defensa, 1921–1930	91.3	153.8
3	Primitiva, 1905–1930	80.1	155.5
3	Salinas, 1910–1930	110.3	216.9

Source: Data calculations by this author, financial statements dataset (March 2003). Data gathered from 795 companies' balance sheets and income statements, 1906–1930, *MSA, BOB, BORA.*

[a] Years that balance sheets and income statements were available.

[b] Group 1 are firms owned, acquired, or purchased by one of the five finance groups under study (see Table 4.1).

[c] Company reported zero value for physical capital.

[d] Group 2 are firms owned by another finance group, foreign or domestic. In parentheses are the origins of initial owners; no parentheses indicate domestic company.

[e] Group 3 are companies owned by independent entrepreneurs.

profit data. A large number indicates that the profit rates are diverse and spread wide around the mean.

The fifty-nine companies were divided into three cohorts on the basis of ownership, to determine whether ownership mattered in profit size and volatility. The first cohort contains twenty-four companies that were owned or acquired by at least one of the leading five business groups under study. These five groups—Tornquist, Bemberg, Devoto, Soulas, and Paper—diversified their holdings in a number of activities and were recognized for their industrial investments. In the second cohort, thirteen companies were owned or acquired by smaller yet important domestic and foreign business groups that had connections to finance and domestic politics. Two companies in this group had a prominent political figure on the directorial board, conceivably helping the company obtain finance capital.[17] Members owning companies in this second cohort could be influential, but they were less known in some cases than the leading groups from cohort 1. Finally, the third cohort gathers the remaining twenty-two companies, which were owned by domestic and independent manufacturers not associated with the other groups under study. The owners of cohort 3 had limited ties to other finance groups, banks, or politics. Con-

Table 5.4. Company Average Profit Rate and Standard Deviation, 1904–1930 (Organized by Ownership Group Category): Yield on Stockholders' Equity

Ownership code	Company name, years[a]	Avg. profit rate (%)	Standard deviation
	GROUP 1[b]		
1	Americana, 1906–1908	7.5	2.4
1	Manufactura Algodonera Argentina, 1925–1929	5.7	2.5
1	Papelera Argentina, 1925–1930	10.3	3.8
1	Compañía Nacional de Tejidos y Sombreros, 1904–1910	3.8	3.9
1	Talleres Metalúrgicos/ TAMET, 1909–1930	5.8	4.7
1	Cervecería Buenos Aires, 1906–1930	10.4	5.0
1	Masllorens, 1924–1930	10.6	6.2
1	Argentina Papel, 1906–1924	11.4	6.3
1	Cervecería Palermo, 1904–1930	10.8	6.6
1	Piccardo Tabacos, 1914–1930	14.5	7.0
1	Cristalerías Rigolleau, 1907–1930	6.3	7.2
1	Hilandera Argentina, 1919–1925	8.1	8.1
1	Introductora de Buenos Aires (cigars), 1904–1930	14.9	8.7
1	Compañía General de Fósforos, 1904–1930	18.7	8.7
1	Tabacalera Argentina, 1914–1930	15.5	9.1
1	Campomar y Soulas, 1922–1930	16.2	9.8
1	Del Norte, 1913–1930	3.1	11.1
1	Cervecería Schlau, 1909–1930	23.0	11.9
1	Compañía de Productos Conen, 1910–1930	9.2	12.1
1	Casati, 1911–1925	6.0	12.6
1	Fenix, 1915–1924	3.9	12.9
1	Ferrum, 1911–1930	23.7	14.0
1	Argentina Quilmes, 1909–1915; 1924–1930	29.1	29.1
1	Anglo-Argentine Iron and Steel Company, 1925–1930	42.6	39.2
	GROUP 2[c]		
2	Argentine Tobacco Company, 1912–1918 (British)	4.6	3.4
2	Cervecería Río Segundo, 1906–1930 (British)	10.7	4.1
2	Unión Fundición y Talleres, 1907–1930 (British)	13.1	4.7
2	Bolsalona, 1921–1930 (Bunge y Born)	8.6	5.0
2	Sedalana, 1925–1930 (domestic banking group)	11.7	5.7
2	Elaboración General del Plomo, 1909–1930 (Spanish)	15.7	6.8
2	Fábrica Argentina de Alpargatas, 1908–1930 (British)	17.3	8.2
2	Cantábrica, 1905–1930 (Spanish)	14.4	15.5
2	Hilanderías Argentina de Algodón, 1906–1912 (British)	−15.0	16.4
2	Cotonificio Dell'Acqua, 1914–1920 (Italian)	9.4	17.8
2	Fosforera Argentina, 1909–1930	10.2	17.9
2	Argentina Cemento Pórtland, 1916–1930 (U.S.)	23.8	24.7
2	LaMetal/Thyssen-LaMetal, 1922–1930	21.6	26.9
	GROUP 3[d]		
3	Argentina de Tejidos de Punto, 1926–1930	4.6	3.7
3	Cervecería Argentina San Carlos, 1914–1930	9.9	5.2
3	General de Tabacos, 1909–1911	21.1	6.5
3	Textil SudAmericana, 1911–1921	−4.1	6.6
3	Ariza Tabacos, 1915–1917	2.5	7.2
3	Acero-Platense, 1905–1911	8.6	8.3
3	Cemento Argentina, 1910–1911	−1.0	9.6
3	Unión Herradores, 1910–1913	5.3	9.6

Ownership code	Company name, years[a]	Avg. profit rate (%)	Standard deviation
3	Argentina de Tejidos, 1921–1924	−11.8	9.8
3	Defensa, 1921–1930	7.8	9.8
3	El Eje, 1905–1930	17.5	10.1
3	Cristalerías Papini, 1913–1930	11.6	11.1
3	Dasso-Crotto, Hilandera Argentina de Sisal, 1923–1929	−26.2	12.4
3	Nacional de Tabacos, 1913–1930	0.7	12.8
3	Del Sel, 1921–1930	−5.2	15.2
3	Textil Argentina, 1919–1927	−4.7	17.8
3	Compañía General de Envases, 1910–1930	21.2	19.0
3	Baibiene y Antonini, 1923–1930	−0.9	20.9
3	Primitiva, 1905–1930	19.2	23.3
3	Buenos Aires, Fábrica de Papel, 1906–1909	−16.1	31.8
3	Union Fósforos, 1909–1910	10.6	35.0
3	Salinas, 1910–1930	17.5	40.4

Source: Data calculations by this author, financial statements dataset (March 2003). Data gathered from 795 companies' balance sheets and income statements, 1906–1930, *MSA, BOB, BORA.*

[a] Years that balance sheets and income statements were available.

[b] Group 1 are firms owned, acquired, or purchased by one of the five finance groups under study (see Table 4.1).

[c] Group 2 are firms owned by another finance group, foreign or domestic. In parentheses are the origins of initial owners; no parentheses indicate domestic company.

[d] Group 3 are companies owned by independent entrepreneurs.

sequently, companies in the third cohort tended to be smaller than those in cohorts 1 and 2.

The results on volatility show clear patterns between a company's profit volatility and ownership (Tables 5.3 and 5.4). Those organized in group 1 had one company failure, but for the most part these companies' profits demonstrated the least volatility. The standard deviation indicates that profit averages of nearly all companies in the first cohort were more stable than those of companies in the other two cohorts (Figures 5.1 and 5.2). Companies in the first cohort had less profit volatility; those in business never had losses and always earned income for each year under study (Figures 5.3 and 5.4). Most companies in group 1 did not have the wide and fluctuating range of profits seen among those in the third cohort.

Only two companies in the second cohort fared poorly. Most were relatively successful, and a few benefited from their connections to foreign finance capital. The canvas textile company Fábrica Argentina de Alpargatas, for instance, was affiliated with the British financial institution Leng, Roberts, and Company (Roberts Group).[18] Directors used this access to foreign capital and network to help their company. In 1921, Fábrica Argentina overextended itself financially with construction of a new building and import of new machinery. Consequently, the Roberts Group negotiated with an affiliated institution to "rescue" the company by buying

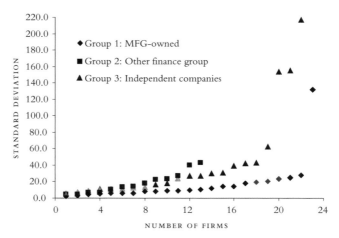

Figure 5.1. Standard Deviation of Individual Companies, Organized in Group Categories for Comparison, 1904–1930:Yield on Capital Stock. *Note:* Data from Table 5.3. Each point represents one company.

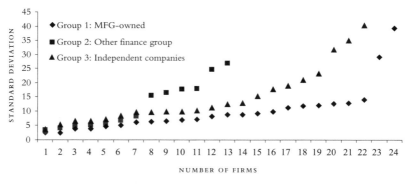

Figure 5.2. Standard Deviation of Individual Companies, Organized in Group Categories for Comparison, 1904–1930: Yield on Stockholders' Equity. *Note:* Data from Table 5.4. Each point represents one company.

the firm's debt at discount.[19] Because Argentina did not have a discount house, it was important for directors to negotiate other ways to transfer or sell debt.

Finally, most of the twenty-two companies in the third cohort had considerable profit volatility. They were particularly vulnerable to economic cycles and other external factors, resulting in volatile profit rates. These rates ranged from negative 27.7 percent to almost 225 percent. Because profits fluctuated wildly, these companies struggled to survive. Companies

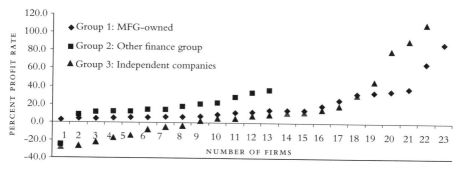

Figure 5.3. Company Profit Averages, Organized in Group Categories for Comparison, 1904–1930: Yield on Capital Stock. *Note:* Data from Table 5.3. Each point represents one company.

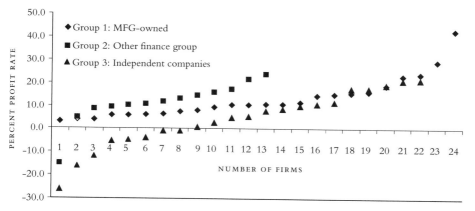

Figure 5.4. Company Profit Averages, Organized in Group Categories for Comparison, 1904–1930: Yield on Stockholders' Equity. *Note:* Data from Table 5.4. Each point represents one company.

in group 3 were most likely to self-finance, so if profits fluctuated widely perhaps it was difficult for managers to operate the company without a steady annual income flow. Nearly half of the firms in the third cohort were acquired, were liquidated, or went bankrupt within ten years of start-up.

Another worthwhile observation of profit averages is that it appears that most companies in group 2 and a few in group 3 had higher profit averages than those in group 1 (Figures 5.3 and 5.4). Group 1 companies had stable, albeit not spectacular, profits, but these companies were in a better position financially and technologically than companies in the other two cohorts. Directors of group 1 companies had the advantage of being able to invest in updated machinery and expand connections to international and domestic finance capital. As discussed in Chapter 4, the leading five groups had access to capital from a variety of sources that helped their companies' remain stable and perform well. Outside capital likely lessened the influence of adverse external factors on profitability.

Groups' investment in physical capital can be assessed from the asset side of the balance sheet and used to estimate yield on capital stock. Return on capital stock was higher than return on equity for most companies because some were not purchasing new equipment and machinery. In such a case, net income appeared larger when divided by the smaller value of capital stock. Smaller firms hung onto aging machinery and equipment to control capital costs; manufacturing corporations that invested little in machinery consistently had a high rate of return on capital stock. For example, the metallurgy company El Eje, founded in 1905, invested regularly in capital improvements until 1912.[20] Then it curtailed operations and investments to reduce debt. Between 1912 and 1930, El Eje's balance sheet showed neither new debt nor capital improvements, and as a result return on capital stock regularly exceeded 10 percent during this period.[21] Similarly, most tobacco companies under study did not replace capital equipment and reported an extremely low value for machinery and buildings. In some cases, tobacco companies allowed their physical capital to depreciate to one peso, in which instance the rate of return on capital stock was inadequate as a measure of performance.

PROFITS AND TARIFFS

Leading groups were aware of their companies' privileged position and sought to maintain it by portraying a hostile and competitive financial environment. By doing so, they hoped to influence the legal climate to help them against foreign competition. For instance, in a public letter by the finance house Ernesto Tornquist y Cía, it heralded itself as "eminently nationalist . . . that fights and continues to fight with the powerful competition from foreign banks."[22] It contended that foreign banks took advantage of Argentina's "deficient banking system" by collecting deposits, taking this capital away from domestic manufacturing, and using it to develop trade and commerce in their own countries.[23]

This image of hostile foreign competition was maintained by leading manufacturers, protectionists, and the UIA to demand protection from the rivalry of foreign manufactured products. Argentine manufacturers often reported that the absence of protective tariff legislation hurt their profitability. The UIA upheld that Argentina's underdeveloped industrial sector was due to the lack of "good legislation to promote industrialization" and the absence of a "true customs law" that would take into account real prices.[24] Protectionists asserted that the "tariff structure was hopelessly inadequate, characterized by protectionism-in-reverse."[25] Some industrial advocates blamed industrial underdevelopment on the government's hostility toward domestic industry.

What were Argentina's tariff rates? Nominal tariff rates were 25 percent ad valorem for most imports of finished consumer goods between 1881 and 1923.[26] There were numerous revisions to the tariff law that increased rates for specific products before 1923. Law 11281 of 1923 raised tariff levels across the board to reflect real market prices. Most products had a rate between 35 and 50 percent, while goods with specific duties had an even higher rate. Another attribute complicating tariff duties was that there was a "tariff rate escalation from raw to finished goods" between 1909 and 1927.[27] The tariff rate was influenced by several factors, such as the strength of competing political players to protect specific goods, the government's need to raise revenue, and the influence of industrial lobbyers. Although the Argentine tariff was not explicitly protectionist, this sentiment appears in the tariff schedule beginning in 1906. For instance, a common practice in Argentina and in protectionist countries was to raise duties on finished products but allow nearly duty-free inputs of raw materials, fuel, and machinery.[28] Also, certain agro-industries such as sugar, flour, and wine enjoyed effective protection. After 1927, the number of activities with such protection increased in Argentina.[29] In the early twentieth century, Argentina's import tariffs were said to be comparable to those of the United States, and at times equal or slightly higher than for France, Germany, or Australia.[30]

How did tariff levels affect profitability between 1904 and 1930? Profit data shows that companies producing goods with high specific duties had better profits than those companies producing items without such duties. For example, the Argentine Congress passed a 40 percent duty on the price of imported burlap sacks and regulated the number of sacks to be produced each year.[31] These measures kept burlap sack prices artificially high.[32] Consequently, the burlap sack industry had some of the highest returns. In 1913, two companies, Primitiva and Salinas, had 41 and 37 percent return on owner's equity respectively.[33] In 1918, a brief economic boom in export trade pushed demand for burlap sacks; in turn, these two companies made triple-digit profits.[34] In that year, Primitiva paid a 100 percent dividend to its ordinary shareholders.[35]

In other instances, directors readily acknowledged that higher tariffs helped raise their profits. During the recession of 1914–1917, the government temporarily increased tariff duties on common consumer goods to raise revenue. The directors of the soap and candle maker Compañía de Productos Conen reported that the higher tariff helped them see higher-than-expected profits. They recorded a 6 percent loss in 1912 but delivered 35 percent return on equity in 1915.[36] This company attributed this dramatic increase to the reduction in imported candles due to the higher tariff.[37] It also reported high profits in 1916, 1918, and 1921 and credited this success to protective tariffs.

Although most manufacturers under study correlated a higher tariff level with sales growth and profitability, three other factors aided the ability to increase sales. First, revision of the exchange rate policy helped to increase sales. In 1914, Argentina went off the gold standard and in 1923 devalued the Argentine peso. The government floated the peso in the 1920s, making the international exchange rate somewhat unstable, and indeed making imported products (at least temporarily) more expensive to domestic consumers. Effectively, the "exchange rate policy from 1906 to 1940 reinforced the protectionist features of the Argentine tariff."[38]

Second, the structure of Argentina's industrial production changed substantially because of rising investment in machinery between 1900 and 1930. As discussed in Chapter 3, manufacturers imported manufacturing machinery worth £66 million (real pounds) between 1890 and 1918.[39] There was a slowdown in investment between 1914 and 1918, but it picked up again in 1919. An impressive 83 percent increase in machine investment occurred between 1919 and 1929, in which manufacturers imported more than £107.2 million (real pounds) of manufacturing machinery. Leading Argentine companies revamped their structure of production through the import of modern machinery.

A third possible reason for increased sales after 1914 was that leading Argentine businessmen tapped into new international sources of investment, and businessmen from the United States were interested in entering Argentine markets.[40] For instance, in 1924 Carlos Alfredo Tornquist sought new agents and foreign investors to help him expand his group's investments. Carlos followed his father's practice of seeking foreign business contacts.[41] He contacted Lockwood, Greene, and Company from Boston regarding his interest in importing cotton manufacturing machinery.[42] Lockwood, Greene responded in a timely manner with a friendly and detailed reply, showing interest in Carlos's idea.[43] It was a reciprocal relationship because U.S. businessmen sought Argentine markets after the start of the First World War.[44] In the 1920s, several British trade agents lamented how U.S. businessmen were leaping at business opportunities in Argentina and established commercial houses beginning in 1914. By 1921, one agent remarked how, within only six years, the National Paper and Type Company of New York had become the sole agent in Argentina for "nearly one hundred manufacturers of printing and allied trades, machinery, and paper."[45]

Despite the importance of these three factors, the tariff issue remained the primary topic of debate between the government and industrialists. The emphasis on raising tariffs was partly due to its ability to benefit both parties. Higher tariff rates could help raise government revenue and increase profits. Most important, manufacturers viewed tariffs as a safety net if their strategies failed to overcome inefficiencies in production and marketing.

Manufacturing Strategies

Manufacturers under study demonstrated the characteristics of vigorous action in the present and planning for the future, but they also sought to profit by concentrating their sector. Industrialists' aversion to risk motivated them to promote strategies that permitted a certain level of flexibility, rewarded investors, and promised higher profits in the future. Three of these strategies were diversification to increase groups' investment, accumulation of reserves, and consistent dividend payments to maintain investor confidence. Two further strategies were to merge with rivals and lobby to raise tariffs. Ultimately, directors under study sought to preserve their wealth and status, and protect their investment by reducing risk.[46]

There were challenges to manufacturing in Argentina, but the degree of the industrial problem was perhaps overestimated. Manufacturers commented on four obstacles that limited their ability to produce at low cost: insufficient demand, unreliable access to inputs of raw materials and fuel, inconsistencies in machinery maintenance, and excessive and hostile foreign competition. These problems were used to justify manufacturers' demand for higher tariffs. Increasing tariff rates became a panacea for some of these broad and diverse obstacles to successful industrialization.

First, manufacturers complained of insufficient domestic demand, noting that imported machinery offered too much productive capacity for Argentina's small domestic markets. In most cases, imported capital-intensive machines were designed to produce for consumers numbering in the tens of millions.[47] Argentina's population was growing, but still relatively small; it was estimated at a mere eleven million by 1930.[48] Despite manufacturers' claims about insufficient market demand, import data show that imports of manufactured goods increased substantially between 1890 and 1930.[49] This could indicate that there was significant demand but imports were satisfying it. Also, if purchasing power was high among consumers, it could be that consumers preferred imports. Indeed, the manufacturers' problem was not necessarily low demand and small markets but rather consumer preference for imports, or more important, directors' deficient mechanisms to accurately determine demand for their product.

Most companies under study used sales and inventories to measure demand, which could be inadequate if not complemented with other measures. For example, Fosforera Argentina followed consumer demand for their product by recording matchboxes sold each month.[50] The company adjusted its monthly output on the basis of sales and inventories. These measures can complement others to assess company performance. But Fosforera's strategy was to use this information to avoid stirring up "competitive tendencies" and unintentionally start a price war with its rival, CGF.[51] The directors' plan was to maintain a nominal sales level and avoid competition (both are measures that would not accurately measure demand).

A second obstacle to industry was input shortages of raw materials and fuel. Manufacturers complained about not having a sufficient supply of affordable raw materials and fuel. In the brewery industry, for example, malts and hops were entirely of foreign origin. Some brewers contended that there were no substitutes for these materials, and they relied heavily on international prices and availability.[52] Directors of the brewery Cervecería Palermo complained that the government should secure low prices for these items and subsidize their costs.[53] Similarly, the iron and steel industry relied on imported iron ore and scrap iron. Directors of the metallurgy company Cantábrica complained that iron shortages raised their overall costs and inhibited their ability to produce efficiently.[54] They blamed lower profit on shortages and the high cost of imported inputs. Manufacturers also blamed factory inefficiency on shortages of inexpensive fuel.

Although shortages of fuel and raw material are indeed a serious obstacle, there were three solutions to reduce the extent of these problems. First, most industries were clustered in Buenos Aires city and the coastal provinces near ports precisely because this gave companies easier access to imported raw materials and fuel. Some factories, such as Quilmes Brewery and Argentina Fábrica de Papel, were purposely located near railroad stations and river ports for greater access to inputs. Second, in 1918 some industrialists started experimenting with seeds to grow needed raw materials. For instance, Quilmes Brewery planted barley seeds to produce the malt needed to make beer.[55] They concluded that high-quality barley could be grown in Argentina and replace its import.[56] But their experiment in barley growing slowed after international trade started again at the end of the First World War; perhaps it was less expensive to import barley and malt than to grow it. Lastly, the government was aware of input inefficiencies and attempted to remedy this problem beginning in the 1910s.[57] For instance, it sponsored mining and fuel expeditions in the interior, hiring geological experts from the United States to survey Argentine soil for any minerals, iron ore, coal, and fuel oil.[58] In 1925, the geologists reported that the cost to mine domestic coal and iron ore would be excessive. The discovered iron deposits were too few, passable only by mule, and too contaminated by silicon dioxide to be useful for industrial use. The expedition, however, found small amounts of crude petroleum in southern Argentina. This was promising, but output could only partially cover national demand. The geologists' recommended that imports of fuel supplement domestic output. They expected that oil plants in Comodoro Rivadavia and La Plata would have an annual output of 730 thousand metric tons, but they were not certain.[59] Author Carl Solberg argued that the government funded petroleum plants exclusively for industrial needs and national security.[60]

A third obstacle and manufacturers' complaint was the inability to properly maintain machinery. Part of the problem was geography; there was a significant delay in importing machine parts from the Northern hemisphere to Buenos Aires. Broken machines could remain idle for a long period until machine parts and trained labor came to the factory. For example, the Unión Sociedad Anónima Cooperativa de Fósforos reported that its business failure was partly due to malfunctioning machinery and the unavailability of trained labor to fix equipment problems.[61] (The company also blamed its poorly trained labor for breaking the machines in the first place.)

Machine breakdowns, however, were likely not any worse in Argentina than elsewhere. Some firms scheduled routine maintenance and repairs. Fosforera Argentina scheduled fifteen days in September for routine maintenance.[62] In most cases, machine maintenance depended on firm size, capital resources, and owners' knowledge of technologies. Most manufacturers had the basic production capabilities to maintain machinery but might not have the funds to afford routine maintenance. Dilmus James argues that neglect of maintenance was an unfortunate but normal occurrence in most Latin American countries as late as the 1970s.[63]

The fourth and final issue commonly voiced by manufacturers was that foreign competition was an obstacle to development of domestic industry.

The UIA asserted that any foreign import of consumer goods was dangerous to local producers. Companies also complained that foreign competition through dumping (sale of foreign manufactured goods well below
cost in Argentine markets) was a serious impediment to local industrial
development. In 1929, directors of the metallurgy company Ferrum complained that they had to lower prices to compete with the "dumping of
cheap imports"; their goal was to increase sales volume while maintaining
profit level.[64]

The story of dangerous foreign competition was somewhat embellished
because before 1930 the government passed policies to protect industry
both directly and indirectly. Congress debated numerous bills as a result of
manufacturers' complaints. Congressmen replied to the demand of manufacturers to stop dumping and control imports of competing products. In
1919, the house of deputies discussed implementing an antidumping bill.
The goal of the bill was twofold: to defend domestic industry from the
"dangers of unfair foreign competition" and to maintain higher prices to
stimulate local investment in manufacturing.[65] This bill was debated in the
1920s.

Whether or not leading groups earnestly believed this image of a hostile
climate is debatable, given their continued investment in manufacturing,
growing contact with outside capital sources, and rising number of manufacturing firms in the 1920s. It is clear, however, finance groups were a
risk-adverse lot that sought government support as a safety net in case their
strategies failed to help them succeed in manufacturing.

Groups under study developed a variety of strategies to deal with industrial obstacles and gain control of their sectors. Two common strategies
were to (1) diversify investment to reduce risk and (2) make regular dividend payments to maintain investor confidence. First, manufacturers diversified their holdings to reduce risk from failure in any one investment.
Their pattern of expansion was to enter into a range of new activities
rather than growing within a single produce line.[66] Groups "were often
willing to take risks, but they generally aimed to preserve a large amount
of flexibility" by owning diverse investment portfolios.[67]

Second, owners paid relatively high dividends to stockholders. The
amount paid per share varied but frequently exceeded 10 percent. For example, in a good year the burlap sack company Salinas Hermanos paid a
70 percent dividend to its ordinary shareholders in 1919. In general, dividends to stockholders were higher than those offered by more traditional
investments such as government and domestic bank bonds. Manufacturers
paid between 6 and 40 percent in annual dividends (ordinary) between

1921 and 1923.[68] Government bonds yielded 2–5 percent and bank bonds yielded 6–10 percent during the same period.[69]

Although high dividends might be said to largely reward the owner-managers because they were typically the major shareholders, managers paid healthy dividends to nonvoting shares and bonds as well, which were typically held by outsiders. Even during a downturn, directors of leading companies such as Cristalerías Rigolleau and Piccardo Tabacos would pay a fixed rate of 7.5 percent on preferred shares to maintain investor confidence. Consistent remuneration assured outside investors that their investment was profitable and they would be rewarded for not diverting their capital elsewhere. The disclosure requirement of all joint-stock companies also permitted managers to report their commitment to reward outside investors. During an upturn, in addition to a dividend directors might also pay special bonuses to all shareholders.

A third strategy was to build an internal capital source by placing net income into a contingency liability fund and a cash reserve. A cash reserve was reported on the asset side of the balance sheet and functioned as a short-term fund. As an asset, this fund was available for immediate needs and was cash-on-hand. Most companies relied on contingent liability funds; these funds were normally reported as liabilities on the balance sheet. The funds were for long-term projects and for use during a downturn, when outside capital sources were difficult to obtain. Some of the numerous short- and long-term uses of this fund were to cover losses, invest in public bonds, finance expansion or improve projects, remunerate directors, and cover worker pensions.[70] Liability funds were also used as valuation reserves or an allowance to cover costs such as depreciation, bad debts, and other accounts receivable. In most cases, firms exceeded the minimum level legally required for contingent liability funds. The Argentine commercial code required that these funds equal 10 percent of shareholder's equity, but some companies held liability funds that accounted for up to 70 percent of owners' equity.[71]

Most companies viewed their contingent liability funds (reserves) as an important source of capital. The cotton textiles company Hilanderías Argentinas de Algodón placed all of its first-year earnings into a liability fund.[72] New companies typically paid lower dividends in order to place more income into reserves. In 1909, directors of Fosforera Argentina discussed paying an 18 percent dividend to their ordinary shareholders.[73] Instead, directors determined that 12 percent was a "sufficient dividend" and allocated the remaining 6 percent to reserves.[74] Company bylaws could also clearly state that profits must first be directed toward building and maintaining reserve funds before distribution to other areas.[75] Leading companies often maintained several reserve funds. Compañía General de Fósforos, for instance, created several funds to cushion profit cycles and cover worker pensions and bad debts.[76]

We analyze companies in the three group categories on the basis of ownership to determine liquidity. A liquidity ratio was determined for all fifty-nine companies under study; liquidity was measured as cash assets and contingent liabilities divided by paid-in equity.[77] The results show that the five leading finance groups typically had significant sums in reserves (group 1 companies). The twenty-four companies in the first cohort had an average liquidity ratio of 51.8 percent. This high liquidity ratio was for two reasons. First, owners had greater access to outside capital that permitted them to devote more earned income to reserves. Second, their risk-averse nature pushed them to maintain higher liquidity in case of some unforeseen distress to the company.

In contrast, companies in the other two cohorts had significantly lower liquidity ratios. The thirteen companies in the second cohort had an average liquidity ratio of 26.2 percent. The twenty-two companies in the third cohort had the lowest average liquidity ratio, 24.6 percent. Lower liquidity ratios were largely due to these companies' using reserves regularly in their business operations. Companies in the second and third cohorts used reserves to self-finance and absorb losses during a downturn. For example, in 1920 Cantábrica began setting aside money to self-finance a ten-year plan to expand operations and update machinery.[78] But by 1929, the directors suspended plans for expansion because of the sliding national economy, and voted to continue holding the money in a reserve fund.[79]

Similar to companies in group 1, directors of the companies in groups 2 and 3 reserved income to provide a safety net during periods of capital shortages. But they dipped into these reserved funds more often, so it was difficult for them to maintain high liquidity. Cristalerías Papini illustrates how smaller companies relied on their reserves to maintain investor confidence and divert bankruptcy. In 1929, Papini used reserves to pay a 6 percent dividend to maintain investor confidence during one of its worst fiscal years.[80] By late 1929, Papini again used its liability fund to absorb a loss of 183,070 paper pesos.[81] Despite these problems, reserve funds helped Papini remain in business during a five-year company recession.[82] But if a downturn was prolonged, a company might exhaust these reserves and become insolvent. Directors of Unión Fósforos blamed their failure on depletion of their reserve fund during a downturn beginning in 1908.[83] Most companies guarded against this risk by regularly placing income in their contingent liability fund.

Reserves were a solution, at the level of the firm, to the lack of estab-lished credit markets for industry. For those companies with limited access to outside capital and long-term credit, it was essential to generate income to create reserves. Managers used these funds to self-finance and protect their companies. For some companies, however, it was difficult to sustain high operating profit every year. Therefore, reliance on reserves was not an ideal solution for a company's long-term financial stability and could not adequately substitute for access to outside capital.

In a fourth strategy, directors sought to collude or merge with rivals to gain control over their respective sectors. The beer sector, for instance, attempted to control prices through a trust. In 1900, the three leading breweries, Quilmes, Palermo, and Bieckert, resolved to fix prices after a series of meetings.[84] The brewers felt justified in this course of action because beer production required substantial investment to import ma-chinery, skilled labor, and raw materials. Beer demand was also highly volatile and peaked during the summer months. They alleged they were competing with wine producers, which had an advantage selling to Span-ish and Italian immigrants who naturally preferred wine. It is unknown if this trust transpired in 1900. Profits show that Palermo's rate remained in the single digits. Bieckert and Quilmes were not obligated to publish their balance sheets because their shares were primarily foreign-owned, and foreign companies were not obligated to disclose statements in 1900.[85]

By 1909, Quilmes, Palermo, and Bieckert again discussed formation of a new beer trust to include Cervecería Buenos Aires (CBA).[86] CBA re-ported that it was not interested in joining this trust. According to CBA, the brewers' goal was to control beer output and set prices. The brewer-ies reported that this was the best way to compete with wine.[87] It is pos-sible that the trust transpired and remained in effect through 1915. The three largest breweries enjoyed double-digit profit rates during a period of national crises. Between 1909 and 1915, Quilmes and Palermo had on average 23.1 and 31.4 percent return on capital stock respectively. Return on equity was on average 38.7 percent and 6.9 percent respectively during this period. CBA, however, had lower profit rates during this same period, 10.6 percent (return on capital) and 8 percent (return on equity). Its lower return on capital could have been because it was not in the cartel, as was claimed.

By 1916, breweries were still complaining of low demand even though the number of breweries had declined and the industry was much more concentrated. The beer trust continued into the 1920s. Bieckert reported to shareholders that the "unprecedented success obtained by the Compa-ny during the past financial year [1919–1920] was due to several causes,"

Table 5.5.   Acquisitions and Mergers, 1888–1927

Primitiva, S.A. (burlap sack)
1889 Merger of Obieta, Torello, y Compañía (SC)[a] and Cramer y Compañía (SC)

Cristalerías Papini, S.A. (glass)
1896 Rafael Papini[b] legally became partnership with limited liability (SC).
1916 Merger of Papini y Compañía (SC); became limited liability joint-stock company. New finance partners: Walter Schorr and Meta Hasenbalg.

Cristalerías Rigolleau, S.A. (glass)
1907 Cristalerías Rigolleau incorporated; finance partners: Jacobo Kade and Banco Francés y Río de la Plata.
1914 Cristalerías Rigolleau expands through finance from Ernesto Tornquist y Cía.

Compañía General de Fósforos, S.A. (matches)
1889 Partnership of Ambrossio Dellacha y Hnos. (SC), Francisco Lavaggi e hijo (SC), and Bolondo y Lavigne (SC). Finance came from Banco de Italia y Río de la Plata.
1906 Acquired Bernal paper factory and phosphoric factory for match production.
1910 Acquired cotton textiles factory for match production.
1916 Acquired printing company.

Thyssen-LaMetal Compañía, S.A. (metallurgy)

1927 Merger of Thyssen, S.A. (foreign-owned) and Lametal, S.A. (domestic).
Ferrum, S.A. (metallurgy—kitchen and bath products)
Began as Oscar Schnaith y Compañía (SC).
1898 Partnership of Oscar Schnaith and Antonio Lavazza.
1911 O. Schnaith y Compañía (SC) partner with Jacobo Kade and Enrique Berduc.
1911 Company becomes Ferrum, S.A.; finance from Tornquist group.
1926 Acquired bathware company.

Talleres Metalúrgicos San Martín, S.A. (metallurgy)
Originally Rezzónico and Ottonello in 1902, became Talleres Metalúrgicos, S.A. in 1908.
1902 Rezzónico, Ottonello, y Compañía (SC); it is the merger of several metallurgy firms: Talleres "El Ancla" (SC), José Ottonello y Luis A. Huergo (SC), Antonio Rezzónico (SP).[d] Merger was financed by Ernesto Tornquist y Compañía.
1909 Additional financing came from Jacobo Kade, E. Berduc, and Ernesto Tornquist y Compañía to incorporate; name change to Talleres Metalúrgicos.
1923 Second major merger with firms Alberto de Bary y Compañía (SC); Zimermann, Noe, y Compañía (SC); Eugenio C. Noe y Compañía (SC); Talleres San Martín, Compañía Mercantil y Rural (SC).
1925 Changed legal name to Talleres Metalúrgicos San Martín, S.A.
1926 Acquired Anglo-Argentine Iron and Steel Company, S.A.

Papelera Argentina, S.A. (paper)
1888 Merger of Maupas, Estrada, Escalada, y Compañía (SC). Finance came from Banco de la Nación Argentina.
1924–1927 Papelera Argentina resulted from the merger and acquisition of the companies Argentina, S.A.; Casati, S.A.; Fenix, S.A.; and Bernal, S.A. Finance came from Banco de la Nación Argentina.
1929 Acquired La Anaíno, Fábrica de papel.

Compañía de Productos Conen, S.A. (soap)
1896 Partnership of José Conen (SP) and José Berisso (SP).
1904 J. Conen y Compañía (SC) legally incorporates. Finance comes from Jacobo Kade, E. Berduc, and Ernesto Tornquist y Compañía

Campomar y Soulas, S.A.
1904 Begins as Campomar Hermanos (SC).
1906 Soulas Financiera partnered with Campomar.

1921 Changed legal status to corporation.
1923 Acquired Masllorens Hermanos (SC).

Manufactura de Tabacos Piccardo y Compañía, Ltda.
1913 Incorporates, finance came from Tornquist Group.
1920 Acquired Compañía Argentina de Tabacos, Ltda.

Sources: Data from *Finanzas, comercio e industria,* 1898–1900 (Buenos Aires); *Álbum Argentina,* 1912; and *Revista Tamet,* Abril–Mayo 1944 (available at BTQ); "Sociedad Anónima de Tabacos Piccardo y Cia, Ltda" *Review of the River Plate,* Nov. 12, 1920, 1293; *Anuario Pillado,* 1898–1900; *Argentine Yearbook,* 1903–1906, 1910–1916.

[a] SP = Sole proprietorship; SC = Sociedad en comandita or partnership with partial limited liability; S.A. = sociedad anónima or limited liability joint-stock company.

among them "the maintaining of prices and a reasonable agreement with competitors in order to avert a reduction in prices which would have been suicidal."[88] Afterward the beer cartel apparently deteriorated on account of suspicion among brewers that others were undercutting the arranged prices. The Anti-Monopoly Law of 1923 that criminalized such arrangements might have also forced these companies to find other ways to control prices.

Leading groups found other ways to control their sector. Some acquired companies to increase the size of existing investments. The process of acquisition was a way to expand existing investments, enter new ones, and find new finance partners and business associates within a relatively short time span (Table 5.5). This technique likely ensured a company's expansion and survival. For the most part, only a few leading groups were able to finance acquisitions and mergers; they developed new ways to finance takeovers, such as offering shares instead of cash payment. In 1903, the Tornquist group purchased the trading and cigar company Introductora. Later in 1910, they used the value of Introductora's shares to purchase the shares of a kitchenware company, O. Schnaith y Cía (renamed Ferrum). The group placed these shares under the ownership of its cigar and import company, Introductora, and the finance house Ernesto Tornquist y Financiera.[89] This same group also expanded its Talleres Metalúrgicos between 1902 and 1926 by offering shares and seats on the board of the newly organized company.[90]

By the 1920s, it became commonplace for leading companies to merge with rivals. The merger to create Argentina's largest paper corporation, Papelera Argentina, illustrates such a case. In 1924, Argentina Fábrica de Papel acquired two medium-scale paper companies, Fenix and Bernal, to create the largest paper corporation in Argentina; its name changed to Papelera Argentina.[91] In 1925, Papelera Argentina reported that acquisition of rival companies was a reliable strategy for growth and profitability.[92] In

1927, the owners purchased another paper company, Casati.[93] The long-term benefits of these mergers, the directors concluded, would be realized through increased market power and profits.[94] Papelera Argentina continued to acquire other paper companies to increase its market share.[95]

In this case, paper manufacturers merged with the explicit intent to concentrate their sector and earn high profits. They felt justified in concentrating the sector because they claimed paper manufacturers had the disadvantage of "low duties" on imported newsprint. Directors explained that lower profit averages were due to low tariffs. According to congressional reports, Congress sought self-sufficiency in newsprint, but at the time the local paper industry was not producing sufficient quantities of newsprint that it could sell at low cost.[96] Congress members lowered duties on newsprint because eliminating imports would hurt consumers and national needs. Part of the problem was that paper manufacturers relied on imported wood pulp. As late as 1931, 54.4 percent of wood pulp was imported to support paper manufacturing. This reliance made it relatively expensive to produce all paper products in Argentina. Congress settled on lower duties for cotton textiles fibers, cloth, thread, carton, and duty-free newsprint because these goods were in high demand and local producers failed to provide them at a low price.[97]

Finally, the leading manufacturers' fifth strategy to ensure profitability was to lobby for protective tariffs. Manufacturers often argued that imports competed with their products and lowered profits. Although tariffs were relatively high and returns were largely satisfactory for most companies under study, manufacturers sought exclusive rights to domestic markets. (All manufactured products were intended for internal markets.) Several scholars have examined why industrialists focused on lobbying for tariff reform rather than other needed reforms such as easier access to industrial credit. This literature demonstrates the complex relationship between the government and industrialists. Rocchi contends that any "state action toward industry was an outcome of general economic policies rather than specific strategies for manufacturing" laid out by a powerful industrial group.[98] Jorge Schvarzer argues that elite industrialists' interests were largely represented before Congress. These industrial elites, represented by the UIA, were politically powerful, but "the absence of open and profound conflict" in Congress was a consequence of industrial elites' social and personal ties to political elites.[99] In congressional debate, leading manufacturers preferred to negotiate the tariff rate rather than introduce entirely new legislation to help industry. It was perhaps easier to pass higher tariff rates than to invent, debate, and pass new industry laws.

The focus on tariff reform was largely because industrialists sought a theme of discourse between government and themselves. They found a politically acceptable topic in tariff reform. Tariff lobbying was a politically motivated strategy that, if successful, would help manufacturers secure domestic markets. Manufacturers and their representative lobby, the UIA, were adamant that competition from imported goods lowered profits. They sought exclusive rights to domestic markets by lobbying to exclude imports of manufactured goods. The UIA argued that high tariffs were necessary to protect domestic manufacturing from unfair competition. According to one UIA report, domestic and foreign producers were not competing on an equal basis because foreign producers had "centuries of experience on how to produce at lower costs."[100] Imported goods were often of better quality and efficiently produced in Western Europe or the United States. Even with moderate tariffs, they were less expensive to produce and were offered at low prices to domestic consumers. Because Argentine manufacturers were new to industrialization, UIA argued, they needed compensation in the form of high tariffs as an incentive to expand industrial investment. UIA asserted that higher prices were temporary until domestic industry could compete on an equal status with foreign-made goods. But there should be no time limits on these tariff measures because domestic producers had a significant gap to close with European competitors.[101]

Leading industrialists could have pushed forth more radical policy changes, but they focused on obtaining government support to protect and subsidize manufacturing because it entailed less dramatic change to the existing economic and financial policies. In most cases, government policies were limited and often reinforced the leading groups' position of market power. Tariff legislation across Latin America was typically a political compromise between parties rather than the outcome of long-standing debate on how to develop a solid industrial plan.[102]

Shortcomings of the Manufacturers' Strategies

The risk-averse nature of the industrialists and the need to control their sectors resulted in strategies that were at times short-sighted and neglected two major issues facing all Argentine manufacturing companies: an inadequate banking and stock market system and the concentrated nature of investment by a few groups.

Argentina's financial system was relatively well developed in comparison with most of Latin America, but underdeveloped in comparison to banks in developed nations.[103] Banks had restrictive lending practices, limiting loan amounts and payment terms. The country had ways to channel and accumulate capital, as through family networks and investment groups; but these groups faced the limitation of having few investors making decisions on what and how much to invest in a venture. Personal capitalism limited how many transactions were made between lenders and borrowers. These informal arrangements, rather than anonymous transactions, put lenders in touch with a limited number of borrowers.

Smaller companies were most likely to bear the consequences of personal capitalism. Without a connection to a bank or finance group, these companies lacked easy access to long-term industrial credit. Most of these companies relied on the slow path of reinvesting profits and building reserves for their growth. Also, small companies in need of finance capital that borrowed from one of the finance groups' financial institutions typically or inevitably rendered some control of their company to the lending finance group.

Argentina's underdeveloped stock market also adversely affected industry in two ways. First, share prices in developed markets can serve as an evaluative mechanism for factory managers.[104] But managers without an adequate stock market lacked a "standard criteria for evaluating their performance, either for purposes of self-assessment or for comparison with rival groups."[105] Without any standard, most directors used profits and sales growth to assess the health of their company. These can be adequate indicators if complemented with other evaluating mechanisms, but biased in an environment of devaluation, recession, or inflation. For example, during a downturn leading large-scale firms increased their sales volume to retain profitability. The owners of Fábrica Argentina de Alpargatas reported increasing sales by 30 percent between 1929 and 1930.[106] But returns failed to increase by the same percentage and had reached only a level similar to the previous fiscal year. Although this may have been a success story given the economic environment of the period, the directors of Fábrica Argentina remained highly concerned as they reported increasing sales in 1929 but without a real or even nominal profit increase.[107]

Also, Argentina's stock market (bolsa) had limited investment opportunities for new and small-scale investors. Although the leading finance groups raised capital on the Argentine stock market, for most owners this was an unreliable way to attract new investors and raise capital. Rocchi contends that part of the problem was the small size of the stock market. When activity happened, it "drove prices well above the nominal value and restrictively beyond the reach of new small-scale investors."[108] Few companies actually incorporated and publicly sold their shares because the Buenos Aires bolsa offered few opportunities to small-scale industrialists seeking a consistent flow of incoming capital. By contrast, in Brazil new urban companies in São Paulo could establish themselves in one year and expand within the next because the Sao Paulo investment community "appears to demonstrate a great deal of impersonal, unrelated investment."[109] In this case, the São Paulo stock market worked as an effective means to raise capital for new companies.[110]

Investment in the most important manufacturing companies was also concentrated in the hands of a few well-known groups. Although leading groups expanded investment, they also tended to create a "situation where a relatively small number of economic agents controlled a large share of private assets in the modern sector of the economy."[111] The five leading groups did not push away new investors, but they created an environment where it was easier to invest or transact a major business deal if a connection existed with a group member. For example, once the merger of Papelera Argentina was completed, the directors were excited to announce the arrival of their new and prestigious director, Hilario H. Leng (who was from the Roberts Groups and accepted the directorship rather than cash payment for his two paper factories) and their new shareholders from CGF.[112] (In 1926, in lieu of cash payment, CGF opted for 82,027 shares, series B, in Papelera Argentina for the sale of their paper company Bernal.[113]) All parties were well known in the financial and business community and associated with a leading and established finance group. All had much to gain by this connection, such as new ties to potential capital sources and dividends from Papelera's expected future earnings. After this transaction and similar ones in other sectors, connections between the most important domestic investors grew closer, concentrating capital and manufacturing firms.

Chapter 6

Political Economy of Industrial Legislation

Believing in a consistent industrial policy that could fill all needs over time defined an ideal goal, but conciliation characterized the debate about developing a long-term industrial policy. Between 1875 and 1930, industrial legislation to protect and promote industry was a recurring discussion in Congress. Adjustment of the tariff rate was viewed as the primary way to develop industry and was often debated among government officials, congress members, industrial advocates, and opponents. Few other topics that were related to industry received the level of attention in Congress the tariff rate did. It remained an important debate in Congress because it did not pose a real challenge to existing economic policies of the period. Also, given the number of tariff revisions, the tariff policy was arguably flexible. It was frequently revised to meet the demands of a selected number of manufacturers at one point in time, but perhaps not all simultaneously.

The debate to increase tariffs gained momentum after the First World War brought on material shortages and economic uncertainty. Supporters of industry underscored the need for economic diversification by developing the industrial sector. They argued that protective tariffs were the means to protect and develop domestic industry. Supporters also sought to achieve national self-sufficiency.

There existed a counterpoint in government, albeit diminished, that stressed the need to foster internal competition. As debate about protective policies grew in the 1920s, some congressional deputies voiced concern about industrial concentration. These congressmen argued that strong protectionism was leading industry toward monopoly and oligopoly. Through their efforts, Congress enacted two laws to ease the entry of small corporations into manufacturing and combat monopolies. It passed the Anti-Monopoly Law of 1923 and the Limited Liability Law of 1932 to simplify incorporation of smaller firms. Both measures were intended to increase competition among domestic firms. But weak enforcement of the Anti-Monopoly Law and the strict regulation of the Limited Liability Law did little to change Argentina's concentrated industrial structure. Instead, these laws helped reinforce the existing noncompetitive structure of small firms working alongside large-scale firms.

Despite growing legislation aimed at protecting and guiding industrial development, these laws did not create a competitive and sustainable industrial sector. Tariff policies in particular were short-sighted and largely enabled established companies to gain greater control over their industrial sectors. After 1930, protective industrial legislation grew. New entrants were small-scale and inefficient producers relying on the government's industrial programs for their survival. Argentine industry developed a structure that endured through the 1980s whereby a handful of modern and large-scale firms that dominated domestic production were surrounded by a constellation of small and inefficient, almost artisan shops.[1]

This chapter examines industrial legislation to demonstrate that its failure to promote successful industrialization stemmed partly from the absence of a well-defined plan from 1900 to 1930. It analyzes how and why tariff protection became closely associated as a necessity for the development of industry. For most of the twentieth century, tariff rate increases were the outcome of compromises among political players, including political parties, regional interests (interior provinces), the industrial lobby, and manufacturers. Each group had its own agenda but expected to benefit, at least partially, from a compromise on tariff levels. For instance, higher tariffs could help the government raise revenue, aid agro-industries of the northwest interior in dominating internal markets, and increase company profits. But if import tariffs were too high the government would not benefit because consumers stopped buying imports. At the same time, other interests sought to lower or eliminate tariffs on raw material, fuel, and machinery inputs for production. In the end, modifications to the tariff rate show the ability of political groups to compromise and find the best politically motivated and short-run solution to industrial development.

Data

The principal sources of data for this chapter are three Argentine serial publications reporting on the congressional deputy minutes, national economic climate, and opinion of the period: the *Diario de sesiones de la Cámara de*

Diputados de la nación, the *Revista de economía argentina,* and the *Anales de la Unión Industrial Argentina.* These sources document the political and economic debate concerning Argentine industrialization.

The *Diario de sesiones* contains the minutes and speeches of the national deputies of Argentina. Through these sources, the *Diario* reflects contemporary political thought on industrialization. The *Revista de economía argentina* was edited and published by the economist and businessman Alejandro Bunge. Its writers were the intellectual supporters of government-supported industry; they articulated the need for state-sponsored manufacturing and influenced a generation of policymakers. They collected data allegedly showing how domestic industry could grow only with the government's support. The final source was published by the leading industrial lobby, the *Unión Industrial Argentina.* The lobby published its reports, debates, and letters in the *Boletín de la Unión Industrial Argentina* (1905–1924) and *Anales de la Unión Industrial Argentina* (1925–1936).[2]

Tariff History, 1875–1914

In 1875, congress members first debated whether tariff rates should protect industry or be solely based on fiscal concerns. A practical issue was that local industry was not ready to replace imports. In that year, Congress compromised and raised tariffs for selected products in specific industries. Deputy Carlos Pellegrini was in the forefront of the protectionist movement; he believed that "all countries should aspire to develop their national industry. [Industry] is the base of a country's wealth, of its power, of its prosperity; and to achieve it she must do all possible, despite the challenges ahead."[3] At that time, however, most deputies were rightly concerned that the nation was not prepared to shut out imports with high tariffs. Beginning in 1876, tariffs on imported goods were reduced, causing deputy members Vicente Fidel López and Miguel Cané to rally against "odious" free trade, which suppressed the development of local manufacturing.[4] In 1881, tariff duties were again increased to 25 percent ad valorem. By 1906, this rate across the board was made law and the general structure of the tariff, albeit with numerous revisions, remained in effect until 1940.

Beginning in the 1880s, the tariff rate issue dominated congressional discussions. Deputies and senators from the conservative political party supported the protection of domestic industries. They were nationalistic and linked their vision of a self-sufficient and strong nation with development of the industrial sector. Other representatives from the interior provinces of Argentina were interested in higher tariffs to protect regional wine and sugar industries. In Congress, the interior was overrepresented with respect to its economic importance.[5] As a result, congressional bills about subsidies and protection of the sugar and wine industries were often discussed.

Beginning in the 1890s, the UIA represented industrialists' interests in Congress and demanded that it raise tariffs to reduce the entry of foreign manufactured goods. UIA often reasoned that the tariff level of 25 percent was based on nominal values rather than real values.[6] Therefore, existing tariffs did not genuinely protect domestic industry from foreign competition. The UIA said it was not requesting a radical change but was demanding that existing tariffs function as expected; that is, they should help local industry fight against foreign competition. The lobby claimed that imports presented an unfair challenge because domestic producers could never compete equally on account of their higher costs of production.[7] The modern production techniques of foreign companies permitted those firms to achieve economies of scale and sell at a lower price. According to the UIA, domestic industry would need a substantial period of protection to catch up with foreign producers' capabilities. Domestic firms were hobbled by high production costs associated with imported raw materials, fuel, and machinery. They argued that manufacturers relied on international prices and supply; shortages and higher prices came unexpectedly and hurt local production.

The UIA maintained that if industry were highly protected, Argentine manufacturers would eventually produce goods equal in quality to imported products. Increased tariffs, the UIA argued, would strengthen domestic industry and reduce the high level of industrial concentration because rising prices would encourage new domestic entrants.[8] The UIA also sought to combat the general perception that protection of industry led to corruption. They asserted that "protectionism was not prohibition" and would not cause shortages of consumer goods.[9] They also acknowledged that, in the past, manufacturers had abused the tariff system by producing low-quality goods or reducing supply to increase prices.[10] The UIA insisted that these were the actions of only a few "disgraceful" manufacturers.

Before 1914, those opposed to raising the tariff rate believed that industry should enjoy some tariffs but not at a protectionist level because domestic industry could not yet efficiently satisfy domestic demand. Some critics also expressed reluctance to support an industry that could function only in a protected environment. In 1910, government officials and leading economic groups helped establish committees in the Chamber of the Buenos Aires stock exchange, the Ministry of Treasury, and the Ministry of Justice to examine the growing manufacturing sector. These committees generally opposed higher tariffs and state intervention to promote industry. In 1911, the chamber's committee on commerce and industry opposed increased state intervention because it believed doing so would reduce industrial efficiency and competition.[11] The committee also noted that high tariffs raised consumer prices and decreased the quality of goods. The committee was particularly concerned that higher prices would decrease the purchasing power of the working classes; it speculated that higher prices could even spark labor unrest.[12] The committee recommended that tariffs remain at the same level. It also recommended that industrialization remain under the control of private enterprise and that national economic policies focus instead on increasing national productivity through exportation of agricultural goods.[13] By 1915, however, this group's recommendations were supported by few people. During the First World War, additional groups came to espouse the idea that economic diversification include the government's promotion of industry.

The Political Economy of the Tariff Debate

The extant literature on the tariff presents opposing views on whether the Argentine tariff was protective or too low between 1900 and 1930.[14] Early works claimed that Argentine industry failed to develop because the government was hostile toward it and aborted any attempt to protect it.[15] Essentially, the government relegated industry to secondary importance behind the agro-export sector. Scholars reasoned that manufacturers and industrial advocates lacked any political clout to push forward protectionist policies. Immigrants dominated in manufacturing but lacked citizenship and political connections. As a result, Congress failed to pass policies to please this group because there was no political benefit in doing so.[16] Another scholar made the case that the industry lobby was politically weak and could not persuade the Radical party, in power from 1916 to 1930, to implement favorable industrial legislation.[17] The Radical party was purported to support only free trade policies, which made Argentina an anomaly because it "adopted only hesitant and limited protection of its manufacturing industries during a period when many other countries were actively building high tariff walls."[18] For these scholars, insufficient government protection was a primary reason industry remained underdeveloped before 1930.

The scholarly literature also asserts that Argentine industry was protected beginning with the late nineteenth century. In a study of long-term tariff rates, for instance, Coatsworth and Williamson found that tariffs were generally high in real values in Latin America, and in Argentina tariffs were quite effective.[19] Colin Lewis contends that previous scholars "may have been excessively influenced by contemporary polemics, accepting uncritically complaints about reduced protection," and failed to take into account more objective sources.[20] Roy Hora asserts that Argentine industry may have been of secondary importance in economic growth but was of primary importance in key political and social circles.[21] Industrial advocates and lobbies had considerable political sway, and their demands for higher tariffs for certain goods and lower tariffs for inputs were commonly realized.[22] According to these scholars, Argentine manufacturing grew behind a wall of protective tariffs and remained underdeveloped precisely because it relied on tariffs and "continued to suck in imports" of inputs for the production processes.[23]

Other scholars reasoned that the Argentine tariff was neither protective nor low.[24] Rocchi contends that the tariff characterized a "midway protectionism whereby "pragmatism dominated in the tariff policy," entailing a balance between extreme groups wanting protection and others seeking very low tariffs.[25]

Discussion of the tariff has produced a rich literature that can be used to assess the implicit and explicit outcomes of the tariff debate. For Congress the goal was to partly help the manufacturing sector through higher tariffs. In particular, they selected specific goods to protect. Implicitly, the focus on the tariff to promote industry was largely accepted because a rate change did not pose a radical change from existing policies. Also, given the numerous revisions to the tariff over time, perhaps it was the most flexible policy. Groups could debate one another and compromise on a rate in exchange for other favors. Over the long run, repeated revisions to the tariff created a complicated "cascading" structure.

The rate was complicated by repeated changes over time and had several protectionist characteristics, but it was not explicitly protectionist across the board. Argentina had both specific duties for individual products and a nominal ad valorem duty between 1890 and 1930. Between 1890 and 1923, the ad valorem duty was 25 percent across the board, but numerous modifications to the tariff resulted in different rates for specific products and industries. Most consumer goods produced in Argentina typically had a higher tariff rate than those products that were not produced within its borders. But this was not a steadfast rule and some goods produced in the country had lower tariffs. Most inputs of raw materials, fuel, and machinery entered with a low tariff or none at all. Selected agro-industries such as sugar, flour, and wine enjoyed effective protection because of the political bargaining between the provinces of the interior and Congress.[26]

How was the rate determined? Was it protectionist? Three factors must be taken into account in assessing how the rate was resolved: exchange rate, the government's revenue needs, and compromises among political players. The exchange rate and government revenue needs played a part in determining the level and effectiveness of the tariff rate. As was stated in Chapter 5, devaluation of the Argentine peso, particularly in the early 1920s, made imported products more expensive to domestic consumers.[27] In that period, it reinforced the protectionist features of the tariff;[28] but the peso gained back some value after 1924.

Revenue concerns also partially determined the tariff rate. Before implementation of the Income Tax Law of 1932, the import tax covered 52 percent of the government's total income in 1900; by 1928, import taxes filled 60 percent of the government's budget.[29] Nevertheless, the government had other sources of income, as through government bonds, foreign direct investment,[30] and foreign loans. During times of crisis, however, foreign loans and investment were difficult to obtain. In such an instance, the government raised tariffs temporarily to increase income and also reduced its spending on public works projects rather than continue to raise tariffs if revenues were insufficient.[31]

Last and most important, compromises among political players helped to determine the tariff rate. These political players were quite diverse: industrial advocates in congress; intellectual groups (for example, Bunge group); the UIA lobby; congress members from the interior with regional interests; and the major critics, Socialist members of Congress who wanted to lower the tariff on imports of consumer goods because it raised prices for basic goods.

Most groups stressed tariffs rather than other policies to develop industry. Members within each group compromised on key issues to present before Congress. For instance, the UIA was structured by two competing groups, small-scale and large-scale industrialists (the UIA was meant to be representative of all industry). Small-scale manufacturers dominated in sheer numbers, but the organization was financed and directed by large-scale industrialists. To avoid a battle or split between the two groups, Schvarzer argues that they conciliated on two key themes to debate in Congress: tariffs and labor.[32]

The tariff rate remained a key topic associated with industry because it was not a radical change from existing policies. Topics that received little attention in Congress were typically those viewed as dramatically shifting away from Congress's stated goals or requiring substantial alteration of existing policies. Some industrial advocates presented other ideas but did not push for them. For example, in 1920 the UIA argued the need for an industrial bank to provide long-term credit. It asserted that Argentine industry was characterized by large firms surrounded by thousands of small shops because of the shortage of industrial credit to small firms. Congress countered that protective tariffs would generate profits sufficient for self-financing and failed to further discuss it.[33] Indeed, it was up to the UIA to pursue their demand for a state-sponsored industrial credit bank. But the tariff rate (and labor issues) remained the UIA's leading agenda item before congress.[34]

Rationale and New Support for Tariff Protection, 1914–1930

After 1914, debate regarding the tariff rate and protection of industry continued from the previous decades but saw greater intensity as the relationship of industrialization to national self-sufficiency gained broader currency. The outbreak of the First World War disrupted Argentina's ties to international markets, reduced its income from exports, and temporarily halted the inflow of European capital into Argentina; 1914 began a period of economic downfall. After the resultant economic crises, several constituencies and interest groups who were previously uninterested in manufacturing came to believe that the economy needed to be diversified and less subject to price fluctuations in international markets. After the war, these groups came to view industrialization as the key to the economic diversification and self-sufficiency that Argentina would need should international economic and political conditions once again create shortages of raw materials, fuel, and finished consumer goods.

The First World War and Argentina's subsequent economic crises marked the beginning of new strategies by pro-industry groups. The UIA and a new group led by Alejandro Bunge became more vociferous in their demand for protection of industry. They expressly linked domestic industrialization with economic self-sufficiency and independence from international markets. The UIA and the Bunge group noted that the number of new manufacturing firms increased during wartime isolation; they used this information as evidence that protectionism would decrease concentration and that the country had the ability to be self-sufficient. For these groups, the emergence of new manufacturing companies signaled Argentina's preparedness to embark on full-scale industrialization of capital and consumer goods. This successful industrialization, they contended, could be realized through heavy state promotion.

Bunge developed the political rationale for protectionism that was adopted by and influenced an entire generation of policymakers and intellectuals. Bunge spoke "in favor of industrialization and economic independence."[35] He was born into a wealthy merchant family and began his public career in 1914.[36] In that year, he began writing a series of books and articles "describing and analyzing the Argentine economic scene"[37]; he wrote on topics ranging from urban wages and housing standards to agriculture efficiency and state-sponsored industrialization. In 1918, he founded the *Revista de economía argentina* to create a forum to write about all economic issues in Argentina. The journal displayed an unusual sophistication for its period thanks to "richness in data," "quality of analyses," and ability to clearly rationalize why Argentina, an agricultural powerhouse, should develop industry.[38] The journal's contributing writers became known as the Bunge group. The Bunge group consisted of leading intellectuals and prominent Argentines who supported state-led industrialization. The group's well-articulated articles offered a clear and convincing rationale for government support of domestic industrialization.[39]

The Bunge group believed that Argentina should emulate the European countries that achieved economic independence through industrialization. In the first issue of *Revista*, a member of the Bunge group announced that Argentina did "not need to invent new theories to advance its national economy" but should merely follow the historical models of advanced countries that developed by protecting domestic industry.[40] The group also argued that in the postwar era "economic nationalism became the norm for all nations of the world."[41] The group noted that tariff and industrial policies in Europe, South Africa, Asia, and other Latin American countries were moving toward protectionism. They asserted that industrial development would inevitably raise technical efficiency, wealth, and living standards.

The Bunge group elevated domestic manufacturing as the key to national self-sufficiency and freedom from crisis in the international economy. For Bunge, sustainable growth could be achieved largely through internal industrial development, not promotion of international commercial trade.[42] He claimed that the United States, England, and Germany enjoyed the "most favorable environment" for their products, but it was time that Argentina "conquered its own markets" and removed the need for imports of consumer goods.[43] He showed that the value of annual imports of manufactured goods exceeded the value of exports, which he cited as evidence of the economy's weakness and vulnerability.[44] He argued that if domestic industry failed to develop, Argentina ran "the risk not of stagnation but of regression, of impoverishment and limited cultural progress."[45]

The UIA was among the leading industrial groups to use the Bunge group's well-crafted rhetoric of "economic nationalism and independence" to place industrial development in the forefront of Argentine politics. The UIA had already adopted a nationalist tone, but the Bunge group's more articulate expressions were widely accepted by legislators and other business interests such as the agrarian and mercantile elites.

Beginning in the late 1920s, the UIA president, Luis Colombo, overtly appealed to those with nationalist tendencies to expand industry's base of political support. He tailored the UIA's objectives to appeal to the growing workers' unions and obtain labor support.[46] Colombo argued that an industrial worker could feel proud to work for a domestic industrial firm that made products specifically for Argentine citizens.[47] In the 1920s, Colombo used radio addresses to argue that the growing labor movement should adapt state-sponsored industrial promotion as part of its agenda.[48] He said that growing unemployment could be reduced through state-backed efforts to increase the number of local manufacturing firms. The notion that greater manufacturing would lead to more employment for the growing urban population came to be one of the UIA's basic and often repeated tenets.[49] Acknowledging that tariffs increased prices for workers, Colombo contended that they would also push workers' wages upward as well.

It is worthwhile to note that although the UIA and the Bunge group argued that a strong industry would also help laborers, they valued workers only as passive commodities. Bunge, for instance, believed that workers who were engaged in "trade unionism were not merely undercutting their own livelihood, but subverting attempts to convert Argentina from a dependency of Europe into an industrial power in her own right."[50] The UIA also opposed labor legislation that cut into companies' profits; it was strictly in defense of manufacturers' rights. When Congress began debate on social welfare legislation such as the eight-hour work day and company-funded pension plans, the UIA immediately attacked these laws as irrational and viable only once Argentine industry fully matured.

In the 1920s, the UIA linked its agenda to what it characterized as the "nation's patriotic needs." In 1920, the UIA led a successful campaign for legislation mandating that Argentine-made goods be imprinted with "Industria Argentina,"[51] arguing that this mark would permit consumers to distinguish between foreign and domestic products. Colombo described purchase of domestically produced goods as an act of patriotism.[52] This demand was made into legislation by 1923,[53] but the UIA continued an appeal for clear labeling and stamping of all products, foreign and national.[54]

In this period, the UIA intensified dissemination of its message that Argentine industry needed protective tariffs to encourage new entrants and promote industrial growth.[55] It argued that protectionism had strengthened the industry and economy of other nations.[56] It further urged that protectionist measures should not be viewed as merely temporary; Argentine industry had a significant gap to close with its European competitors. Domestic industry could be successful only if it remained protected and had exclusive access to domestic markets. According to the UIA, only the government with its control over tariffs and economic policy could sustain domestic industry. The period around the First World War demonstrated local producers could successfully replace imports of manufactured goods. The UIA asserted that if consumer goods could be produced locally, imports should not be permitted to compete with these nascent local industries.[57]

The UIA also sought other measures to push industry. It demanded a long-term guarantee for duty-free imports of raw materials and machinery, subsidized fuel, reduced rail freight charges to ease internal transport, liberal credit terms, and antidumping legislation to control the entry of inexpensive imports.[58] Dumping was often referred to as "disloyal competition" as foreign companies sold products below cost.[59] The UIA contended that foreign companies kept their costs down by devaluing currency, maintaining low wages, and reducing shipping costs.[60] Dumping was viewed as particularly threatening because Argentine companies had higher costs of production and could not effectively compete with these imports. The UIA also urged more liberal credit availability for industry, claiming this would "stimulate overall economic growth and wealth for the nation."[61] It actively sought increased government contracting and procurement with local industry; such activity would serve as a large-scale buyer for domestic products. It lobbied for reduced corporate taxes and establishment of import quotas if tariffs proved insufficient. Although the UIA brought these issues before Congress, the primary topic of discussion was to increase tariffs.

Between 1916 and 1930, the political party in power, the Radicals, did not oppose protection of domestic industry and actually debated several industrial bills in Congress. But President Hipólito Yrigoyen often "vacillated between raising tariffs to placate industry and to realize additional government revenues, and lowering them to strengthen his hold on urban consumer markets."[62] In one speech, the president suggested that Argentina should research Brazilian industrial legislation to ascertain how Argentina could strike a balance between free market efficiency and the growth of domestic industry.[63] President Yrigoyen's ambivalence partly stemmed from his skepticism about Argentina being able to effectively produce high-quality goods at low cost. He seems to have believed that Argentina should aspire to develop an efficient industrial sector capable of exporting its manufactured goods in competition with other nations.[64] During this period, Yrigoyen publicly acknowledged the importance of domestic industry. In 1917, he noted that the number of small-scale industrial firms grew significantly during the First

World War, when the Argentine Congress temporarily increased tariffs to increase government revenue. He attributed this growth to isolation from world markets and higher tariffs. But Yrigoyen cautioned against maintaining high tariffs after the war; he believed that free markets were still the best insurance of increased economic efficiency. Also, growth in small-scale firms did not change the concentrated manufacturing environment. These firms depended on higher prices to remain in business and did not constitute significant competition for existing and established large-scale firms.

Despite the moderate approach voiced by the president, after 1918 the industrial cause gained new support from leading economic groups, politicians, and Congress members. Legislators, leading entrepreneurs, and landowners were deeply alarmed when the postwar economy became far more unpredictable than before the war. Agricultural prices for beef "sagged" between 1920 and 1924, causing an "acute exchange shortage."[65] International wheat prices also declined in the 1920s. Although Argentina's wheat yield "rose 33 percent over the previous decade," farmers could not achieve the sales and growth of the Belle Époque.[66] European economies were in disarray, and agricultural prices continued to decline. As a result of these conditions, promotion of domestic industry came to be collectively recognized as a prescription for economic diversification. It was also viewed as a way to decrease dependence on agricultural exports as a source of national income. These groups called on the Argentine government to promote and protect industry.

Beginning in 1919, members of the influential Buenos Aires stock exchange and the elite landowners' club, Sociedad Rural Argentina, partnered with UIA members and government officials to create the Argentine Confederation of Commerce, Industry, and Production. The confederation sponsored a series of national conferences to examine the postwar national economy and acted as a think tank on how to revive the Argentine economy.[67] Initially, the group championed efforts to sell more wheat in international markets, but prices remained volatile and low at times. The value of imports also continued to exceed the value of export receipts.

After the first national conference of the confederation in 1919, a special committee was formed in Congress to examine industry. This commission's pivotal 1919 report recommended a large number of new industrial policies and sweeping changes to existing industrial codes. The recommendations included tax reduction for industry, extended tariff protection for new industries, special rates for internal transport of domestically produced goods, liberalization of industrial credit, development of export facilities for industry, antidumping laws, and subsidies for factories using domestic raw materials.[68] The commission also concluded that the Tariff Law of 1905 (repeatedly revised until then) did not offer effective protection in real terms. Although the committee underscored industrial problems, it failed to supply a well-defined plan on how to effectively implement solutions to these problems. Stimulated by the committee's recommendations, Congress soon convened to discuss industry's problems. Again, the tariff rate adjustment received the highest priority as a way to develop industry.

By 1922, manufacturers and pro-industry groups proposed additional policies that would bar certain imports outright and give existing and new industries a broader array of privileges. In 1922, Javier Padilla, general director of commerce and industry, presented one industry bill that encapsulated industry's aspirations.[69] The bill called for creation of a new government department, the Industrial Development Committee (IDC), which would implement a number of initiatives: (1) tax deferral or reduction of up to 50 percent for domestic manufacturing; (2) permanent duty-free imports of raw materials; (3) special rates for transport of goods within Argentina; (4) guaranteed yields of 6 percent for up to ten years; (5) government assistance with exporting or buying excess inventories; and (6) compelling the Banco de la Nación Argentina to lend to domestic manufacturers at a low fixed rate determined by the IDC.[70] Although the bill was not enacted into law in the 1920s, these policies influenced legislation for the next three decades. Most of these measures passed in the 1930s and 1940s.

The Argentine Confederation of Commerce, Industry, and Production also agreed that new protectionist polices were needed to foster a strong industrial sector. Arguing that Argentine industry had many systematic weaknesses but insisting that shaky technical capability or inadequate capital markets was not the principal problem, the confederation identified industry's greatest challenge as lack of adequate government support and tariff protection. They recommended that the administration pursue "clearly active and definite" policies in favor of national industries. The confederation clearly stressed that agro-industries in particular should be heavily protected.[71]

Another important set of industrial allies were the legislators and governors of the interior provinces. They were largely concerned with protecting their regional industries; publicly they advocated that support of agro-industry (particularly sugar, flour, and wine production) as a means for the underdeveloped interior regions to prosper. In the late nineteenth and early twentieth centuries, the liberal export boom mainly benefited the littoral regions, widening the income gap between the prosperous littoral and impoverished interior provinces. During the colonial period, the northwest of Argentina had been one of the richest regions of the republic thanks to its strong ties to the Peruvian silver economy. After independence, however, the region declined economically. The interior region's poverty was largely a result of environmental degradation from excessive irrigation, clear cutting of forests, and water pollution.[72]

Roy Hora argues that legislators from the interior were overrepresented in Congress, which explains the extensive debate regarding protection of the northwestern agro-industries. Buenos Aires province contained 30–40 percent of the Argentine population and had sixteen representatives in Congress. Three minor provinces, in terms of population and economic importance, also had sixteen representatives (Santiago del Estero had seven; Tucumán five, and Catamarca four).[73] These northwestern legislators helped push forward their regional demands for industrial protection in Congress. Interior legislators had a substantial amount of leverage, guaranteeing them favorable political exchanges. For instance, José Sánchez Román claims that the deputies and senators representing the interior provinces successfully delayed an income tax system that was favored by littoral politicians until Buenos Aires deputies agreed to support subsidies for industries of the interior.[74]

By the 1920s, it was suggested that the growing economic divide between the prosperous Pampas regions and the impoverished interior could pose a threat to the sustained political unification of Argentina achieved some sixty years earlier. Mindful of the social and political implications of the interior's underdevelopment, by the early 1920s Congress debated how to effectively promote sugar, wine, cotton textiles, and tobacco production in the interior.[75] The support for protective tariffs suggests that it might have been a quid pro quo for subsidies of regional products.

Congress considered generous subsidies and incentives for the sugar industry in the interior. In one bill, they proposed that the government guarantee an annual return on investment of 6 percent to each sugar mill during its first fifteen years of operation (the bill seemed very similar to the guarantees offered to railroad companies at the turn of the century).[76] The stipulations of this sugar bill were that a mill must produce fifteen thousand tons of sugar each year and in return the government would guarantee returns to the mill, but the total amount offered was limited to five million pesos. Other bills sought promotion of cotton textile production in the interior. In 1921, the minister of agriculture commissioned engineer Julio Sánchez to acquire textile machinery from Belgium and use it to establish factories in the impoverished northwest regions of La Quebrada and La Puna in Jujuy province.[77] For particularly impoverished areas such as Catamarca province, Congress considered whether to directly fund establishment of a new cotton textile factory.[78] Cotton textile production was considered a promising way to help

Argentina's poorest regions by fostering jobs for impoverished women and children. Congress also discussed bills to train rural and poor women for productive work through special training centers, the National Institutions for Rural Women.[79] The mission of the institutes was improvement and growth of the agricultural sector and agro-industries through improved health and sanitation methods in rural areas.

Congressional debate of the time demonstrated relatively amicable exchanges between politicians of the interior and littoral. Peter Smith's original dataset on voting patterns suggests political cooperation among groups.[80] Sánchez Román also shows that during the interwar years and crisis periods, political and economic groups negotiated and preferred to cooperate over diverse issues, leading to creation of numerous ad hoc advisory councils within Congress.[81] Part of the exchange was to pass legislation based on a set of compromises agreed on by the involved parties.

The government's decision to promote and protect manufacturing activity in the interior was a political compromise between the impoverished interior provinces and the wealthier littoral provinces and territories. Industries and raw material programs based in the interior provinces were among the first to receive protective tariffs and subsidies. The raising of these tariffs, however, cannot be accurately viewed as congressional acquiescence to the agenda of industrial advocates of the nation. Instead, national deputies from the littoral provinces realized that to mitigate political and social tensions between the littoral and interior regions, the former would be required to offer subsidies and protection of the agro-industries of the interior provinces.

For diverse political, intellectual, economic, and social reasons, increased protection came to be accepted as a political necessity as of the early 1920s. In 1922, a bill was discussed to increase tariffs on all manufactured imports. The compromise was the tariff law of 1923, which raised tariffs on most (though still selective) consumer goods. It was yet another revision that resulted from political bargaining and compromises. Machinery, raw materials, and other products needed for industry remained duty-free. The appeal to economic nationalism and internal unity succeeded in overcoming Argentina's historical orientation as an exporter of agricultural commodities and importer of finished manufactured goods.

By the late 1920s, Argentina's political, mercantile, and agrarian elites were willing to support government promotion of industry for three reasons. First, they believed that industry and agriculture could be interdependent and equal promoters of the economy. The agricultural sector could produce the raw materials needed in manufacturing processing; they believed this interdependence could be achieved within a generation.[82] Second, they appear to have accepted, to varying degrees, the "historically based thesis" that industry was the "natural stage" following agricultural expansion. They believed in the strong parallels in Argentina's historical and economic evolution with that of advanced European nations such as Britain and France rather than the rest of Latin America. In these European nations, the historical pattern was that industry became the "obvious and natural stage" after agrarian expansion.[83] Last, they concluded that a capacity to satisfy domestic demand for manufactured products was essential to making the domestic economy "more secure, more independent, and less affected by crisis in international markets."[84]

Critics of Protectionism

Although sentiment in favor of protectionism grew in the 1920s, several groups remained opposed to the trend. The most vocal opponents of increased tariffs were the Socialists. In 1919, the Argentine Socialist party rejected increased tariffs because they would raise prices for basic consumer goods. The Socialists argued tariffs merely permitted large-scale industrialists to enjoy oligopoly rents at the expense of poor and working-class consumers.[85] President Marcelo T. de Alvear (1922–1928) also toned down the rhetoric of protection and at least publicly espoused laissez-faire principles after 1923. By 1924, his uncertainty about the development of local industry labeled him a traitor of protection in some of the scholarly literature.[86]

In the early 1920s, critics argued that there were two major adverse effects of increasing protectionism. First, more protection drove up the size of established firms. They argued there was a rise in trusts, cartels, and monopolies in Argentina, particularly in the manufacturing sectors located in the interior. Second, these policies encouraged foreign companies to start factories within the Argentine borders. Indeed, some foreign companies began "opening factories in Buenos Aires to secure a place in the market."[87] The Socialists indicated that foreigners were setting up factories in Argentina and enjoying protective tariffs. In particular, they admonished the North American cement company Argentina de Cemento Pórtland for beginning to take control of this sector.[88]

Critics also argued that competition among domestic companies was essential to combat concentration and monopolies. In the postwar period, Congress debated policies to increase the number of local firms and create internal competition. Two bills that passed into law were the Anti-Monopoly Law of 1923 and the Limited Liability Partnership Act of 1932, to simplify incorporation of smaller firms and raise the number that could compete with each other.

The antitrust and monopoly bill stirred contentious debate in Congress between 1918 and 1922. It arose from numerous allegations of monopolies, cartels, and consolidation of large firms. In 1919, the Argentine Congress set up the first investigative committee on trusts; it concluded that trusts and monopolies were clearly present in the sectors of wine, sugar, rice, flour, beef, and petroleum.[89] Several members of Congress defended the cartels. Ernesto Padilla, a deputy from Tucumán province, argued that monopolists were actually "capitalists." Without "ultra-protectionism like in Brazil," Padilla asserted that the rice industry would find itself competing with imports and must form cartels to become larger and compete effectively.[90]

The Anti-Monopoly Law passed in 1923, but it was difficult to establish occurrence of violations.[91] The law largely functioned as a warning; no one was indicted before 1930. The law classified violations as either per se or contrary to the rule of reason. Per se violations were defined as certain acts of conduct that were deemed patently anticompetitive. It was difficult to catch explicit agreements between two competitors to set prices, create a pact, or fuse capital for the purpose of sustaining a monopoly. In contrast, the rule of reason applied to certain practices whose anticompetitive effects were questionable and therefore best judged case by case. Because rule of reason was a somewhat gray area, the law identified certain acts that could cause probable action by a prosecutor. For example, if a director were suspected of having fixed prices, destroyed goods for the purpose of raising prices, purposely shut off machines, abandoned fields, or created regional monopolies, then the case went to trial.[92]

The antimonopoly law failed to realize its intended outcome because of lax enforcement and specific legal wording that made it difficult to enforce. For example, in 1925 Deputy José Amuchástegui called for a congressional investigation to modify it by removing the stipulation that companies must have "criminal intent."[93] He argued that although violations of price fixing and trusts were numerous, they were nearly impossible to prosecute thanks to broad legal jargon and specific criteria that could not be met. Amuchástegui cited recent appeal of the federal capital's Cámara del Crimen that repealed the judgment against the bakers' society, Centro de Patrones Panaderos. The criminal appeals court repealed the judgment against the bakers' price-fixing arrangement because it could not find criminal intent.[94]

In 1929, Congress debated another new bill to ease legal requirements for incorporation and capitalization. They sought to increase the number of small-scale firms. This bill was influenced by a similar law passed in Germany in the late nineteenth century. According to congressional members, the German outcome was the growth of a large number of competitive firms.

The Argentine bill called for easing regulation to transfer partnerships into limited liability firms.[95] Before this bill, only joint-stock companies enjoyed the full benefits of limited liability. This new bill was intended to give limited liability to smaller firms. In 1932, the bill passed into law as the Limited Liability Partnership Act.[96] It was strictly limited to partnerships of no more than twenty investing in commercial and manufacturing activity.[97]

Although the 1932 law helped to increase the number of small firms, these new small-scale companies were not competitive. They had high costs stemming from labor-intensive methods. Most of these small firms resembled their predecessors of the late nineteenth century, which used labor-intensive methods and supplied manufactured goods to a limited clientele. Most could also operate only in a highly protected environment.

Shortcomings of Industrial Legislation

Industrial legislation did very little to create an efficient and sustainable manufacturing sector. Most legislators failed to develop a long-term and coherent plan for sustainable industrialization. In the postwar period, Congress had extensive discussion and debated several bills with the intent of creating an ideal environment for manufacturing. Most bills had been influenced by legislation passed in Germany, the United States, and England. European industrial legislation offered examples for building legislation in Argentina, but this legislation failed to address issues specific to Argentine industry. For instance, some was clearly created by developed nations to encourage greater development in established fields of technology and machine making. Such fields were undeveloped in Argentina, but bills of this sort came before Congress. Some "borrowed" bills that were argued in Argentina pertained to encouraging indigenous technology, as in Europe and the United States, through easing patent regulation, awarding cash prizes for new inventions, and easing credit terms for inventors of machinery.[98] The goal of these policies, however, was not necessarily to emulate the machine making that took place in the early industrial phases of the United States, England, and Germany. But rather they encouraged the transfer of technology; foreigners were treated as equals in patent legislation and the revised law encouraged them to patent their machinery in Argentina. Other bills debated nationalization of oil because the government wanted to heavily subsidize the fuel needed for industry.[99] Although this legislation had worked well in other regions, it was not a guarantee of working well in Argentina given its specific problems.

Despite these bills, the tariff debate remained in the forefront. Increasing tariff rates solidified the inward-oriented nature of Argentine manufacturing and hurt its overall development in two ways. First, the tariff structure protected domestic manufacturers from importers of competing products of low-cost items for immediate consumption. The goods produced in Argentina were admittedly of lower quality than imports and intended for a mass working-class market. Once leading manufacturers captured a market, however, they did not typically improve their product or expand into producing high-quality items. Production of higher-quality products required additional capital for machinery and new inputs. In the glass industry, for example, the top three national glass manufacturers failed to produce high-quality glass (such as crystal or windows) even though there was a lucrative market for these items.[100] Instead, most large flat glass or glass for windows was imported. Regarding the making of fine crystal goods, such products were more expensive to produce and required more expensive machinery and skilled labor than production of simpler or cruder items. By the 1920s, foreign companies set up factories in Argentina because they found a niche in producing finer products. The U.S. glass firm American Industries set up a factory in Argentina to produce its patented high-quality clear crystal.[101]

Second, the tariff debates and increase of the 1920s established a presumption among government leaders that more protection, rather than efficiency-increasing measures, was the best way for government to aid industry. Protectionism became a panacea that pushed aside other potential government-based solutions. As stated earlier, in 1920 the UIA lobbied for an industrial bank to provide long-term credit to manufacturing, arguing that the thousands of small artisan shops were characteristic of Argentine industry because of the lack of industrial credit to expand operations and firm size. Congress rejected their proposal, responding that protective tariffs would generate increased profits sufficient for self-financing.[102]

Congress failed to develop the ideal manufacturing sector through tariff legislation because it was a short-term and political solution. Decisions to raise tariffs were not the outcome of longstanding dialogue about multiple options to promote industry. Instead Congress raised tariffs because it was the best political compromise and less cumbersome than committing to a long-term industrialization plan. Revisions to the tariff created a complicated and badly organized structure.

Chapter 7

Conclusions

Early twentieth-century Argentina rebukes the conventional wisdom on industrialization and development. Outwardly, Argentina had many of the prerequisites for successful industrialization: a growing agro-export sector, burgeoning population, an expanding transport system, and a developing banking system. Once manufacturing started in the late nineteenth century, it brought new technologies, opened new investment opportunities, and generated skilled and unskilled jobs for the thousands of new immigrants who settled in the cities. Because consumer, labor, and finance markets were nearly all located in Buenos Aires city and surrounding provinces,[1] manufacturing factories concentrated in this region had easy access to markets and shipping ports.

Manufacturing grew significantly; it went from no representation at all in the first census of economic activities in 1869 to become the second most important economic activity by 1930.[2] In the 1920s, industry's fast growth prompted one leading proponent of Argentine manufacturing, Alejandro Bunge, to comment that the country could become a truly industrialized nation within twenty years.[3] The standard view of industrialization holds that it brings numerous opportunities for advancement across social and economic sectors.

As of 1930, however, Argentine manufacturing was inefficient and concentrated. Industry was constrained because of numerous economic and noneconomic obstacles. Was Argentine industry bound to fail? Alan Taylor remarks that Argentina's "history provides a more complex story than the simple two-period framework of success followed by failure."[4] Rather, the outcome of industrialization must be examined as a product of its economic and political environment, as well as its business culture. For the most part,

127

industrial cycles followed economic cycles, showing fast growth in the beginning, dipping dismally during the First World War, and picking up again after 1918. After a four-year financial depression (1914–1917), Argentina's economic growth resumed during the 1920s[5] because the agro-export sector flourished again. The country diversified and expanded its output of maize, linseed, and cereals.[6] Through most of the twentieth century, industry never led overall economic growth, but it became and remained the second most important economic sector. It performed well or poorly, following the cycles of the overall economy.[7] Industry failed to surpass the economic importance of the agricultural sector largely because of the latter's incredible high-level performance. Agricultural productivity increased over time because of technical advancements in agricultural machinery, cattle breeding, and seeding methods.

But why did Argentine industry fail to become a sustainable and developed sector? The dominant tendency in the literature on industrialization is to blame the state or industrialists for underdevelopment. In the 1940s, Adolfo Dorfman first examined Argentine industry to answer why it failed to become a leading economic sector despite government intervention and private and public investment.[8] Thereafter, numerous studies offered theories and ideas to explain industry's underdevelopment, truncation, and unfulfilled potential.[9]

Regardless of the origins of these studies, most shared a similar conclusion: Argentine manufacturers and the government failed to develop a sustainable industrial sector capable of surpassing the economic importance of the agriculture sector. These scholars explained industry's shortcomings by identifying who or what was to blame for industrial underdevelopment. It was assumed that manufacturers and the government inherited the responsibility to create the correct type of industrialization but failed to do so because manufacturers were inept and rent-seekers and the government was not interested in aiding industrial development.

This book has endeavored to show that an explanation for unmet promise is best found in analysis of firm-level data and microanalysis of decision making and policy making at the company and government levels. Such an inquiry shows that manufacturers' strategies were in response to inadequacy in the nation's financial and political institutions. First, policymakers followed standard practices of conciliation among diverse interests groups, political parties, and other government officials when they created industrial policies.[10] As a consequence, industrial legislation was poorly construed. Congress debated numerous industrial bills, but few catered to taking concrete steps toward long-term industrial planning. Bills to increase tariff rates dominated congressional debate because they were the most politically acceptable topic of discussion. The outcome—laws increasing tariff rates—was largely a political compromise rather than the result of thoughtful debate about how to develop a sustainable industrial sector.

Second, banking institutions were well developed in Argentina, but lending practices were rather stringent, limiting a manufacturer's access to capital. The importance of personal connections to credit markets also prevailed through 1930. Argentina had an adequate number of banks, but they adhered to restrictive lending policies that created a scarcity of long-term credit. Only the five leading finance groups under study obtained sufficient capital through their informal financial sources and personal lending networks. The absence of impersonal capital markets for long-term lending limited the size of existing manufacturing firms and posed a barrier to new entrants. For most small and medium-size companies, manufacturing finance came from small, short-term loans and operating reserves. Reinvestment of profits constituted a major though inadequate source of finance for most companies under study. This lack of long-term credit remained a persistent problem well beyond the formative stage of Argentine industry. In their study of industrialization between 1940 and 1980, Jorge Katz and Bernardo Kosacoff found that there were "major difficulties in the links between manufacturing firms and the sources of finance for their long-term development."[11] Even during the heyday of the government's promotion of industry, they observed "the almost complete absence of medium and long-term capital markets" for industry.[12]

In response to the obstacles of industrialization, leading manufacturers developed strategies that actually contributed to the problem. They were essentially a risk-averse lot, willing to take on risk but within limits. Managerial practices were beneficial for short-term survival and helped local companies in a closed economy, but they lacked any long-term goal for international competitiveness.

Previous scholarship has blamed the anticompetitive strategies of the nation's leading entrepreneurs for industrial underdevelopment. Scholars argued that these entrepreneurs were shortsighted in their choosing to pursue high rents, which were used to purchase luxury items and display wealth through conspicuous consumption. But was the Argentine capitalist indifferent to the development of industry beyond his own immediate self-interest?[13]

Between 1890 and 1930, Argentina's manufacturers acted in a rational and self-interested manner on the basis of limited information in a volatile investment climate. Their strategies sometimes helped the longevity of their companies. But the basic problems of industry persisted because they were never addressed directly, as in the case of imported machinery. Manufacturers' continued reliance on imported manufacturing machinery through the 1920s perpetuated their problems with dependence on imported raw materials, fuel, and skilled engineers. Also, machines in certain industries required high-grade inputs that were available only abroad; for example, in brewing, cotton textiles, and paper production the specifications of imported machinery called for precise types of wood pulp, malts, hops, and long staple cotton available only outside Argentina. By the 1920s, the Argentine government began subsidizing domestic oil and training local engineers to work on foreign machines. But these things were costly to start up and maintain, requiring a substantial and consistent flow of finance capital.

Manufacturers focused on capturing a large share of the Argentine consumer goods market to protect their companies and investments. Among their strategies were price-fixing arrangements through trusts, merging with or acquiring rivals, and lobbying for increased tariff protection. Evidence from the firms under study demonstrates that owners were not fixated on immediate profits to fund conspicuous consumption. Instead they appear to have been more directed toward ensuring the longevity of the firm. They took a personal interest in the operation and investment of their company.

But owner-managers' personal interest in their company created some discrepancies with the concept of the modern, large-scale firm. Some managers exerted too much control in daily company matters, managing the companies almost as if they were family-run.[14] Successful finance groups operated the modern large-scale and capital-intensive firms that dominated their sectors. These owner-managers adopted the latest foreign technologies, and a few even expanded production to neighboring countries (for example, Compañía General de Fósforos and Fábrica Argentina de Alpargatas established factories and offices in Montevideo, Uruguay and São Paulo, Brazil). But owner-managers continued to place family members and close associates in key management and board positions to dominate in management decisions and hold the majority of voting stock. It would be difficult to have an efficient hierarchal management system if one owner-manager was involved at all levels, not permitting nonassociated men to help manage the company. In such manner, the advancement of the firm was limited to the vision of a few major stockholders and owners.

The availability of finance capital was also an issue limiting the size and number of manufacturing enterprises. Entrepreneurs used their net income in a number of ways. They built large cash reserves and contingent liability funds so as to self-finance expansion and absorb volatile market shifts. They paid out dividends to maintain investor confidence. Company reports show that directors carefully contemplated how to allocate reserves and redistribute profits. In developed economies with efficient capital markets, large company reserves could indicate that a firm anticipated a court judgment or bad debt, or that the company was hoarding rather than investing funds. In Argentina, however, large contingency funds indicated that directors were careful managers, concerned about the survival of their company in a fluctuating and capital-scarce economy.

Manufacturers' strategies to control their industrial environment may have been rational, but they were also self-serving in seeking a nearly risk-free industrial environment. The risk-averse nature of Argentine manufacturers compelled them to remove even the threat of competition by merging, creating trusts, and lobbying for higher tariffs. Although companies may have needed higher profit to self-finance and endure volatile profit cycles, the profit data showing double-digit (and in a few cases triple-digit) rates indicate that entrepreneurs were also rent seekers, rewarding themselves on their capital investment. For the most part, their strategies were a short-term response to the existing or anticipated external economic environment. In the end, they contributed to the concentrated nature of domestic industry because only a few manufacturers could successfully sustain these strategies.

Manufacturers sought higher rents by lobbying for higher tariffs to shut out imports of competing manufactured goods. But the laws to increase tariffs passed only in small part because of manufacturers' lobbying. The Unión Industrial Argentina lobbied for significant tariff protection for nearly four decades but made only incremental advances. In the political climate of the post-1914 period, Argentine legislators and other important economic groups believed that development and economic recovery would occur through promotion of domestic industry. Argentine legislators and intellectuals were not unique in this belief. Solberg argues that Argentina was among the few countries to be still debating protective tariffs for manufacturing between 1916 and 1930. By the 1920s, most European countries had raised tariffs to protect their industries.[15]

By the mid-1920s, industrialization was clearly considered by many to be, as *La Nación* put it, Argentina's "new source of wealth."[16] Industry, however, was not a new source of wealth barely developing in the 1920s; it had been on the rise since the late nineteenth century. The new policies of the 1920s did not help to build a strong industrial sector. Instead, they preserved patterns established in the late nineteenth century. By 1930, leading manufacturers benefited from a concentrated structure of industry.

Government's primary response to the structural problems facing manufacturing was to increase tariffs and potentially close markets to imported manufactured goods. The goal of state-sponsored industrialization was to build an industry that could supply consumer goods for internal markets. These political outcomes were accepted by the majority of political players. The act of raising tariffs did not commit the government to any long-term agenda. In the 1920s, the government erected high tariffs as a blanket response to all of manufacturing's problems rather than passing particularized legislation to address the structural problems of imported raw materials and machinery, or to analyze financial and industrial regulations.

A primary problem with tariff legislation was that it lacked a long-term agenda to examine how higher tariffs and profits might actually lead toward the progress of industrial development. By 1931, the government's protective tariff legislation had helped solidify an inefficient, inward-oriented industrial sector. Such a structure remained intact through most of the twentieth century. For the most part, the post-1930 bills and policies largely followed the model set forth in the first forty years of industry (1890–1930).

Reference Matter

Potential Bias in the Census Data

The manuscript census of 1895 was not without flaws. First, the question of representation should be addressed. The number of firms and workers from the 1895 manuscript census was compared to that reported in the industrial census published in the same year. The published census did not report output values and excluded some industries. The manuscript census surveys fairly represented the firms and workers listed in the published census. The published number of firms in six activities was 96 *alpargaterías*, 61 breweries, 128 textile and clothing shops, 2,265 foundries and machine shops (forges included), 152 soap and glycerin companies, and 584 tobacco manufacturers.[1] I compared these published numbers with those in the manuscript census. As a percentage of the total published number, the manuscript surveys for alpargatas shops represented 47 percent of the total published number of firms; metallurgy 24 percent; soap industry 51 percent; cotton, wool, and mixed textiles 28 percent; and tobacco 35 percent.[2] I also compared the published number of workers with what was in the manuscript census. The manuscript surveys amounted to 39 percent of the total number workers in alpargatas, soap industry 36 percent, tobacco 41 percent, and burlap sack 30 percent.

A second flaw with the 1895 manuscript census was inconsistent reporting of material costs on the part of companies. Although most reported both value of output and material costs, some firms reported only gross output. This had an effect on estimations using value added, which was calculated as the value of gross output minus material costs. Firms failing to report material costs were biased upward with respect to those disclosing material costs. To address this problem, I used both value of output and value added in running estimations of concentration ratios, labor, and total factor productivity. In most cases, the results from value added and value of output followed the same trends.

A third potential problem was using firm-level data from the manuscript census of 1895 alongside the sector-level data in the published censuses of 1914 and 1935. I used these censuses to compare labor productivity between census years. There could be bias upward in 1895 because the firms that appear in the 1895 manuscript census were a smaller proportion of the total number of those listed in the published census of 1895. This bias could affect the results between 1895 and 1914.

Despite these biases or errors, the estimated results using census data reflected patterns that also appeared in the secondary literature and in primary sources such as company annual reports. The firm-level data from the manuscript census permitted quantitative and statistical analysis of industry before the turn of the century. These analyses had not yet been done for Argentina and were necessary for a better understanding of early Argentine industrialization. The published and manuscript censuses were not without their problems, but together they helped to fill in gaps about the structure of industry.

Census Survey Forms

Survey Form 1

Segundo Censo de la República Argentina
Fábricas de Cerveza

Provincia o territorio de _____ Departamento o Partido de _____
Pedanía, distrito o sección_____ Pueblo o ciudad de _____
Nombre o razón social del establecimiento_____
Nombre de sus propietarios_____
¿Cuál es la nacionalidad del dueño?
¿Cuál es el capital total invertido, en pesos nacionales de curso legal?
De ese capital ¿cuánto tiene:
      a) en inmuebles? (casa, edificio, terreno)
      b) en máquinas y herramientas?
      c) en materia elaborada y por elaborar?
¿Qué clases de cervezas fabrica?
¿Cuántos litros de cerveza fabricó en todo el año 1894?
¿Qué valor calcula que tiene el total de cerveza que fabricó en 1894?
¿Qué clase de agua emplea? Decir si emplea agua de río, pozo, algibe, etc., y en
      el primer caso el nombre del río o arroyo.
¿Cuál es el valor calculado de la materia prima empleada en el año 1894 en el
      establecimiento:
      a) de procedencia argentina?
      b) de procedencia extranjera?
¿Qué número de máquinas de vapor tiene el establecimiento?
¿Cuántos caballos de fuerza representan las máquinas?

Si tiene máquina de fabricar hielo ¿cuántos kilos puede producir en 24 horas?

¿Cuántas máquinas de toda otra clase tiene el establecimiento?

¿Cuántos hervidores tiene?

¿Qué capacidad suman en litros o decímetros cúbicos?

¿Emplea envases del país o extranjeros? Indicar las clases de envase y su procedencia, por ejemplo: si son botellas o barriles, y si están hechos en el país o en el extranjero. Si los barriles son del país, decir que madera.

¿Cuántos carros tiene para el servicio de la fábrica?

¿Cuántas personas trabajan en el establecimiento?

De estas personas ¿cuántos son:

    a) Varones?

    b) Mujeres?

    c) Argentinos?

    d) Extranjeros?

Firma de la persona que llenó este boletín: _____

Este boletín fue llenado el día _____de _____ de 1895

Survey Form 2

Segundo Censo de la República Argentina

Boletín Industrial

Provincia o territorio de _____ Departamento o Partido de _____

Pedanía, distrito o sección_____ Pueblo o ciudad de _____

Nombre o razón social del establecimiento_____

Nombre de sus propietarios _____ .

A. ¿Qué industria se ejerce en el establecimiento?

B. ¿Cuál es la nacionalidad del dueño?

C. ¿Cuál es el capital total invertido, en pesos nacionales de curso legal?

D. De ese capital ¿cuánto tiene:

    a) En inmuebles? (casa, edificio, terreno)

    b) En máquinas y herramientas?

    c) En materia elaborada y por elaborar?

A. ¿Cuál es el valor calculado de las mercaderías elaboradas en el año 1894?

B. ¿Cuál es el valor calculado de la materia prima empleada en el año 1894 en el establecimiento:

    d) De procedencia argentina?

    e) De procedencia extranjera?

C. ¿Qué número de máquinas de vapor tiene el establecimiento?

D. ¿Cuántos caballos de fuerza representan las máquinas?

E. ¿Cuántas máquinas de toda otra clase tiene en el establecimiento?

F. ¿Cuántas personas trabajan en el establecimiento?

G. De estas personas ¿cuántos son:
   a) Varones?
   b) Mujeres?
   c) Argentinos?
   d) Extranjeros?

Firma de la persona que llenó este boletín _____

Este boletín fue llenado el día ____de _____ de 1895

Survey Form 3

Segundo Censo de la República Argentina
Sociedades anónimas

Provincia o territorio de:

Departamento o partido de:

Distrito, Pedanía, o sección de:

Ciudad o pueblo:

1. ¿Cuál es el nombre de la sociedad?

2. ¿Cuál es el objeto de la sociedad?

3. ¿En qué año se fundó en ese pueblo?

4. ¿Es casa central o sucursal?

5. Si es casa central, ¿cuál es el capital incluyendo el de todas sus sucursales en la república?

6. Si ha dado dividendo correspondiente al año 1894 ¿cuánto %?

7. ¿Cuál es el valor actual, %, de sus acciones, según las últimas ventas, cotización o apreciación equitativa?

8. Remitir el último balance:

Este boletín fue llenado el día ____ de ____ de 1895

Firma del empadronador_____

Firma del gerente o encargado de la sociedad _____

Appendix C

Data and Methods of Argentine Machine
Investment, 1890–1930

Chapter 3 traces fourteen categories of machinery, parts, and fuel for machinery exported from four countries—Great Britain, the United States, Germany, and France—to Argentina from 1890 to 1930: (1) agricultural machinery, implements, and their components; (2) steam engines and machinery (excluding locomotives); (3) electrical machinery for industry; (4) glass-making machinery; (5) metal-working machinery; (6) wood-working machinery; (7) textiles machinery; (8) paper-making machinery; (9) sugar refining machinery; (10) brewing equipment; (11) cement-making machinery; (12) other unspecified industrial machinery; (13) replacement, spare parts, and belts for machinery; and (14) fuel investment.[1]

The export trade statistics from these four principal export countries had varying characteristics that must be taken into account. The first issue is to reconcile changes in categories across countries; they were matched as closely as possible. A second issue to consider is possible inclusion of an indefinite amount of miscellaneous machinery. For instance, the British and French data reported machinery exports in categories such as "industrial machinery, not specified." Whenever possible, I sought qualitative data describing machinery exported to Argentina to determine machine type.

The export trade data from the United Kingdom is complete from 1893 to 1930. UK data has a general category, "Machinery, Not for Locomotive," and does not separate industrial machinery by subcategories. The British data are particularly important because of the close trading relationship between Argentina and Britain in the early twentieth century. Britain was the main consumer of Argentine agricultural and beef products. It was also Argentina's principal supplier of industrial machinery and fuel (coal) before 1914.

As with the British data, French trade data list all manufacturing machinery in a general category, "machines et mécaniques." This issue must be taken into account when examining the data. French data are available from 1897 to 1915 and from 1925 to 1928. Before 1897, the French data reported only quantities exported to Argentina and failed to give values. After 1897, however, quantities and values of export trade are both available. The French data were interrupted during the First World War and its aftermath; there were no export statistics separated by country from 1915 to 1921. Data were also incomplete between 1923 and 1925; this export trade series ends in 1928.

The U.S. data were the most complete, with detailed subcategories between 1890 and 1930. Beginning in the late 1910s, the United States replaced the United Kingdom as the main supplier of industrial machinery to Argentina. During most of the period, the United States was its chief supplier of agricultural machinery and implements. A reason for this shift toward U.S. goods may have been that U.S. manufacturers were more responsive to the need for simpler and lower-maintenance machines in Argentina. For instance, inexpensive internal combustion engines with simpler designs from the United States "had distinct advantages over the more expensive and durable engines produced [by the UK]."[2] U.S. engines were easily replaced for less than the cost of sending a British service engineer to overhaul and recondition a UK-produced engine.[3]

Export data from Germany was well organized in explanatory categories and subcategories. Germany was one of Argentina's most important supplier of machinery, competing for second or third place as machine exporter. German trade statistics, however, were interrupted during the First World War and immediately thereafter. Between 1914 and 1919, Germany reported the value of exports but failed to separate these values by country. Between 1920 and 1922, Germany reported only weight of exported machinery and not the currency values. The country's period of extraordinarily high inflation (1923–24) made exports practically gratis after the German mark was converted into real pounds. Unfortunately, between 1914 and 1924 it was not possible to determine the value of machinery exported from Germany to Argentina.

There are two limitations to using export data. They cannot, for instance, show the reuse of second-hand machinery within Argentina. Most small companies that could not afford to import machinery typically purchased second-hand machinery from larger domestic companies. Another issue is underreporting of investment in machinery because this export trade series cannot measure Argentine investment in domestically produced machinery. By the 1920s, Argentines machine makers were producing simple machines and replacement parts. But without sufficient and reliable domestic data it is difficult to assess how much was invested in locally produced machines and replacement parts.[4]

Despite these limitations, export data are useful in developing estimates of machine investment and in calculating the rate of growth in manufacturing investment over time. The series is intended to be an approximate estimation of machine investment and is not yet meant to be a complete picture of investment in machinery.

Appendix D

Data and Methods for Profit Calculations

Accounting is not a static phenomenon; companies change methods over time. This appendix describes the financial statements and methods used to estimate profit rate and other calculations. Although there may still be inconsistencies in the financial statements, the information from these statements added enormous value and depth to this book.

In preparing estimates, I used several accounting guides that were specific to Argentine accounting practices in the early twentieth century. They were Ministerio de Justicia, Inspección General de Justicia's *Nueva fórmula obligatoria para balances de sociedades anónimas, nacionales y extranjeras*; Gerhard G. Mueller, *Accounting Practices in Argentina*; and Interpretación del formulario de balances para las sociedades anónimas," *Guía de sociedades anónimas* (1929).

Cost-Accounting Methods

I used two cost-accounting methods to calculate company profits.[1] The first estimate is return on stockholder equity (ROE), which is net income divided by stockholder equity. Argentine manufacturers reported net income as the sum of all gross income minus reported costs of operation, raw material costs, and money held for reserves. Gross income includes all money that came in from sales, holdover income from previous years, interest from other investments, and rents. Owner's equity is the sum of paid-in capital and reserves. Both equity and reserves are located on the liability side of the balance sheet. To obtain an accurate account of net income, I calculate gross income as sales, interest, and rents. Holdover income from previous years is not added in as net income because holdover income has already been calculated in profit from previous years. Thus it is removed to avoid double counting of income. It is also done this way to focus on the company's current earnings for better assessment of current annual performance.

The second calculation is return on physical capital (ROK), which is net income divided by physical capital. ROK is the economic return on the physical capital invested in the firm. Physical capital is located on the asset side of the balance sheet; it is the sum of the depreciated value of all fixed properties such as buildings, factories, machinery and installations, accessories, furniture, vehicles, raw materials, work animals, and tools. It also includes the historical or current value of land, current value of cash and foreign currency on hand, and all other negotiable currency. These are all included on the asset side of the balance sheet.

Working capital such as inventory and accounts receivable is excluded from the calculation of ROK. Argentine manufacturing companies typically had a large amount of working capital that varied widely from year to year. Including working capital would have inflated the asset side and undermined profit ratios. Moreover, working capital was an unstable value. For instance, companies sold their working capital at discount or wrote it off as a loss or debt whenever the value of inventory or accounts receivable grew too large.[2]

In these two profit calculations, I adjusted the cost side of the income statement because many manufacturers withheld income, placed it in special reserve funds, and labeled this as a cost. The owners' goal was to deflate current profits and shift them to a later period when the need would be greater. Profits that were held for reserves were not truly a cost in the sense that the money was needed to cover expenses in a current financial year. The money was not being used for current needs but for contingent liabilities, future depreciation costs, future projects, and possible bad debts. Removing retained earnings from the cost side and placing them back on the income side where they truly belong should permit more accurate profit ratios.

ROE was calculated in this way:

Return on stockholder equity (ROE) =
$$\frac{(\text{Gross income} - \text{Current costs}) - \text{Holdover income}}{\text{Paid-in capital} + \text{Reserves}}$$

Equity is calculated as all paid-in capital in preferred and common stock. It may seem more appropriate to consider only ordinary shareholders; they were the ultimate risk bearers. But in Argentine firms the major owners of both classes of shares were the same people in most cases. Reserves were collected and became company equity. Adding reserves as equity in the calculation tends to understate rather than overstate the level of profitability.

Return on physical capital (ROK) was also estimated, and ROK was calculated in this manner:

Return on physical capital (ROK) =
$$\frac{(\text{Gross income} - \text{Current costs}) - \text{Holdover income}}{\text{Physical capital}}$$

I also calculated leverage, which is a coefficient estimating debt divided by equity.[3] I estimate debt to equity ratios to determine if companies under study are taking on debt or relying on annual income for their companies' operations. I wish to know when debt is being accrued. Generally, if a company takes on debt it is assumed that it does so to improve and expand its capital stock or organization. Doing so in a highly leveraged company or one that carries substantial debt and little equity could indicate poor money management. The company is considered a risky investment because if (when) there is an economic downturn the company could fail and investors lose their investment. But having no long-term debt could indicate that the company is highly profitable and using only net earnings to finance its growth and development.[4] If the company is not especially profitable, this implies that managers do not finance through debt or have profits to invest in new technologies and organization; this latter situation is not considered a desirable investment.

Normally, the debt-to-equity ratio is estimated using only long-term debt. I included short-term and long-term debts. Long-term debt (a contract for more than one year) was not a common form of debt among Argentine manufacturers between 1890 and 1930. Even manufacturing bonds, which are normally considered long-term debt, were a short-term investment maturing within one year. Generally, manufacturing companies with collateral could take on short-term loans from banks, to be repaid within six months. One exception to long-term loans was mortgages, which could have a long repayment schedule. Not all firms took on mortgage debt, however. It was also possible to extend repayment on a short-term loan by continuously renewing it. An official short-term debt could in practice become a long-term loan, but only under special circumstances.

The ratio is calculated in this manner:

Debt-to-equity ratio:

$$\frac{\text{Short-term debt} + \text{Long-term debt}}{\text{Paid-in capital} + \text{Reserves}}$$

The final ratio that was calculated is liquidity, or liquid assets divided by deposits. Typically, banks perform this ratio to test if an investment is a credit risk. I used it to test whether the companies in my study possessed a high level of liquidity, potentially to protect the firm from bankruptcy. I measured reserves as liquid assets because firms under study used them this way. I used paid-in capital as deposits; this is money that is deposited and paid for by the investors and cannot be quickly liquidated under normal circumstances.

The ratio is estimated as:

Liquidity ratio:

$$\frac{\text{Cash (asset side)} + \text{Reserves (liability side)}}{\text{Paid-in capital (deposits)}}$$

Depreciation of Physical Capital

One observation from Table 5.1 merits some discussion, to explain why the rate of return on stockholder's equity was typically lower than return on capital stock.[5] The depreciation value is the initial value of the item less the portion representing services of the asset already used. In several cases, firms depreciated all at once in a single year. This practice would make profits appear lower in prior years and then suddenly larger in the year in which the firm depreciated all at once. Before 1923, a few companies under study lumped all physical assets together on one accounting line, making it difficult to distinguish between machinery, buildings, and land. Depreciation schedules varied depending on asset type. In 1923 the Inspección General de Justicia (IGJ) set minimum accounting standards for depreciation. The minimum depreciation cost of furniture, fixtures, work animals, and vehicles was 10 percent annually over the initial value, and 10 percent annually over acquisitions made during the financial year. The minimum depreciation cost of machines was 5 percent annually over the initial value. Installations, tools, and materials were to depreciate at a rate of 20 percent per annum over the initial value, or in five segments so that within five years the value would be zero. When possible, I adjusted capital stock by following the minimum depreciation schedule set forth by the IGJ, and I also calculated ROE to get a clearer profit assessment over time.

Notes

The following abbreviations are used in the Notes:

AGN   Archivo General de la Nación de Buenos Aires, Argentina
BOB   *Boletín oficial de la bolsa de comercio de Buenos Aires*
BORA   *Boletín oficial de la República Argentina*
BTQ   Archive of the Biblioteca Tornquist, Buenos Aires, Argentina
BUIA   *Boletín de la Unión Industrial Argentina*
MSA   *Monitor de sociedades anónimas*
REA   *Revista de economía argentina*
RRP   *Review of River Plate*
UIA   Unión Industrial Argentina

Chapter 1

1. "Los primeros defensores de la producción nacional," *Revista de economía argentina,* Jan.–June 1925, *14, 342.*

2. No author, "Porqué y cómo somos proteccionistas," *Boletín de la Unión Industrial Argentina*, Apr. 15, 1914, *28*(544), 2

3. After 1862, the government began the processes of regulating the money supply and stabilizing currency. In 1891, administrators created the conversion house to give the federal government exclusive control over issuance of currency. Though only briefly adopted in 1881, the gold standard was put into effect in Argentina from 1894 to 1895, and between 1899 and 1914. In 1899, the conversion board stabilized the gold-to-paper rate at 0.44 paper pesos to 1 gold peso; this exchange rate remained in effect until 1935. Between 1900 and 1935, Argentina had two currencies, paper pesos and gold pesos. Both were supported by gold. Gold pesos were used for international accounts and paper pesos were for domestic exchange. For a discus-

sion of the gold standard in Argentina, see A. G. Ford, *The Gold Standard 1880–1914: Britain and Argentina* (New York: Garland, 1983). In addition to these policies, the nation developed a whole new set of institutions to reduce financial uncertainty, which increased the country's credibility to creditors and investors. For discussion of the politics of money before 1900, see Jeremy Adelman, "The Politics of Money in Mid-Nineteenth Century Argentina," in John Harriss and others (eds.), *The New Institutional Economics and Third World Development* (New York: Routledge, 1995).

4. David Rock, *Argentina 1516–1987* (Berkeley, University of California Press, 1987), 169.

5. The Commercial Department of the Ministry of Agriculture reported investment capital; they were part of the Income Tax project in 1917 and wanted to assess capital inflows. *Argentine Annual* (1921), 133.

6. Ernesto Tornquist y Co., Ltda., *Economic Development of the Argentine Republic in the Last Fifty Years* (Buenos Aires: Ernesto Tornquist y Co., Ltda., 1919), xvii.

7. Jeremy Adelman, *Frontier Development: Land, Labour, and Capital on the Wheatlands of Argentina and Canada, 1890–1914* (Oxford: Clarendon Press, 1994), 1.

8. *Times Book on Argentina* (London: Times, 1927), 4.

9. Overall GDP grew at an average annual rate of 5.2 percent between 1875 and 1914. Roberto Cortés Conde, *La economía argentina en el largo plazo* (Buenos Aires: Universidad de San Andrés, 1997), 19.

10. Carlos Díaz Alejandro, *Essays on the Economic History of the Argentine Republic* (New Haven, Conn.: Yale University Press, 1970), 3.

11. *Anuario geográfico argentino* (Buenos Aires, 1941), 186.

12. Ibid., 157–159.

13. José Moya, *Cousins and Strangers: Spanish Immigrants in Buenos Aires, 1850–1930* (Berkeley: University of California Press, 1998), 1.

14. Victor Bulmer-Thomas, *Economic History of Latin America* (Cambridge: Cambridge University Press, 1994), 86. For additional population information, see also Moya, *Cousins and Strangers*.

15. Bulmer-Thomas, *Economic History*, 86.

16. Buenos Aires city grew from having 187,346 persons, as reported in the 1869 national census, to more than two million in the 1936 city census. *Anuario geográfico argentino*, 157.

17. Díaz Alejandro estimated that two million people per annum were economically active between 1900 and 1904, an annual average of three million between 1910 and 1914, and nearly five million between 1930 and 1934. Díaz Alejandro, *Ensayos sobre la historia económica argentina* (Buenos Aires: Amorrortu editores, 1976), 389.

18. Alan M. Taylor, "Capital Accumulation," in Gerardo Della Paolera and

Alan M. Taylor (eds.), *A New Economic History of Argentina* (Cambridge: Cambridge University Press, 2003), 179. This argument was initially made in Alan Taylor, "External Dependence, Demographic Burdens, and Argentine Economic Decline After the Belle Époque," *Journal of Economic History,* Dec. 1992, 52(4), 907–936.

19. Quantities imported by unit (kilogram, bottle, ton, and so on). *Anuario de la Dirección General de Estadística* (Buenos Aires: Compañía Sud-americana de Billetes de Banco, 1892–1914); Argentina, Dirección General de Estadística y Censos, *Anuario del comercio exterior de la República Argentina* (Buenos Aires: Dirección General de Estadística de la Nación), 1915–1935.

20. By comparison, manufacturing value added accounted for 12.3 percent of GDP in Mexico and 12.1 percent in Brazil (1970 U.S. prices). Bulmer-Thomas (1994), 137.

21. These figures come from Cortés Conde's estimates of industrial production. The Economic Commission for Latin America (CEPAL) calculated that Argentina's industrial production grew on average 5.4 percent per year between 1900 and 1914, and at an average 4.1 percent annually between 1914 and 1935 (three-year averages). Cortés Conde (1997), 207.

22. The 1935 census takers took into account technology changes between 1914 and 1935 in order to compare these two years. The published censuses of 1895 and 1914 included industrial activities that no longer existed by the time of the 1935 census because of improved technology. Industrial activities operating in 1935 did not exist in earlier census years. Also, the number in 1935 includes both state-owned and private enterprises. Dirección General de Estadística de la Nación, *Censo industrial de 1935* (Buenos Aires: Ministerio de Hacienda, 1937), 21.

23. Capital stock is the sum of physical and working capital: offices, buildings, property, inventories, machines, tools, and accessories. Data for capital, labor, and value of output came from three censuses: *Segundo censo nacional: Censo de las industrias 1895, Vol. 3* (Buenos Aires: 1898); Ministerio de Hacienda, *Tercer censo nacional: Censo de las industrias 1914,* Vol. 7 (Buenos Aires: Talleres Gráficos de L. J. Rosso y Cía., 1917); and *Censo industrial de 1935* (1937).

24. The manufacturing sector was not recorded in the census of 1869. The value of output was not available in the 1895 published census and was not compared in this instance.

25. Capital stock and value-added were converted to real paper pesos (1920 = 100). Real pesos were determined by using the wholesale price index calculated by Leonard I. Nakamura and Carlos Zarazaga, "Economic Growth in Argentina in the Period 1900–1930: Some Evidence from Stock Returns" (Table 9.1, Price Indexes), in John H. Coatsworth and Alan M. Taylor (eds.), *Latin America and the World Economy Since 1800* (Cambridge, Mass.: Harvard

University Press, 1998), 254. To obtain the years before 1900 and after 1930, I consulted Carlos Zarazaga, who kindly submitted his data sources to expand this price index. Sources for the price index are Gerardo Della Paolera, "How the Argentine Economy Performed During the International Gold Standard: A Reexamination," Ph.D. dissertation, University of Chicago, 1988, for the years to 1914; and after 1914, Roberto L. Domenech, "Estadísticas de la evolución económica de Argentina, 1913–1984," *Estudios de IEERAL,* 1986, *9*(39): 103–185.

26. Bulmer-Thomas (1994), 144–145.

27. Ibid.

28. Stephen H. Haber, "Assessing the Obstacles to Industrialisation: The Mexican Economy, 1830–1940," *Journal of Latin American Studies,* Feb. 1992, *24*(1), 2.

29. Jeremy Adelman, *Frontier Development,* and Roy Hora, *The Landowners of the Argentine Pampas: A Social and Political History, 1860–1945* (Oxford: Clarendon Press, 2001).

30. Stephen Haber, "The Political Economy of Industrialization," 537–584, in Victor Bulmer-Thomas, John H. Coatsworth, and Roberto Cortés Conde (eds.), *The Cambridge Economic History of Latin America: The Long Twentieth Century,* Vol. 2 (Cambridge: Cambridge University Press); María Inés Barbero and Fernando Rocchi, "Industry," 261–294, in Della Paolera and Taylor (eds.), *New Economic History of Argentina*; Fernando Rocchi, *Chimneys in the Desert: Industrialization in Argentina During the Export Boom Years, 1870–1930* (Palo Alto, Calif.: Stanford University Press, 2006).

31. Haber, "Assessing the Obstacles," 3.

32. John Coatsworth, "Obstacles to Economic Growth in Nineteenth-Century Mexico," *American Historical Review,* Feb. 1978, *83*(1), 80–100; Haber, "Assessing the Obstacles."

33. Jorge G. Fodor y Arturo O'Connell, "La Argentina y la economía atlántica en la primera mitad del siglo XX," *Desarrollo económico* Apr. 1973, *13*: 3–65. Argentina was a major exporter of agricultural products; between 1909 and 1914, it produced 12.6 percent of the world's wheat exports. Adelman, *Frontier Development.*

34. The Argentine tariff is a valuation tariff and not based on the actual value of the articles imported. Articles were subject to a duty of 25 percent ad valorem "but provided different rates of ad valorem duty for certain articles." The law of 1923 raised tariff levels to reflect real market prices. See Frank Rutter (U.S. Department of Commerce), *Tariff Systems of South American Countries,* tariff series no. 34 (Washington, DC: U.S. GPO, 1916), 47–50. See also custom duty and tariff laws: law 2766 of 1891; law 2923 of 1892; law 3050 of 1894; law 3672 of 1898; law 3890 of 1900; law 4933 of Dec. 20, 1905; law 10220 of 1917; law 10362 of 1918; law 11022 of 1920; and law 11281 of Dec.

6, 1923. Duty is 25 percent, unless noted in custom laws number 3050, 4933, 10362, and 11281.

35. Although the tariff law of 1923 was not explicitly intended to be protectionist, Argentina's tariff levels were high by international standards, exceeding those of Canada, France, and Germany. Its rates were described as "clearly protectionist." Roy Hora, "Terratenientes, empresarios industriales y crecimiento industrial en la Argentina: los estancieros y el debate sobre el proteccionismo (1890–1914)." *Desarrollo Económico,* Oct.–Dec. 2000, *40*(159), 487.

36. For early studies on entrepreneurs' influence and development, see Fleming, "The Cultural Determinants of Entrepreneurship and Economic Development"; and Thomas C. Cochran and Ruben E. Reina, *Entrepreneurship in Argentine Culture; Torcuato Di Tella and S.I.A.M.* (Philadelphia: University of Pennsylvania Press, 1962).

37. Juan Carlos Korol and Hilda Sábato, "Incomplete Industrialization: An Argentine Obsession," *Latin American Research Review*, 1990, *25*(1), 7–30.

38. André Gunder Frank, *Capitalism and Underdevelopment in Latin America: Historical Studies of Chile and Brazil* (New York: Monthly Review Press, 1967).

39. Ricardo Ortíz, *Historia económica de la Argentina* (Buenos Aires: Ultra Plus, 1974; Aldo Ferrer, *The Argentine Economy* (Berkeley: University of California Press, 1967).

40. Prebisch argued that the core-satellite model subjected Latin American countries to domination by European markets.

41. Helen Shapiro and Lance Taylor, "The State and Industrial Strategy," *World Development* (1990) *18*(6): 861–878, 862.

42. Colin M. Lewis, "Latin American Business History, c. 1870–1930: Recent Trends in the Argentinian and Brazilian Literature," *América Latina en la historia económica; boletín de fuentes* (July–Dec. 1995): 89–110, 91.

43. Rory Miller, "Latin American Manufacturing and the First World War: An Explanatory Essay," *World Development,* 1981, *9*(8), 707–716.

44. Carl Solberg, *Oil and Nationalism in Argentina: A History* (Palo Alto, Calif.: Stanford University Press, 1979), 25.

45. Juan Carlos Korol and Hilda Sábato, "Incomplete Industrialization: An Argentine Obsession," *Latin American Research Review,* 1990, *25*(1), 23.

46. Geller first applied the theory of staple growth to the Argentine case. Lucio Geller, "Un teorema y un comentario sobre el efecto del crecimiento económico sobre el comercio internacional," *Desarrollo económico,* Jul.–Sep. 1970, *10*(38): 293–304; Korol and Sábato (1990), 22; Ezequiel Gallo, "Agrarian Expansion and Industrial Development in Argentina, 1880–1930," Buenos Aires: Instituto Torcuato Di Tella, Centro de Investigaciones Sociales, 1970.

47. Gallo (1970), 11.

48. Ibid.

49. This argument is summarized in Paul H. Lewis, *The Crisis of Argentine Capitalism* (Chapel Hill: University of North Carolina Press, 1990), 4.

50. Shapiro and Taylor, "The State," 364.

51. For example, Jagdish N. Bhagwati, "Directly Unproductive, Profit-Seeking (DUP) Activities," *Journal of Political Economy* (Oct. 1982), *90*(5): 988–1002.

52. Alfred Chandler, *The Visible Hand: The Managerial Revolution in American Business* (Cambridge, Mass.: Harvard University Press, 1977); Joseph A. Schumpeter, *The Theory of Economic Development* (New York: Oxford University Press, 1961).

53. Frits Wils, "The Theoretical Frame of Reference," *Industrialization, Industrialists, and the Nation-State in Peru: A Comparative Sociological Analysis* (chapter 1), Berkeley, Calif.: Institute of International Studies, 1979.

54. Mark Casson, "Entrepreneurship and business culture," in Jonathan Brown and Mary B. Rose (eds.), *Entrepreneurship, Networks, and Modern Business*. Manchester: Manchester University Press, 1993: 30–54; Mark Granovetter, "Coase Revisited: Business Groups in the Modern Economy," *Industrial and Corporate Change*, Vol. 4, no. 1 (1995): 93–130.

55. María Inés Barbero,"Treinta años de estudios sobre la historia de empresas en la Argentina," *Ciclos*, First semester 1995, *5*(8), 179–200; Raúl García Heras, "Historia empresarial e historia económica en Argentina: un balance a comienzos del siglo XXI." Historia del Desarrollo Empresarial, Monografías de Administración, Universidad de los Andes, April 2007.

56. Solberg (1979), 4.

57. Korol and Sábato (1990), 11.

58. Roy Hora, "Landowning Bourgeoisie or Business Bourgeoisie? On the Peculiarities of the Argentine Economic Elite, 1880–1945," *Journal of Latin American Studies,* 2001, *34*(3): 587–623, 589.

59. Hora (2001a), 600.

60. Hora found that most were heavily invested in real estate (mainly rural, but also urban) between 1880 and the First World War. Hora (2001a), 609.

61. Hora, "Empresarios y política en la Argentina, 1880–1916," unpublished work, paper presented at Panel 46, Thirteenth Congress of the International Economic History Association, Buenos Aires (July 2002), 11–12.

62. Hora (2002), 14–15.

63. Korol and Sábato (1990), 10.

64. Hora (2002), 12.

65. Della Paolera and Taylor (2003), 1.

66. An example is Della Paolera and Taylor (2003).

67. Barbero and Rocchi, "Industry," 268.

68. Argentina, *Anuario de la Dirección General de Estadística* (Buenos Aires: Compañía Sud-americana de Billetes de Banco, 1892–1914); Argentina, Dirección General de Estadística y Censos, *Anuario del comercio exterior de la República Argentina* (Buenos Aires: Dirección General de Estadística de la Nación, 1915–1930).

69. These companies represented a range of small to large corporations of that time. The industries are (1) beer, (2) cement, (3) paper, (4) tobacco, (5) burlap sack, (6) cotton and wool textiles, (7) glass, (8) metallurgy, (9) matches, and (10) soap.

70. Law 5125 of 1907 required foreign and domestic corporations to submit company balance sheets and financial information each trimester to the Ministry of General Justice for publication. Failure to do so was under penalty of a fine between two hundred and one thousand pesos for each violation.

71. Joint-stock companies were under the jurisdiction of the Argentine Ministry of Justice (General Inspection Division). The ministry collected accounting records, enforced compliance of legal obligations, and set standards for all legal procedures regarding the corporations. There are no single proprietorships, family-owned firms, or simple partnerships examined in this book. Such enterprises were not obligated to publish a balance sheet or declare their earnings, and I was unable to calculate their performance. Corporations with a short operating history owing to dissolution or acquisition are also not prominent among my sources.

72. Barbero and Rocchi (2003); Solberg, "Tariffs and Politics in Argentina, 1916–30," *Hispanic American Historical Review,* 1973, *53*(2); Díaz Alejandro (1970); Donna Guy, "La industria argentina 1870–1940: Legislación comercial, mercado de acciones y capitalización extranjera." *Desarrollo Económico,* Oct.–Dec. 1982, *22*(87): 351–374; Jorge Schvarzer, *La industria que supimos conseguir: Una historia político-social de la industria argentina* (Buenos Aires: Grupo Planeta Editorial, 1996); and Solberg (1979).

73. Data come from company reports, balance sheets, and income statements belonging to the fifty-nine manufacturing firms between 1904 and 1930. These financial statements were largely gathered from two finance journals of the time: *Boletín oficial de la bolsa de comercio de Buenos Aires* and *Boletín oficial de la República Argentina*. Financial records were also available in individual company pamphlets intended for investors of that time. I employed two cost-accounting methods to calculate profits: rate of return on capital stock and rate of return on owners' equity.

74. Luis Colombo and Unión Industrial Argentina, "El problema actual," *BUIA*, Feb. 1931, *44*(746), 25–27.

75. Unión Industrial Argentina, "Por qué la Argentina es un buen mercado: una política librecambista mantiene a la Argentina abierta a los productos extranjeros con un mínimo de competencia local," *BUIA*, Dec. 1927, *41*(708), 762.

76. Luis Colombo and Unión Industrial Argentina, "El problema nacional del petróleo: conferencia de nuestro presidente," *BUIA*, Oct. 1928, *41*(718), 1451–1454.

77. Unión Industrial Argentina, "La racionalización industrial: la normalización," *BUIA*, Feb. 1931, *44*(746), 3–9.

Chapter 2

1. Manuel C. Chueco, *Censo 1889. Estudio sobre los resultados del censo de las industrias* (Buenos Aires: Compañía Sud-Americana de Billetes de Banco, 1890).

2. Barbero and Rocchi argue that this growth rate was attributable to several factors such as new protective tariffs and opening of credit markets. Barbero and Rocchi, 2003, 261–294.

3. A number of authors discuss some of the obstacles to industry: Ferrer, *The Argentine Economy*; Adolfo Dorfman, *Historia de la industria argentina* (Buenos Aires: Escuela de Estudios Argentinos, 1942); Ortíz, *Historia económica de la Argentina*; Díaz Alejandro, *Essays on the Economic History of the Argentine Republic*; and Schvarzer, *La industria que supimos conseguir.*

4. Firm-level data from the manuscript industrial census of 1895 was also used because the 1895 published census failed to report costs and value of output.

5. See "Censo social e industrial de 1895," manuscript (Buenos Aires: Archivo General de la Nación, 1895).

6. Additional information about the census data is available in Appendixes A and B.

7. Real pesos were determined by using the wholesale price index calculated by Nakamura and Zarazaga, "Economic Growth," 254. To obtain values for the years before 1900 and after 1930, I consulted Zarazaga, who kindly submitted his data sources to expand this price index. Sources for the price index are Della Paolera, "How the Argentine Economy Performed," for the years up to 1914, and for after 1914, Roberto L. Domenech, "Estadísticas de la evolución económica de Argentina, 1913–1984." *Estudios de IEERAL,* 1986, *9*(39), 103–185.

8. Number of workers was used as a proxy for labor input in Stephen Haber, Armando Razo, and Noel Maurer, "Political Instability and Economic Performance in Revolutionary Mexico" in *Political Economy of Institutions and Decision* (Cambridge: Cambridge University Press, 2002); and in Kenneth L. Sokoloff, "Productivity Growth in Manufacturing in Early Industrialization: Evidence from the American Northeast, 1820–1860." In Stanley L. Engerman and Robert E. Gallman (eds.), *Long-term Factors in American Economic Growth.* Chicago: University of Chicago Press, 1986, 679–736.

9. "Censo social e industrial de 1895"; *Censo industrial de 1935;* Ministerio de Hacienda, *Tercer censo nacional: Censo de las industrias 1914,* Vol. 7 (Buenos Aires: Talleres Gráficos de L. J. Rosso y Cía., 1917).

10. "Censo social e industrial de 1895."

11. The varying work productivity for adult male, adult female, and child labor was discussed in Claudia Goldin and Kenneth Sokoloff, "Women, Children, and Industrialization in the Early Republic: Evidence from the Manufacturing Censuses," *Journal of Economic History,* Dec. 1982, *42*(4), 741–774; Sokoloff, "Productivity Growth."

12. "La historia de industria en la República Argentina en el siglo pasado," (pamphlet; Buenos Aires, 1930). For further discussion on mid-nineteenth-century soap and candle production techniques, see Campbell Morfit, *A Treatise on Chemistry Applied to the Manufacture of Soap and Candles* (Philadelphia: Parry and McMillan, 1856).

13. Morfit, *Treatise.*

14. Ibid.

15. *Album argentina de industrias* (Buenos Aires, 1910), Available at Biblioteca Tornquist.

16. Rutter, 1916, 47–92.

17. Blanca Sánchez-Alonso, "Labor and Immigration," in Victor Bulmer-Thomas, John H. Coatsworth, and Roberto Cortés Conde (eds.), *The Cambridge Economic History of Latin America: The Long Twentieth Century.* Cambridge University Press, 2006, 382 and 409.

18. Sánchez-Alonso, "Labor and Immigration," 409.

19. Ibid., 409.

20. Dimas Helguerra, *La producción Argentina en 1892, Descripción de la industria nacional—su desarrollo y progreso en toda la República* (Buenos Aires: Goyoaga y Cía, 1893), 169–170.

21. Ibid.

22. Unión Industrial Argentina debated the iron policy (*política del hierro*) before the Argentine congress. Big industrialists lobbied Congress to protect their interests in metallurgy. Metallurgy series, in *Boletín de la Unión Industrial Argentina.*

23. H. Foster Bain, C. E. Williams, and E. B. Swanson, *Las posibilidades de la manufactura de hierro y acero en la Argentina* (Buenos Aires: Talleres Gráficos del Instituto Geográfico Militar, 1925); Solberg, *Oil and Nationalism* (1979).

24. República Argentina, Departamento nacional del trabajo, División de estadística, *Industria textil: capacidad normal de trabajo de los obreros, especialmente mujeres y menores,* Informe del Dr. José Figuerola (Buenos Aires, 1939).

25. Alberto Oscar Petrecolla, "Prices, Import Substitution, and Investment in the Argentine Textile Industry (1920–1939)," Ph.D. dissertation,

Columbia University, New York, 1968, 59; Departamento Nacional del Trabajo, *Industria textil.*

26. Departamento Nacional del Trabajo, *Industria textil*, 38.

27. Cortés Conde shows that it was not until 1919 that industrial production surpassed that for 1913. After 1919, industrial production continued to grow but was somewhat volatile. See Table A5, "Producto Industrial, 1900 = 100," in Cortés Conde, *La economía argentina,* 236–237.

28. In 1904, on average workers had a nine-hour work day and labored on Sunday. In a municipal study of average hours per worker in 1904, 7,323 establishments of the industries under study stated that 97.8 percent of their workers labored between eight and ten hours per day. Of these workers, 37.3 percent regularly worked on Sundays. "Horas de trabajo en los establecimientos industriales," in Buenos Aires (Argentina). Dirección general de estadística municipal, *Censo general de población, edificación, comercio é industrias de la ciudad de Buenos Aires, Levantado en los días 11 y 18 de septiembre de 1904 bajo la administración del Sr. Don Alberto Casares*, por Alberto B. Martinez, director de la dirección general estadística municipal (Buenos Aires: Compañía Sud-Americana de billetes de Banco, 1906).

29. Law 11317 of 1924.

30. Law 11371 of 1924 replaced law 5291 of 1907. It increased the working age from ten to twelve and set literacy requirements. Law 5291 is reprinted in Matilde Alejandra Mercado, *La primera ley de trabajo femenino, "La mujer obrera" (1890–1910)* (Buenos Aires: Centro Editor de América Latina, 1988), 72–74.

31. Article 11 lists activities where working women are prohibited: shipping, mining, construction, machinist (machine operator), working with weapons, cleaning machinery while in motion, tinting and leatherworking, glassblowing, blacksmithing, etc. Law 11317 of 1924.

32. "La mujer en la industria, Cristalerías Papini," 1933, Public relations photographs, Archivo General de la Nación, sección fotos, caja 774, sobre 26, file no. 146,196.

33. The manuscript census of 1895, "Censo social e industrial," offers firm-level data on capital stock and the number of workers for the first half of 1895 and the value of output for the entirety of 1894. The capital stock for the first half of 1895 includes physical capital such as buildings, land, other properties, fixed assets, machinery, and tools. Physical capital is a measure of stock and is needed for only one point in time. The number of workers employed during the first semester of 1895 was used for labor input. Output, however, is a "flow" generated by the stocks of capital and labor. The value of output for the whole year of 1894 was required and used for statistical analyses.

34. The general form of a production function is $Q = f(L, K)$, where Q is output, L is Labor, and K is capital. Output is a function of labor and capital.

The form of the Cobb-Douglas production function is:

$$Q = ß1 \times K^{b2} \times L^{b3} \times e^{ui}$$

Output equals the intercept multiplied by capital raised to the beta coefficient one, multiplied by labor raised to the beta coefficient two. This is not a linear relationship and is thus written in log form.

35. Damodar N. Gujarati, *Basic Econometrics*, Third Edition (New York: McGraw-Hill, Inc., 1995).

36. $ß0 = \ln ß1$ and $ß2$ is the partial elasticity of output with respect to capital input, holding the labor input constant. $ß3$ is the partial elasticity of output with the respect to labor input. It measures the percentage change in output. Gujarati, *Basic Econometrics*, 215.

37. Alpargatas are canvas shoes with rubber bottoms.

38. There were insufficient observations to do statistical analyses of the paper and cement industries. The published census of 1895 failed to report any data for the cement and paper industries, perhaps because these activities had fewer than three firms in each industry.

39. Alan M. Taylor, "Peopling the Pampa: On the Impact of Mass Migration to the River Plate, 1870–1914." *Explorations in Economic History,* Jan. 1997, *34*(1), 100–132: 124–125.

40. Sebastián Galiani and Pablo Gerchunoff, "The Labor Market," in Della Paolera and Taylor (eds.), *New Economic History of Argentina*, 149–151.

41. A price-taking firm cannot influence the prices of its outputs or inputs because it is too small in relation to the total market. Dominant firms set prices because they are large in relation to the total market; price-taking firms adjust their prices accordingly.

42. Helguerra, *La producción Argentina en 1892* (1893), 146.

43. Economies of scale are simply the decline in long-run average cost as a firm increases all inputs and expands its scale of production.

44. *Boletín Industrial* (Buenos Aires, 1900).

45. Equity in this case referred to paid-in capital. Ricardo Pillado, *Anuario Pillado de la deuda pública y sociedades anónimas establecidas en las repúblicas Argentina y del Uruguay para 1899–1900* (Buenos Aires, 1900), 345.

46. Barbero, "Argentina: Industrial Growth and Enterprise Organization, 1880s–1980s," in Alfred Chandler, Jr., Franco Amatori, and Takashi Hikino (eds.), *Big Business and the Wealth of Nations* (Cambridge: Cambridge University Press, 1997), 369.

47. In obtaining HHI, the individual market share of each firm in fractional terms must be squared. The HHI is given by the sum of these squared terms; thus $H = s_i^2$, where s_i is the market share of the ith firm. HHI takes into account both the number of firms in an industry and their differences.

48. "Censo social e industrial."

49. Ibid.

50. Stephen Haber, Armando Razo, and Noel Maurer, *The Politics of Property Rights: Political Instability, Credible Commitments, and Economic Growth in Mexico, 1876–1929* (Cambridge: Cambridge University Press, 2003).

51. "Censo social e industrial."

52. By 1922, both firms reorganized and incorporated into joint-stock companies. The Campomar Woolen Textiles Company became Campomar and Soulas, Ltda., S.A.

53. These firms failed to report material costs in the manuscript survey of 1895.

54. Fábrica Argentina de Alpargatas failed to report material and operating costs; therefore only value of output could be used. (Fábrica Argentina de Alpargatas operated under this name until the 1990s.)

55. I used value of output because Primitiva failed to report costs in the manuscript census survey of 1895.

56. Bieckert was not among the breweries studied because its financial records were not readily available through published sources. Only partial records were published in Argentina's journals of that time, in the *Economist* and *Review of the River Plate*. These records were insufficient to do a full company study. All CR4 results are from four-firm estimations using "Censo social e industrial."

57. Ibid.

58. One hectoliter equals one hundred liters. Dirección General de Estadística de la Provincia de Buenos Aires, *Anuario estadístico de la Provincia de Buenos Aires, 1896, Vol. 3* (La Plata: Talleres de Publicaciones del Museo, 1898), 133.

59. Ibid.

60. Ibid., 133.

61. "Censo social e industrial"; *Segundo censo nacional*; *Censo industrial de 1935*, 44; "Cerveza," *MSA*, 1916, vol. 22, 69–70; *Estadística industrial de 1935* (1937).

62. "Cerveza," *MSA*, 1916, vol. 22, 69–70.

63. Ibid., 70.

64. Letter from Javier Padilla to Minister of Agriculture Honorio Pueyrredón, in *Datos estadísticos referentes a la industria cervecera* (Buenos Aires, May 15, 1917), 5–6.

65. Data on capacity utilization was not available. *Anuario Estadístico de la Provinicia de Buenos Aires, 1896*.

66. The number in each box was estimated between two and four dozen sticks, depending on the type of match.

67. Tariff codes for years 1894, 1905, and 1918.

68. *Censo social e industrial, 1895*; "Fósforos" *MSA*, 1916, *22*, 74; *Estadística Industrial de 1935* (1937).

69. A horizontal merger is the merging of companies that produce and sell a similar product.

70. Argentina's legal entity *sociedad en comandita* was modeled after the *société en commandite* in the French commercial code. It was a legal arrangement that permitted partnerships some limitation on personal liability and the right to sell shares on the Buenos Aires stock exchange. But this form did not enjoy all the privileges associated with the limited liability joint-stock company.

71. *Boletín Industrial* (1894); *Anuario Pillado* 1900.

72. *Finanzas, comercio e industria en la República Argentina de 1899* (Buenos Aires: Imprenta "Roma" de Juan Carbone, 1900), 142.

73. Ibid.

74. Ibid., 139.

75. Ibid.

76. *Anuario de la Dirección*; *Anuario del comercio exterior de la República Argentina*, 1915–1930.

77. *Anuario geográfico argentino* (1941), 333; Petrecolla; Barbero and Rocchi, "Industry."

Chapter 3

1. Beatriz Sarlo, *La imaginación técnica: Sueños modernos de la cultura argentina* (Buenos Aires: Ediciones Nueva Visión, 1992); Robert Arlt, *The Seven Madmen*, translated by Nick Caistor (London: Serpent's Tail, 1998).

2. Calculated using adjusted values of industrial product; Cortés Conde, *La economía argentina*, 230–231.

3. Dorfman, *Historia de la industria argentina*; Carl Solberg, "Tariffs and Politics in Argentina," *Hispanic American Historical Review*, May 1973, *53*(2), 260–284; Díaz Alejandro, *Essays*; Donna Guy, "Carlos Pellegrini and the Politics of Early Argentine Industrialization, 1873–1906," *Journal of Latin American Studies*, 1979, *2*(1), 123–144; Schvarzer, *La industria que supimos conseguir* ; Solberg, *Oil and Nationalism*.

4. Guido Di Tella and Manuel Zymelman, *Los ciclos económicos argentinos* (Buenos Aires: Editorial Paidós, 1973), 170–171.

5. Isabel Sanz-Villaroya, "Economic Cycles in Argentina: 1875–1990," *Journal of Latin American Studies*, Aug. 2006, *38*(3), 549–570.

6. André Hofman, *The Economic Development of Latin America in the Twentieth Century* (Northampton, Mass.: Edward Elgar Press, 2000), 36.

7. The U.N. Economic Commission on Latin America created indices of machine imports for Argentina, but only after 1945. Jorge Katz and Bernardo Kosacoff, "Import-Substituting Industrialization in Argentina, 1940–1980: Its Achievements and Shortcomings," in Enrique Cárdenas, José Antonio Ocampo, and Rosemary Thorp (eds.), *An Economic History of*

Twentieth-Century Latin America. Vol. 3: Industrialization and the State in Latin America: The Postwar Years (New York: Palgrave, 2000), 282–313.

8. Data reporters presented a formula for correctly adjusting tariff values because tariffs on goods depended on numerous factors: weight, country of origin, port destination, current tariff laws. *Anuario de la Dirección General de Estadística; Anuario del comercio exterior de la República Argentina.*

9. Wilson Suzigan, *Indústria brasileira: Origem e desenvolvimento* (São Paulo: Brasiliense, 1986).

10. Available at University of California Los Angeles and Dartmouth College.

11. The index came from Feinstein, *Statistical Tables,* T136–T138. See Appendix C of this book, "Data and Methods of Argentine Machine Investment, 1890–1930," for full explanation and references.

12. For a detailed discussion of technological problems associated with sugar production in Argentina's interior, see Donna J. Guy, "Refinería Argentina, 1888-1930: límites de la tecnología azucarera en una economía periférica," *Desarrollo económico,* Oct.–Dec. 1988, *28*(111), 353–373.

13. Sanz-Villaroya, "Economic Cycles," 562.

14. From 1919 to 1932, investment represents 16 percent of GDP and "its correlation with GDP is 0.88, greater than that of any other variable." Ibid., 564.

15. Ibid., 562.

16. The Caja fixed the rate of one British pound to 5.04 Argentine gold pesos. The paper peso was pegged to the Argentine gold peso at a rate of 2.27, or 11.45 paper pesos equivalent to one British pound. Argentina had a two-currency system; the paper peso was used for domestic trade and the gold peso for international trade.

17. Adelman, chapter 7, "Technical Change on the Frontier," *Frontier Development.*

18. "La industria argentina: lo que dicen las cifras." *Boletín de la Unión Industrial Argentina,* Jan. 15, 1909, *22*(481), 1–2.

19. Sánchez-Alonso, "Labor and Immigration," 377–426.; Taylor, "Peopling the Pampa."

20. Taylor, "External Dependence."

21. Suzigan, *Indústria brasileira.*

22. Southern cone region refers to the southernmost areas of South America, Argentina, Chile, Uruguay, and the southern parts of Paraguay and Brazil.

23. Ford.

24. By 1926, for example, Argentina's railroad network accounted for 43 percent of railroad track in South America. *Times Book on Argentina,* 4.

25. Cochran and Reina.

26. Otto Eduardo Bemberg studied at Arcueil et Institute Tannenberg (France) and Weihenstephan (Germany). *Quien es Quien* (1939).

27. Company machine report, "Compañía General de Fósforos: Gastos de maquinaría para la fábrica en Uruguay" (1929).

28. Sanz-Villarroya; Cortés Conde.

29. Suzigan, 85.

30. Suzigan, 85–86.

31. "Premios a la elaboración de hierro." In *Diario de sesiones de la Cámara de Diputados: Sesiones extraordinarias,* Jan. 8, 1919, 5, 45–51.

32. "Prestamos a establecimientos industriales," *Diario de sesiones de la Cámara de Diputados,* Jul. 4, 1919, 2, 682–683.

33. Hora, "La política económica del proteccionismo en Argentina, 1870–1914," paper presented at the XIV International Economic History Congress, Helsinki, Finland, Aug. 2006.

34. Sergio Berensztein and Horacio Spector, "Business, Government and Law," 324–368. In Della Paolera and Taylor (eds.), *A New Economic History of Argentina,* 325.

35. Di Tella and Zymelman, 172–173; the law 11281 of 1923 raised tariffs across the board for all finished consumer goods produced in the country. The rate varied according to product (35–50 percent); some products had specific duties resulting in an even higher rate.

36. The bill stated that government's only interest in the oil industry was to provide fuel for railroads, public utilities, merchant marine, and domestic industry. "Proyecto de ley." In *Diario de sesiones Cámara de Diputados, sesiones ordinarias,* Aug. 19, 1920, 4, 285.

37. J. A. Massel, "Markets for Machinery and Machine Tools in Argentina." *Special Agent Series,* no. 116, Department of Commerce (Washington: U.S. GPO, 1916); Frank H. von Motz, "Markets for Agricultural Implements and Machinery in Argentina," *Special Agent Series,* no. 125, Department of Commerce (Washington, DC: U.S. GPO, 1916).

38. "Lockwood, Greene, y Co., Inc. a Carlos A. Tornquist," Letter dated Aug. 13, 1924, available at BTQ, file no. industrias 144-8271.

39. Department of Overseas Trade, "The Market for Paper and Paper Products in the Argentine Republic" (London: HMSO, 1920), 11.

40. Fodor y O'Connell, "Argentina y la economía atlántica," 7.

41. Albert O. Hirschman, *The Strategy of Economic Development* (New Haven, Conn.: Yale University Press, 1958).

42. Roderick Floud, *The British Machine-Tool Industry, 1850–1914* (Cambridge: Cambridge University Press, 1976).

43. Alexander Gerschenkron, *Economic Backwardness in Historical Perspective: A Book of Essays* (Cambridge, Mass.: Harvard University Press, 1962).

44. Hirschman, *Strategy,* 99–101.

45. Haber, *Industry and Underdevelopment: The Industrialization of Mexico, 1890–1940* (Palo Alto, Calif.: Stanford University Press, 1989); Edward Beatty, *Institutions and Investment: The Political Basis of Industrialization in Mexico Before 1911* (Palo Alto, Calif.: Stanford University Press, 2001).

46. Ibid.

47. Adelman, *Frontier Development; Anuario Geográfico* indicates that between 1857 and 1930 only 53 percent of all immigrants entering Argentina actually remained in the country. *Anuario geográfico Argentina* (Buenos Aires, 1941), 186.

48. Adelman, *Frontier Development*.

49. Luis Alberto Romero and Hilda Sábato, "Between Rise and Fall: Self-Employed Workers in Buenos Aires, 1850–1880," in Jeremy Adelman (ed.), *Essays in Argentine Labour History, 1870–1930* (Oxford: St. Anthony's College, 1990), 52–72.

50. Cortés Conde and Cornblit discuss the immigrants' role in industry. Roberto Cortés Conde, "Problemas del crecimiento industrial (1870–1914)," in Torcuato Di Tella (ed.), *Argentina, sociedad de masas.* (Buenos Aires: Editorial Universitaria de Buenos Aires, 1965), 70; Oscar Cornblit, "Inmigrantes y empresarios en la política Argentina," *Desarrollo Económico,* Jan.–Mar. 1967, *6*,(24), 667–668.

51. Haber, "Political Economy of Industrialization," 537–584.

52. Katz suggests that Argentine industry developed a structure that endured through the 1980s whereby a handful of modern and large-scale firms that dominated domestic production were surrounded by a constellation of small and inefficient, almost artisan, shops. Jorge Katz, *Structural Reforms, Productivity and Technological Change in Latin America* (Santiago: United Nations Economic Commission for Latin America and the Caribbean, 2001).

53. Dutrénit argues that "the ultimate achievement is to be a 'technologically mature firm' with the ability to 'identify a firm's scope for efficient specialization in technological activities, to extend and deepen these with experience and effort, and to draw selectively on others to complement its own capabilities'." Gabriela Dutrénit, "Building Technological Capabilities in Latecomer Firms: A Review Essay," *Science, Technology, and Society*, Jul.–Dec. 2004, *9*(2), 212–213.

54. Dutrénit, "Building," 209–241, 212–213.

55. Kim analyzed Korea's successful move toward industrial innovation between 1962 and 1995. Linsu Kim, *Imitation to Innovation: The Dynamics of Korea's Technological Learning* (Boston: Harvard Business School Press, 1997), 4.

56. Kim, 5.

57. Kim, 13.

58. Dutrénit, "Building," 220.

59. Martin Bell and Keith Pavitt, "Technological Accumulation and In-

dustrial Growth: Contrasts Between Developed and Developing Countries," *Industrial and Corporate Change*, 1993, *2*(2), 157–210.

60. Alfred Chandler and Herman Daems, "Administrative Coordination, Allocation, and Monitoring: Concepts and Comparisons," in Alfred Chandler and Herman Daems, *Managerial Hierarchies: Comparative Perspectives on the Rise of the Modern Industrial Enterprise* (Cambridge, Mass.: Harvard University Press, 1980), 28–48.

61. Casson, "Entrepreneurship and Business Culture," 43.

62. On networks, see María Inés Bárbero, "Treinta años de estudios sobre la historia de empresas en la Argentina," *Ciclos*, First semester 1995, *5*(8), 179–200.

63. Group categories varied slightly before 1909, but for this project the collected information came from the categories of mechanical equipment, machinery, and motors. From 1909 to 1930, these categories were in group 4 (all mechanical equipment , subdivided in classes 44–53) and group 5 (machines and motors, subdivided in classes 58–71). Classification was determined by the Argentine Ministry of Agriculture, Division of Patents and Trademarks.

64. Kim.

65. Edward Beatty, "Patents and Technological Change in Late Industrialization: Nineteenth Century Mexico in Comparative Context," *History of Technology*, Vol. 24 (2002): 121–150.

66. Lewis contends that one way to determine if tariff rates were effective is to examine the number of foreign manufacturers establishing companies within Argentina; the entry of several foreign manufacturers after 1923 signaled that tariffs were keeping out their exports. Colin M. Lewis, "Immigrant Entrepreneurs, Manufacturing and Industrial Policy in the Argentine, 1922–28." *Journal of Imperial and Commonwealth History*, Oct. 1987, *16*(1), 77–108.

67. Haber, Razo, and Maurer, *Politics of Property Rights*; Alfred D. Chandler, *Scale and Scope: The Dynamics of Industrial Capitalism* (Cambridge, Mass.: Harvard University Press, 1990).

68. Sebastián Galiani and Pablo Gerchunoff, "The Labor Market," 122–169. In Della Paolera and Taylor.

69. In congressional debates, it seems there was an implicit fear that women might find work more easily than men because they were paid significantly less than males. Perhaps the Argentine government sought to ensure male employment by reducing the competition of female labor.

70. Additional explanations for slow growth in female-dominated activities are shortages in financing and production inputs.

71. *Anuario Geográfico Argentino* (1941), 333–334; Petrecolla, "Prices"; "Nature and Scope of the Argentine Economic Recovery, 1937," *Revista de economía argentina* (Aug. 1937), *6*(230), 228.

72. By contrast, Brazil and Mexico had large cotton textile sectors. The Brazilian cotton textile industry grew through the expansion of cotton production and finance. In 1880, Brazil had forty-three cotton textile mills and more than 80,000 spindles. By 1930, there were 354 active cotton mills, more than 2.5 million spindles, and 78,000 looms. Stephen Haber, "Industrial Concentration and the Capital Markets: A Comparative Study of Brazil, Mexico, and the United States, 1830–1930," *Journal of Economic History,* Vol. 51, no. 3 (Sept. 1991), 573. The number of spindles in Mexico reached nearly 250,000 as early as 1888 and grew to more than 800,000 by 1930 and 862,303 by 1933. Haber (2003), 269.

73. Marcela Nari, *Políticas de maternidad y maternalismo político, Buenos Aires, 1890–1940* (Buenos Aires: Editorial Biblos, 2004), 217.

74. Keith Pavitt, "Technologies, Products, and Organisation in the Innovating Firms: What Adam Smith Tells Us and Joseph Schumpeter Doesn't," *Industrial and Corporate Change,* 1998, 7: 433–452, 439.

Chapter 4

1. Andrés M. Regalsky, "Banking, Trade, and the Rise of Capitalism in Argentina, 1850–1930." In Alice Teichova, Ginette Kurgan-van Hentenryk, and Dieter Ziegler (eds.), *Banking, Trade and Industry: Europe, America and Asia from the Thirteenth to the Twentieth Century* (Cambridge: Cambridge University Press, 1997), 359–377.

2. These were private, national, and foreign banks. Andrés M. Regalsky, "La evolución de la banca privada nacional en Argentina (1880–1914): Una introducción a su estudio," in Pedro Tedde and Carlos Marichal (eds.), *La formación de los bancos centrales en España y América Latina. Vol. 2: Suramérica y el Caribe* (Madrid: Banco de España, 1994), 35–59; Charles Jones, "The Transfer of Banking Techniques from Britain to Argentina, 1862–1914," *Revue Internationale d'histoire de la banque* ,1983, 252–264; Rocchi, "Money and Factories: The Myths and Realities of Industrial Financing" (chapter 6), in *Chimneys.*

3. Haber, Razo, and Maurer, *The Politics of Property Rights,* 81.

4. Jones, "The Transfer of Banking," 262–263.

5. Ibid.; for explanation of discounting, see Haber et al., *Politics,* 82.

6. For purposes of this work, I used the term *merchant finance groups* because of these groups' background in merchant trading and financing. In the extant literature, such groups are known as business groups, *grupos económicos,* merchant finance groups, and *financieros.* In other regions, the Korean *chaebol* and Japanese intermarket groups have characteristics similar to these Latin American groups. For a study of business groups across regions, see Mark Granovetter, "Coase Revisited," 93–130.

7. Haber, *Industry and Underdevelopment;* Henry Kirsch, *Industrial Develop-*

ment in a Traditional Society: The Conflict of Entrepreneurship and Modernization in Chile (Gainesville: University Presses of Florida, 1977); Alfonso Quiroz, "Financial Leadership and the Formation of Peruvian Elite Groups, 1884–1930," *Journal of Latin American Studies*, 1989, 20, 49–81; María Inés Barbero, "Mercados, redes sociales y estrategias empresariales en los orígenes de los grupos económicos: De la Compañía de Fósforos al Grupo Fabril (1880–1929)." *Estudios Migratorios Latinoamericanos*, 2000, 44, 119–145.

8. For further discussion on groups' networks and international connections see Jorge Gilbert, "El grupo Tornquist entre la expansión y las crisis de la economía argentina en el siglo XX," *Ciclos en la historia, la economía, y la sociedad*, First and Second semesters 2003, *13*, (25–26), 65–92; María Inés Barbero, "Grupos empresarios, intercambio comercial e inversiones italianas en la Argentina: El caso de Pirelli (1910–1920)," *Estudios Migratorios Latinoamericanos*, 1990, *5*, (15–16), 311–341; Barbero, "Mercados, redes sociales y estrategias empresariales en los orígenes de los grupos económicos: De la Compañía de Fósforos al Grupo Fabril (1880–1929)," *Estudios Migratorios Latinoamericanos*, 2000, *15*, (44), 119–145.

9. Noel Maurer and Tridib Sharma, "Enforcing Property Rights Through Reputation: Mexico's Early Industrialization, 1878–1913," *Journal of Economic History*, 2001, *61*(4), 950–951.

10. These groups are known by other names too. The Devoto group, for instance, has received myriad names from authors such as Demarchi and Italian. Also, the Paper group had members on its directorial board who belonged to a well-known group of French industrialists; they are known as the French group or grupo del Banco Francés.

11. Examples of other finance groups invested in large-scale industries are Bunge and Born, Portalis/Bracht, Di Tella, and Grupo Roberts. The Bunge and Born group were a significant merchant financier family. By the 1920s, Born and Bunge expanded their investments to include finance, agricultural, and nonagricultural ventures (Bolsalona, *Memoria del Presidente de Bolsalona*). Marichal identified Bunge and Born and Portalis/Bracht, among others. See also Barbero, "Mercados." Charles Jones discusses the importance of British capital and the existence of British mercantile and banking groups in Argentina and the River Plate region. Jones, "The State and Business Practice in Argentina, 1862–1914," in *Latin America, Economic Imperialism and the State: The Political Economy of the External Connection from Independence to the Present*, edited by Christopher Abel and Colin M. Lewis (London: University of London, 1985), 184–197; and "Institutional Forms of British Foreign Direct Investment in South America," *Business History*, 1997, *39*(2), 21–41. The Grupo Roberts (or Leng and Roberts Compañía) is discussed in several places and had connections with other merchant finance

groups. Rubén Bozzo and Horacio Mendoza, "Grupo Roberts," *Realidad económico*, 1974, *18*, 50–63. Although all of these groups and foreign capital are worthy of discussion, this chapter is limited to the five groups.

12. For a historical guide to Argentina's "pioneers of industry," see Americo R. Guerrero, *La industria Argentina: su origen, organización y desarrollo* (Buenos Aires: Plantie, 1944); María Susana Azzi and Ricardo de Titto, *Pioneros de la industria argentina* (Buenos Aires: Editorial El Ateneo, 2008).

13. Naomi Lamoreaux, "Banks, Kinship, and Economic Development: The New England Case," *Journal of Economic History*, Sept. 1986, *46*(3), 647–667.

14. Ibid., 667.

15. Ibid.

16. Information for this dataset of 1,282 directors comes from a variety of primary and secondary sources. All fifty-nine companies under study were public corporations whose records were available in business and finance journals of the time. The most important among these records were company by-laws, directors' and stockholder reports, and financial statements. These records are available in three publications: *Monitor de sociedades anónimas; Boletín oficial de la bolsa de comercio de Buenos Aires;* and *Boletín oficial de la República Argentina.* Other important sources included the *Nomina de diputados de la nación por distrito electoral, período 1854–1991 (Hasta el 31–5–1991)* (Buenos Aires: Dirección de Archivo, Publicaciones y Museo, Subdirección de publicaciones e investigaciones históricas, 1991); *Diario de sesiones de los diputados de la nación*; and Peter H. Smith's original dataset for *Argentina and the Failure of Democracy*, Smith, "Argentine Chamber of Deputies Roll Calls, Sessions 1904–1955," deposited at the Data and Program Library Service, University of Wisconsin-Madison (Apr. 1974).

17. "Bolsa de comercio de Buenos Aires: Historia de la jurisdicción y practicas comerciales desde la época del Virreynato," donated by Luis Colombo to Biblioteca Nacional, 1935; British Chamber of Commerce in the Argentine Republic (Incorporated), *Annual Report,* for years 1920–1930.

18. *Quien es quien en la Argentina: Biografías contemporáneas* (Buenos Aires: Guillermo Kraft, 1939).

19 Cortés Conde, "Problemas del crecimiento industrial," 59–83; Cornblit, "Empresarios," 641–691.

20. Ibid.

21. Donna Guy, "La industria argentina, 1870–1940: Legislación comercial, mercado de acciones y capitalización extranjera." *Desarrollo Económico,* Oct.–Dec. 1982, *22*(87), 351–374.; Barbero, "Argentina: Industrial Growth," 368–393. Jorge Gilbert, "El Grupo Tornquist, 1906–1930" (unpublished manuscript), XVI Jornadas de Historia Económica, Asociación Argentina de Historia Económica, Universidad Nacional de Quilmes, 1998.

22. Rory Miller, "Business History in Latin America: an introduction,"

In Carlos Dávila and Rory Miller (eds.), *Business History in Latin America: The Experience of Seven Countries* (Liverpool, England: Liverpool University Press, 1999), 14.

23. Barbero, "Grupos empresarios, intercambio comercial e inversiones italianas en la Argentina: El caso de Pirelli (1910–1920)," *Estudios Migratorios Latinoamericanos*, 1990, *5*(15–16), 311–341. Barbero, "Mercados," 123.

24. The legal requirement was that one shareholder could not represent more than one-tenth of the votes conferred by all shares issued, or represent more than 20 percent of the votes present at the meeting. Argentine Commercial Code of 1889, Article 354.

25. Hora, "Landowning Bourgeoisie"; Jorge Sábato, *La clase dominante en la Argentina moderna: Formación y características* (Buenos Aires: Imago Mundi, 1991).

26. Cochran and Reina, *Entrepreneurship in Argentine Culture.* See also William J. Fleming, "The Cultural Determinants of Entrepreneurship and Economic Development: A Case Study of Mendoza Province, Argentina, 1861–1914," *Journal of Economic History*, Mar. 1979, *39*(1), 211–224.

27. *Anuario geográfico argentino* (1941).

28. *Finanzas, comercio e industria en la República Argentina de 1898* (Buenos Aires: Imprenta "Roma" de Juan Carbone, 1899), available at Biblioteca Tornquist, Buenos Aires, Argentina (hereafter BTQ).

29. *Finanzas* (1899).

30. Tariff laws and modifications of no. 3050 of 1894, no. 4933 (Dec. 20, 1905), and no. 10362 (1918).

31. These four leading directors were (1) Julian Balbin, on the directorial boards of Banco de la Provincia de Buenos Aires and Argentina Fábrica de Papel; (2) Angel Estrada, president of the Banco de la Nación from 1900 to 1910 and a director in the paper company; (3) Tomás Estrada, on the board of Banco de la Nación and Argentina Fábrica de Papel; (4) Indalecio Gomez, on Argentina Fábrica de Papel's board and director of both Banco de la Nación and Banco de la Provincia de Buenos Aires. Source: dataset of 1,282 directors and data collected from *Monitor de sociedades anónimas* (hereafter *MSA*), *Boletín oficial de la bolsa de comercio de Buenos Aires* (hereafter *BOB*), and *Boletín oficial de la República Argentina* (hereafter *BORA*).

32. Angel Estrada was president of the Banco de la Nación from 1900 to 1910. Tomás Estrada was also a voting member of the bank's board. Banco de la Nación Argentina, *El Banco de la Nación Argentina en su cincuentenario, 1891–1941* (Buenos Aires: Impreso en la Argentina, 1941).

33. Credit data collected from the transaction books of the Archivo del Banco de la Provincia de Buenos Aires (1906–1916) and Banco de la Nación Argentina (1892–1896). Also Rocchi, chapter 6 in *Chimneys*.

34. Dataset of 1,282 directors; Regalsky, "La evolución."

35. U.S. Bureau of Statistics, *Special Consular Reports,* 39.

36. Ibid.

37. Argentina had a sheep wool industry, but Masllorens imported higher-quality merino wools and cashmere from Spain. *Finanzas* (1899).

38. Argentina Código de Comercio de 1889 required that corporations must initially form with a minimum of ten shareholders.

39. In company elections, shareholders representing at least 75 percent of the subscribed capital and the affirmative vote of shareholders representing at least half of the subscribed capital were required for passing any resolution. Company resolutions were issues pertaining to any change to the company: anticipated dissolution, prolongation of company life span, merger, reduction of capital, reinstatement or increase of capital, change or modification in the statutory objects of the company, and other modification to the company's statutes. *Código de comercio de 1889,* articles 335–345 (1889).

40. "Baibiene y Antonini," company bylaws, *MSA* (1922).

41. A son and nephew were both directly involved in his businesses. Cervecería Quilmes, *Quilmes Cerveza: Quilmes Centenario.* (Buenos Aires: Quilmes, 1990) (document available at office of Quilmes Brewery, Quilmes, Buenos Aires province); dataset of 1,282 directors.

42. Initially, lawyers of Quilmes Brewery wanted the case dismissed, arguing that Baenninger's wife and children failed to show evidence proving the legal marriage and legitimacy of his children. Carlos Silveyra, *Sucesión Baenninger versus Cervecería Argentina Quilmes*, printed civil suit case regarding inheritors' rights to a private company's shares and bonds. (Buenos Aires, 1925), 4–6 (document available at Biblioteca Nacional, Buenos Aires, Argentina).

43. Silveyra, *Sucesión*.

44. Juan Baenninger received 3 percent per year during his tenure with the company. Silveyra, 3, 15–16.

45. Casson argues that succession to eldest son is a common attribute among business network cultures. Casson, "Entrepreneurship and Business Culture," in Jonathan Brown and Mary B. Rose, *Entrepreneurship, Networks, and Modern Business* (Manchester: Manchester University Press, 1993), 34.

46. Bemberg initially went to Brazil in 1850 on medical orders to help his asthmatic condition. While in Brazil, he planned to visit Buenos Aires. Before embarking to Buenos Aires, he obtained a "letter of introduction" from the Prussian minister in Rio de Janeiro to present to high society in Buenos Aires. In 1853, Bemberg married a daughter of a wealthy Ocampo family. (A "porteño" is a resident of the port city, Buenos Aires.) Cervecería Quilmes.

47. Cervecería Quilmes, 15.

48. Ingrid Fey, "First Tango in Paris" (Ph.D. dissertation, University of California Los Angeles, 1996).

49. Cervecería Quilmes.

50. Fey.

51. Otto Eduardo studied at Arcueil et Institute Tannenberg in France. Cervecería Quilmes, 18–19.

52. Clifford Kono, Donald Palmer, Roger Friedland, and Matthew Zafonte, "Lost in Space: The Geography of Corporate Interlocking Directorates," *American Journal of Sociology,* Jan. 1998, *103*(4): 869–911.

53. Kono et al.

54. In 1830, the finance house Bunge, Bornefeld y Cía. was the predecessor to the finance house Altgelt, Ferber y Cía., which eventually through marriage ties became the finance house Ernesto Tornquist y Cía. Ernesto was hired by Altgelt, Ferber, y Cía. He later married the daughter of Adan Altgelt. Ernesto Tornquist y Cía, Limitada, *Ernesto Tornquist y Compañía, Limitada, 1874–1924: En occasion del cincuentenario de la existencia de nuestra casa bajo el nombre Ernesto Tornquist y Cía, Ltda., y en homenaje a su ilustre fundador Don Ernesto Tornquist* (Buenos Aires: La Compañía, 1924), 9.

55. Ernesto Tornquist y Cía, 3–8; for further discussion on Tornquist investments see Jorge Gilbert, "Los negocios del holding Tornquist," in José Villarruel (ed), *Prosperidad y miseria. Contribuciones a la historia económica argentina,* Chapter 4 (Buenos Aires: Editorial Al Margen, 2004); Gilbert, "El Grupo Tornquist" (2003).

56. "Compañía Nacional de Sombreros," *MSA* (1912).

57. "Compañía Nacional de Sombreros," *MSA* (1911), 368–369.

58. Sábato argues that elites shifted investment rather frequently to avoid failure in any one venture.

59. Roberts, Leng y Cía reportedly had international connections to the Baring Brothers and finance house Morgan from New York. *Guía descriptiva de las industrias* (Buenos Aires, 1895), available at Biblioteca Tornquist; "Fábrica Casati de San Nicolás," bylaws (June 23, 1910); "Fenix Fábrica de Papel," *MSA,* 1913, *6,* 151–153.

60. These results come from measures of annual return on capital stock and return on equity; "Fenix" and "Casati."

61. As president and major shareholder of the companies, Leng had substantial control. "Casati" and "Fenix Fábrica de Papel," *BOB* (Nov. 29, 1926), 1146.

62. "Papelera Argentina," bylaws, *BOB* (1924).

63. Jean Tirole, "A Theory of Collective Reputations," *Review of Economic Studies,* 1996, *63,* 1–22.

64. Gilbert, "El grupo Tornquist entre la expansión."

65. Also, he was assigned a special diplomatic mission to survey the possibilities of potential foreign investment in Argentina. Ernesto Tornquist y Cía (1924), 18.

66. Ernesto Tornquist y Cía (1924), 12–13.

67. "En todos los grandes problemas de la economía argentina, [Ernesto] Tornquist adopta como solución, la acción." Ernesto Tornquist y Cía (1924), 6.

68. It is not unusual in business networks to have "dominant personalities" who personify the corporate cultural norms. Casson, 43; Cochran and Ruben.

69. Illuminating examples are "Piccardo Tabacos" photo album (ca. 1930), "Rezzónico, Ottonello y Cía" photo album, file no. (album industrias 14, BTQ), and "Ferrum" photo album (ca. 1940), *Revista TAMET* (albums available at BTQ); "Quilmes" pamphlet (1949) and Quilmes company history and album (1990).

70. "Quilmes," *La Nación,* 1919 (BTQ).

71. In 1919, thirty-six hundred workers went on strike at Quilmes Brewery to protest directors' rejection of their demands for a "20 percent increase in salaries; eight hour day; abolition of overtime; waterproof clothing of cellar workers; and rubber shoes for operatives in the bottling department." "Note on News: Quilmes Brewery," *Review of the River Plate*, Nov. 12, 1920, 1285.

72. "Correspondencia enviada por la secretaria general de la Liga de las Naciones al Señor Carlos Alfredo Tornquist, delegado por la Argentina, a la conferencia financiera internacional," letter dated June 30 1920, available at BTQ, file no. Finanzas 1052–1.

73. "Cervecería Palermo," directors' report, *MSA* (1921), 150.

74. Ibid.

75. *Boletín industrial* (Sept. 21, 1893), Biblioteca Nacional.

76. The three match shops were Bolondo, Lavigne y Cia., A Dellacha y Hermanos, and Francisco Lavaggi e hijo. Pillado, *Anuario Pillado* (1899), 221–222.

77. "Las industrias nacionales: hilandería de lanas peinadas y fábrica de tejidos de Campomar y Soulas," *La Epoca*, Oct. 16, 1918 (available at BTQ, file no. industria 332).

78. "Masllorens," company bylaws, *MSA* (1919); Masllorens financial statements, *BORA* (1921–1930).

79. From 1902 to 1917, there were between seven and twenty-six chartered banks in Argentina. *MSA* listed operating banks every month.

80. Dirección General de Estadística Municipal, Municipalidad de la Capital, República Argentina. *Anuario estadístico de la Ciudad de Buenos Aires* (Buenos Aires: Compañía Sudamericana de Billetes de Banco, 1903–1915) contains information on banks' deposits and savings; also, *MSA* published monthly banking information (I looked at October and December of every year 1915–1929); "Estado de los bancos según sus balances al 31 de octubre

de 1915" and "Estado de los bancos según sus balances al 31 de octubre de 1916" *MSA*, 1916, *22,* 128–129; "Estado de los bancos según sus balances al 31 de octubre de 1917" *MSA*, 1917, *24,* 112; "Estado de los bancos según sus balances al 31 de diciembre de . . ." *MSA* 1918–1929, Vols. 26–48.

81. Exchange rate: 1 British pound = 5.14 Argentine gold pesos. "Cristalerías Rigolleau," company reports and balance sheets 1914–1917, *BOB* (1914–1918).

82. Return on equity was 1–3 percent annually. *BOB* (1914–1918). "Cristalerías Rigolleau," balance sheets 1914–1917.

83. "Cristalerías Rigolleau," bylaws, *BOB* (first semester 1908), 473–477.

84. There is no 1919 balance sheet because directors and shareholders suspended financial activity temporarily to reorganize bylaws and manage debt. Special shareholder meeting, 807–810, in "Renovación de obligación hipotecaria otorgada por la sociedad anónima 'Cristalerías Rigolleau' y la fideicomisaria sociedad anónima 'Financiera, Comercial, e Industrial Ernesto Tornquist y Compañía, Ltda,'" *BOB* (May 15, 1922), 807–816.

85. "Cristalerías Rigolleau," new mortgage terms, *BOB* (1919).

86. Each bond was sold for 1,000 gold pesos each, and accrued 8 percent interest per year. The actual loan was reduced to 600,000 gold pesos because land valued at 150,000 gold pesos was part of the contract. "Renovación de obligación hipotecaria," 814–816.

87. Debenture holders were known as trustees of the company. Debenture Law, law no. 8875, Feb. 23, 1912, articles 1–36.

88. Reserves were money from profits collected annually and held in a contingency fund on the liability side of the balance sheet.

89. Compañía General de Fósforos, balance sheets and income statements (1904–1930).

90. Piccardo Tabacos, balance sheets and income statements.

91. "Talleres Metalúrgicos," director's report, *MSA*.

92. "Talleres Metalúrgicos," special report, *BOB*.

93. "Talleres Metalúrgicos," special stockholder's meeting report and revised company bylaws, *MSA* (1921–1922).

94. The merger was a way to consolidate resources and reduce the number of competitors.

95. *Código de comercio de 1889,* artículo 318 (1889). Equity is reserves and paid-in capital. Both are located on the liability side of the balance sheet.

96. This is based on the profit-and-loss calculations made for the fifty-nine companies under study.

97. According to Argentina's bankruptcy laws, a joint-stock company could dissolve for any number of reasons. The law stated specifically that if at any time during the firm's life it had a loss amounting to 50 percent of its subscribed capital, the firm was obligated to inform the legal commercial courts

and publish their near-bankrupt status in the local newspapers. (Subscribed capital is the monetary amount of shares still owed to the company by shareholders.) If the loss amounted to 75 percent of the company's paid-in capital, then liquidation was compulsory (the exact term used is "disolución ipso jure"). Isaac Halperín, *Manual de sociedades anónimas por Juez de la Cámara Nacional de Apelaciones en lo comercial* (Buenos Aires: Roque de Palma, 1961), 374.

98. Also, companies could forestall creditors or make special payment arrangements if they declare bankruptcy. Archivo General de la Nación Argentina, "Las resoluciones, memorias, disolución y retiro de personería jurídica de La Unión Sociedad Anónima Cooperativa de Fósforos, 1908–11" (Manuscript) Buenos Aires: Archivo General de la Nación-Tribunales comerciales, hereafter Fósforos-AGN. This manuscript had company information such as bylaws, credit sheets, inventories, invoices, balance sheets, and final bankruptcy report.

99. "Cervecería del Norte," balance sheet and income statements.

100. "Cervecería del Norte," director's reports, *MSA* (1913–1922).

101. In the early twentieth century, most brewers were located in Buenos Aires province. Beer making and transport required constant refrigeration and was costly. Prior to low-cost refrigerated railways and trucks, there was a risk that beer would spoil; the costs to transport it across the large geographical region from Buenos Aires to Tucumán were relatively high.

102. "Quilmes y Del Norte," anniversary issue of Bemberg's breweries (1940), BTQ.

103. "Estado de los bancos según sus balances al 30 de noviembre de 1929," *MSA,* 1929, *48,* 166.

104. Regalsky; Taylor.

105. "Elaboración General del Plomo," director's report, *BOB,* 1916.

106. "Elaboración General del Plomo," financial statements and director's reports, *BOB,* 1924–1928.

107. Rocchi, in *Chimneys,* 197.

108. Fósforos-AGN.

109. "Unión Fósforos," balance sheets (1909–10).

110. Fósforos-AGN.

111. "Baibiene y Antonini," balance sheets, *BORA* (1923–1930).

112. "Baibiene y Antonini," *MSA* (1925–1930).

113. "Fosforera Argentina," stockholder report, *MSA* (1927).

114. Specific examples include Primitiva, Baibiene y Antonini, Chientelassa Hermanos, and Cervecería Buenos Aires. Court archives Letras B, C, and L, available at Tribunales Comerciales, Archivo General de la Nación, Buenos Aires, Argentina (hereafter AGN).

115. "Baibiene y Antonini contra Morini," Letra B, legajo no. 70, año 1912. Buenos Aires: Departamento comerciales tribunales, AGN (litigation, manuscript).

116. Write-offs appear on the liability side of the balance sheet or income sheet.

117. This company was later acquired by British investors and renamed Unión Fundición y Talleres.

118. "Chientelassa Hermanos," Letra C, legajo no. 2, 1891–1896. Buenos Aires: Departamento comerciales tribunales, AGN, 1898 (litigation, manuscript).

Chapter 5

1. Quiroz, "Financial Leadership," 56.

2. The law classified violations as either "per se" or contrary to the "rule of reason." Per se violations were defined as certain acts of conduct that were deemed patently anticompetitive. In contrast, the rule of reason applied to certain practices whose anticompetitive effects were questionable. These were judged case by case, but rule of reason was somewhat of a gray area, and in per se it was difficult to catch explicit agreements between two competitors. Argentine law number 11210, passed Aug. 28, 1923.

3. *Boletín oficial de la república Argentina* (hereafter *BORA*) published balance sheets and income statements beginning in 1910. *Boletín oficial de la bolsa de comercio de Buenos Aires* (hereafter *BOB*) began publishing balance sheets and income statements in 1905. The number of annual balances in my possession varies from three to twenty-seven years per company. The variation is partly due to companies' going bankrupt after only a few years in business. For three companies, I have fewer than five years of financial statements. They are the cement manufacturer Cemento Argentina, the match firm Unión Fósforos Cooperativa, and the metallurgy company Unión Herradores. I included these companies because part of the goal of this book is to compare the performance of both failed and successful companies.

4. They contain data on physical and working capital, short- and long-term debt, owner's equity, sales, costs, retained earnings, profit, and loss. I estimate profits, debt-to-equity, and liquidity to assess firms' performance from 1904 to 1930.

5. Haber, *Industry and Underdevelopment*. See also A. J. Arnold, "Innovation, Deskilling, and Profitability in the British Machine-Tools Industry: Alfred Herbert, 1887–1927." *Journal of Industrial History,* 1999, *2*, 50<=–71"; and Margaret Levenstein, *Accounting for Growth: Information Systems and the Creation of the Large Corporation.* Palo Alto, Calif.: Stanford University Press, 1998.

6. See Chapter 4 for additional information about this dataset.

7. *Memorias del directorio* or annual directors' reports were located in *BOB* beginning in the 1910s. I also located memorias, companies' histories and records in several nonserial publications beginning in 1898, at the Biblioteca

Tornquist, Buenos Aires (hereafter BTQ). Memorias were also published in *Anuario Pillado* 1898–1900, *Anuario Kraft* 1895–1930, *BOB*, and *Monitor de sociedades anónimas*, 1899–1930 (hereafter *MSA*).

8. Among the earliest scholarly works to discuss Argentina's fluctuating cycles was Guido Di Tella and Manuel Zymelman, *Las etapas del desarrollo económico argentino* (1967).

9. David Joslin, *A Century of Banking in Latin America to Commemorate the Centenary in 1962 of the Bank of London and South America, Limited* (London: Oxford University Press, 1963), 25–27.

10. See Cortés Conde, *La economía argentina*; Adolfo Sturzenegger and Ramiro Moya, "Economic Cycles," in Della Paolera and Taylor; and Arturo O'Connell, "Argentina into the Depression: Problems of an Open Economy," in Rosemary Thorp (ed.), *An Economic History of Twentieth-Century Latin America, Vol. 2* (Oxford: Oxford University Press, 2000), 165; Di Tella and Zymelman, *Las etapas*.

11. O'Connell, "Argentina into the Depression."

12. Sturzenegger and Moya, "Economic Cycles," 87.

13. Economic downturns resulted in the insolvency of a significant number of small and medium-scale retail and manufacturing companies. *MSA* reported general bankruptcy figures. The finance journals *Cronista comercial* and *Avisador mercantíl* reported company names and amounts lost in bankruptcy. These sources are located at BTQ; in *Cronista comercial,* look under Indice estadístico de las convocatorias, quiebras, concursos, civiles y arreglos desde el primero de enero al 30 de septiembre, 1920–1940.

14. T. R. Ainscough, "Growing Money in Argentina: A Concise Guide to Capital Investment for All Classes," *Review of the River Plate,* June 8, 1928, *65,* 26–27, 29 (hereafter RRP).

15. "International stock dividends," weekly and monthly series, *Economist,* 1900–1930.

16. Bank data determined from Banco El Hogar Argentino, Banco de Galicia y Buenos Aires, and Banco Popular Argentino. "Informaciones," series, *MSA,* 1916, *21,* 126–127; *22,* 39; and 1917. For the years 1918–1929, sources were *BOB* and *BORA*.

17. Two companies had leading political figures on their directorial board: Benito Villanueva sat on the board of Fosforera Argentina and Carlos Pelligrini (descendent of Former President Carlos Pelligrini) sat on the board of LaMetal/Thyssen.

18. Before 1900, this company had a financial relationship with the Baring Brothers and J. P. Morgan Co. *Guía descriptiva de las industrias.* Buenos Aires, 1895, available at BTQ.

19. "Fábrica Argentina de Alpargatas," company report, *MSA,* 1921, *31,* 122.

20. "El Eje," balance sheets and income statements, *BORA* and *BOB*, 1905–1930.

21. A small amount of debt was listed in 1921 but apparently quickly paid off because debt returned to zero in 1922.

22. "Compañías de Ernesto Tornquist y Cía," letter (six pages), dated February 1930, available at BTQ, document no. Misc 130–20.

23. Ibid.

24. "El auge de importaciones de posguerra," *Boletín de la Unión Industrial Argentina*, Apr. 15, 1924 (664) (hereafter *BUIA*).

25. Mark Falcoff, "Economic Dependency in a Conservative Mirror: Alejandro Bunge and the Argentine Frustration, 1919–1943," *Inter-American Economic Affairs*, 1982, *35*(4), 64.

26. The Argentine tariff is a valuation tariff and not based on the actual value of the items imported. Rutter, *Tariff Systems*, 1–62: 47–50, 55. See also custom and tariff laws: law 2766 of 1891; law 2923 of 1892; law 3050 of 1894; law 3672 of 1898; law 3890 of 1900; law 4933 of Dec. 20, 1905; law 10,220 of 1917; law 10,362 of 1918; law 11,022 of 1920; and law 11,281 of Dec. 6, 1923, in effect 1924.

27. Julio Berlinski estimated that "for cotton, wool, and silk, the tariff rates for spun fibers varied between 5 and 14 percent, the rates for cloth varied between 23 and 46 percent while the rates for finished produced varied between 40 and 46 percent." Berlinski, "International trade," in Della Paolera and Taylor, 203 and 207.

28. Díaz Alejandro, "The Argentine Tariff, 1906–40," *Oxford Economic Papers*, Mar. 1967, *19*(1), 84.

29. Ibid., 86–88.

30. See Rocchi, *Chimneys*, 204, for description of early works on the tariff.

31. James R. Scobie, *Revolution on the Pampas: A Social History of Argentine Wheat, 1860–1910* (Austin: University of Texas Press, 1977), 96.

32. Ibid.

33. "Primitiva" and "Salinas," balance sheets, *BOB* (1913).

34. "Primitiva" and "Salinas," balance sheets, *BOB* (1918–19). Moya and Sturzenegger calculated a GDP growth rate of 13.3 percent in 1918. Moya and Sturzenegger, "Economic Cycles," 97.

35. Between 1890 and 1925, Primitiva was reported to have paid 637 percent in dividends, averaging 18.2 percent per annum. T. R. Ainscough, "Growing Money," 19.

36. Profit rates for Compañía de Productos Conen are my estimation.

37. "Compañía de Productos Conen," stockholder's meeting, *MSA* (Apr. 27, 1916), *21*, 95.

38. Díaz Alejandro, "Argentine Tariff, 1906–1940," 90.

39. See Chapter 3 for description of data and methods.

40. Andrea Lluch, "La inversion extranjera directa norteamericana en Argentina (1900–1930)" Paper presented at the Fifth Colloquium on the History of the Firm, Universidad de San Andrés, Mar. 2007.

41. Before his death in 1908, Ernesto went on a special mission abroad to survey the possibilities for foreign investors.

42. "Lockwood, Greene, y Co., Inc. a Carlos A. Tornquist," letter dated August 13, 1924, available at BTQ, file no. industrias 144–8271.

43. Ibid.

44. "U.S. banks were not allowed to invest in Latin America until just before the First World War." Bulmer-Thomas (2003), 97.

45. Department of Overseas Trade, prepared by the Anglo-South American Bank, *Report on the Market for Paper and Paper Products in the Argentina Republic* (London: His Majesty's Stationary Office, October 1921), 36–37.

46. Oligopoly tendencies were common among other groups in Latin America as well. Quiroz, "Financial Leadership," 59–60.

47. Haber, *Industry and Underdevelopment.*

48. Several organizations estimated the population size on the basis of city censuses, population density, and immigration statistics between the censuses of 1914 and 1935. Alejandro Bunge, *Población total de la Argentina: Razón de su crecimiento* (Buenos Aires: Oceana, 1917). See also "Argentina's Population," *RRP* (July 5, 1929), *67*, 51.

49. *Anuario de la Dirección General de Estadística; Anuario del comercio exterior de la República Argentina.*

50. "Fosforera Argentina: Fósforos en gruesas de 4–40 hechos y vendidos," *Boletín Industrial,* 1910.

51. "Fosforera Argentina," stockholder report, *MSA* (1927).

52. Honorio Pueyrredón, Ministry of Agriculture, "La industria cervecera," letter, Buenos Aires, May 15, 1917, available at BTQ.

53. "Cervecería Palermo," *Argentine Yearbook* (1903), 448; balance sheet June 30, 1902; "Cervecería Palermo," stockholder's meeting, *MSA* (1918), 134.

54. "Cantábrica," memoria del directorio, *BOB* (Oct. 10, 1927), 838–839.

55. Cervecería Argentina Quilmes, *Cebada cervecera: instrucciones para cultivar con éxito su semilla* (Buenos Aires: Casa Jacobo Peuser, Mar. 1918).

56. Ibid., 4.

57. Solberg, *Oil and Nationalism.*

58. Bain, Williams, and Swanson, *Las posibilidades.*

59. Bain et al., *Las posibilidades,* 33–34.

60. Solberg, *Oil and Nationalism.*

61. "La Unión Sociedad Anónima Cooperativa de Fósforos limitada,

1906–1912," manuscript available at Departamento comerciales tribunales, Archivo general de la Nación de Argentina, Buenos Aires, Argentina (hereafter Fósforos-AGN).

62. "Fosforera Argentina," 1910.

63. Dilmus James, *Used Machinery and Economic Development* (East Lansing, MI: Michigan State University, 1974).

64. "Ferrum" *BOB*, Director's report, Jan. 20, 1930, 174.

65. "Defensa de la industria nacional (contra dumping)." *Diario de sesiones, Vol. 4* (Sept. 18, 1919), 815–818.

66. Barbero, "Mercados."

67. Miller and Dávila, "Business History in Latin America," 13.

68. These estimates were based on a cross-section of companies taken between 1921 and 1923: Compañía General de Fósforos, Cristalerías Rigolleau, Fosforera Argentina, Compañía General de Envases, Cristalerías Papini, El Eje, Ferrum, Cervecería Río Segundo, Cervecería Palermo, Introductora, Piccardo Tabacos, Elaboración General del Plomo, and Campomar y Soulas. Monthly data reported in "Crónica de asambleas," *MSA*, 1921–1923.

69. *The Economist*, 1900–1930, for government bond yields. Bank data came from Banco Escolar Argentina, Banco el Hogar Propio, Banco Popular Argentino, Banco de Italia y Río de la Plata, Nuevo Banco Italiano, and Banco de Galicia y Buenos Aires. Monthly data reported in "Crónica de asambleas," *MSA*, 1921–1923.

70. Guidelines recommended 5 percent to a reserve fund, 10 percent to a contingent liability fund, 10 percent to the directorial board, 2 percent to the auditors, and any remainder to be distributed to shareholders. Ministerio de Justicia, Inspección General de Justicia, *Nueva fórmula obligatoria para balances de sociedades anónimas, nacionales y extranjeras. Decreto aprobatorio del Ministerio de Justicia e Instrucción Pública*, "Edición especial del Monitor de sociedades anónimas y patentes de invención," (Buenos Aires, 1925).

71. The Argentine Commercial Code declared that a reserve fund should be formed by at least 2 percent of realized net profits each year until such fund amounted to a minimum of 10 percent of the capital stock of the company. Some companies held reserves well beyond the basic requirements. Argentina Ministerio de Justicia, *Argentine Commercial Code of 1889* (1889), article 369.

72. In this legal case, Manuel Chueco was suing the company for his share of 2 percent of annual profits for serving as auditor for one year. He claimed that because all the profits were designated to reserve funds, he received no compensation for his services. "Manuel Chueco versus Hilanderías Argentinas de Algodón, 1906," *MSA*, 1909, 7, 126–129.

73. "Fosforera Argentina," stockholder's meeting, *MSA*, Dec. 27, 1909.

74. Ibid.

75. In 1911, President Hilario Leng wrote the bylaws of his paper firm, Casati, which clearly stated that the annual profits were to be distributed first to reserve funds, second to bondholders, and last to dividend payments. "Fábrica de Papel Casati," company bylaws, *MSA* (1911).

76. "Compañía General de Fósforos," balance sheets and income statements, *BOB*, 1918–1929.

77. I used paid-in capital as deposits because this is money deposited and paid for by the investors and cannot be quickly liquidated under normal circumstances.

78. "Cantábrica" memoria del directorio, *BOB* (1920).

79. "Cantábrica" memoria del directorio, *BOB* (1930).

80. "Cristalerías Papini," memoria del directorio, *BOB* (Apr. 15, 1929), 854–855.

81. "Cristalerías Papini," memoria del directorio, *BOB* (June 2, 1930), 1496, and *BOB* (June 8, 1931), 706; "Cristalerías Papini," income statement (1929).

82. "Cristalerías Papini," June 2, 1930, 1496; and June 8, 1931, 706.

83. AGN, Unión Fósforos.

84. Archivo del Instituto Ravignani, Universidad de Buenos Aires," Memoria y balance general, Cervecería Palermo, 30 de Junio de 1900," Box 17, Buenos Aires, Argentina.

85. Bieckert was primarily owned by British investors, and Quilmes stock was listed on the Parisian stock exchange.

86. "Cervecería Buenos Aires," stockholder's meeting, *MSA* (1909) *8*, 264–265.

87. "Cerveza," *MSA* (1916), *22*, 69.

88. "Annual general meeting of shareholders of the Bieckert Brewery Company," *RRP* (Nov. 19, 1920), 1363.

89. "Ferrum," company bylaws, *MSA* (1910).

90. Tornquist group began in 1902 when they bought shares in the sociedad en comandite Rezzónico y Ottonello. They acquired and merged with three metallurgy firms, El Ancla, José Ottonello y Luis A. Huergo, and Antonio Rezzónico, to create Talleres Metalúrgicos. In 1909, they changed the company's legal status to that of a limited liability joint-stock company. From 1923 to 1926, they organized a great merger of five metallurgy firms (1923–1926) to create the largest metallurgy corporation in Argentina, Talleres Metalúrgicos San Martín. The five merging firms were Alberto de Bary y Cía.; Zimmerman, Noe, y Cía., Eugenio C. Noe y Cía; Mercantíl y Rural (1923); and the Anglo-Argentine Iron and Steel Company. *Album Argentino* (Buenos Aires: BTQ, 1909); Talleres Metalúrigicos, antes Rezzónico, Ot-

tonello, y Compañía, *MSA* (1909), 7, 81–82. *Revista Tamet* (Buenos Aires: BTQ, Abril–Mayo 1944).

91. Before this, in 1910 Argentina Fábrica de Papel acquired the assets of two dissolved companies, Buenos Aires and Americana, to increase its physical capital. Americo E. Rava, "Historia y estado actual de la industria del papel en la Argentina." In Centro Argentino de Ingenieros (eds.), *Los ingenieros argentinos en la industria nacional* (Buenos Aires: El Centro, 1941), 123–138.

92. "Papelera Argentina," memoria del directorio, *BOB* (Oct. 31, 1927), 1005.

93. Ibid.

94. "Papelera Argentina," memoria del directorio, *BOB* (Oct. 31, 1927), 1005–1006.

95. "Papelera Argentina," memoria del directorio, *BOB* (Nov. 11, 1929), 1371.

96. "Derechos al papel,"*Diario de sesiones de la Cámara de diputados, Sesiones extraordinarias* (Jan. 13, 1915), 7, 437–444; "Derechos de importación de papel, Proyecto de Ley," *Diario de sesiones de la Cámara de Diputados, Sesiones ordinarias* (Sept. 5, 1916), 2, 1779–1781.

97. See source for import duties, note 49.

98. Rocchi, *Chimneys*, 205.

99. Schvarzer, *Empresarios*, 43.

100. Unión Industrial Argentina, *Texto del memorial con que la Unión Industrial Argentina respondió a la consulta que le formulara la Comisión de Presupuesto y Hacienda de la H. Cámara de Diputados sobre el actual estado económico del país* (Buenos Aires: L. J. Romo, 1922), 1–62: 5; UIA and Guillermo Padilla, *La Unión Industrial Argentina ante el Honorable Senado de la Nación* (Buenos Aires: Tipo-Litografía "La Buenos Aires," 1920), 1–20.

101. UIA and Guillermo Padilla, *La Unión Industrial Argentina ante*; UIA, *Texto del memorial*, 6.

102. Haber, "Political Economy."

103. Bulmer-Thomas, *Economic History*, 97–98.

104. Nathaniel Leff, "Industrial Organization and Entrepreneurship in the Developing Countries: The Economic Groups," *Economic Development and Cultural Change* (Jul. 1978) 26(4), 671.

105. Ibid., 670–671.

106. "Fábrica Argentina de Alpargatas," director's report, *BOB* (1929).

107. "Fábrica Argentina de Alpargatas," director's report, *BOB* (Apr. 7, 1930), 919.

108. Rocchi, *Chimneys*, 193.

109. Anne G. Hanley, *Native Capital: Financial Institutions and Economic*

Development in São Paulo, Brazil, 1850–1920 (Palo Alto, Calif.: Stanford University Press, 2005), 105, 106–109.

110. Hanley, *Native*, chapter 4, "The Republican Revolution and the Rise of the Bolsa."

111. Nathaniel H. Leff, "'Monopoly Capitalism' and Public Policy in Developing Countries," (Research Working Paper, Graduate School of Business, Columbia University, May 1979) 7.

112. "Papelera Argentina," bylaws, *BOB* (1924); "Compañía General de Fósforos," director's report, *BOB* (July 4, 1927), 49.

113. Compañía General de Fósforos, director's report, *BOB* (July 4, 1927), 49.

Chapter 6

1. Katz, *Structural Reforms*.

2. These sources are located in Argentina and in various libraries in the United States. The *Revista de economía argentina* (hereafter, *REA*) is located in the Baker Library at Harvard Business School and at Ohio State University. The *Diario de sesiones* is accessible in various forms; the entire collection is available in most research libraries in the United States. Several years of the *Boletín* and *Anales* of the Unión Industrial Argentina are located at the Science, Industry, and Business Library in New York City. Complete series are available at BTQ.

3. "Los primeros defensores de la producción nacional," *REA,* Jan.–June 1925, *14,* 342.

4. Ibid., 343–344.

5. Hora, "La política económica."

6. There are many examples of this argument in the literature. Unión Industrial Argentina, "Defensa industrial," *REA,* Jan.–June 1922, *8,* 246–248.

7. Unión Industrial Argentina, *Texto del memorial,* 5.

8. Ibid.; Unión Industrial Argentina, *Texto del memorial,* 6.

9. "Porqué y cómo somos proteccionistas," *Boletín de la Unión Industrial Argentina* [hereafter *BUIA*], Apr. 15, 1914, *28*(544), 1

10. Ibid., 2–3.

11. Congreso Nacional del Comercio, "Consideraciones sobre la industria nacional," *BOB,* Oct. 23, 1911 (341), 535–537.

12. Ibid., 533.

13. Ibid., 534.

14. Díaz Alejandro, "The Argentine Tariff, 1906–1940," 76.

15. Dorfman, *Historia de la industria argentina*; and Ferrer, *La economía argentina.*

16. Cornblit, "Inmigrantes y empresarios"; Schvarzer, *Empresarios del pasado,* 31–32.

17. Eugene Sharkey, "Unión Industrial Argentina, 1887–1920: Problems of Industrial Development." Ph.D. dissertation, Rutgers University, New Jersey, 1977."

18. Solberg, "The Tariff and Politics in Argentina," 260.

19. John Coatsworth and Jeffrey G. Williamson, "Always Protectionist? Latin American Tariffs from Independence to Great Depression," *Journal of Latin American Studies,* May 2004, *36*(2), 205–232.

20. Lewis, "Immigrant Entrepreneurs," 99–100.

21. Hora, "La política económica del proteccionismo."

22. Hora, "La política"; Schvarzer, *Empresarios.*

23. Lewis, "Immigrant Entrepreneurs," 83; Hora, "Terratenientes, empresarios industriales," 470–471.

24. Díaz Alejandro, "Argentine Tariff, 1906–1940," 307.

25. Rocchi, "The Empire of Pragmatism: Politics and Industry in the Period 1880–1930" (chapter 7 of *Chimneys*).

26. As stated in previous chapters, law 11281 of 1923 raised tariff levels across the board for all finished consumer goods produced in the country. The rate varied according to product. It was between 35 and 50 percent; some products had specific duties resulting in an even higher rate.

27. Díaz Alejandro, "The Argentine Tariff, 1906–1940."

28. Ibid., 90.

29. José Antonio Sánchez Román, "Shaping Taxation: Economic Elites and Fiscal Decision-Making in Argentina, 1920–1945," *Journal of Latin American Studies*, Feb. 2008, *40*(1), 83–108; Sánchez Román, "Economic Elites, Regional Cleavages, and the Introduction of the Income Tax in Argentina," Paper presented at the XIV International Economic History Congress, Helsinki, Finland, Aug. 2006.

30. Argentina benefited from receiving a substantial amount of foreign investment in infrastructure.

31. Andrés M. Regalsky, "Financiamiento e inversión pública en la transición hacia el Estado empresario, Argentina 1900–1935," Paper presented at the XIV International Economic History Congress, Helsinki, Finland, Aug. 2006.

32. The labor issue was important because Congress was passing a number of labor laws to protect women and children, reduce labor hours per week, set minimum wages, create pension funds, and so on. Manufacturers alleged that these laws lowered labor productivity, resulting in inefficient production. Schvarzer, *Empresarios*, 50.

33. "El crédito industrial," *BUIA*, Aug. 15, 1920, *33*(620), 5.

34. Ibid.

35. Falcoff, 59.

36. Falcoff, 60–61.

37. Ibid., 61.

38. Ibid., 61–62.

39. Claudio Belini, "El Grupo Bunge y la política económica del primer peronismo, 1943–1952," *Latin American Research Review,* Feb. 2006, *40.*

40. R. A. Ramm Doman, "Librecambio, proteccionismo, y prohibicionismo," *REA,* July–Dec. 1918, *1,* 142.

41. Ramm Doman, "Política comercial y económica en el mundo después de la guerra," *REA,* Jan. 1922, *8*(43), 43.

42. Bunge, "Nueva orientación de la política económica argentina: Introducción al estudio de la industria nacional," *REA,* 1921, *6,* 452.

43. Ibid., 455.

44. Ibid., 451–452.

45. Falcoff, 63.

46. Falcoff, 65; "Los proyectos de ley de la diputación socialista sobre jornada legal de ocho horas y 'semana inglesa'," *BUIA,* Aug. 15, 1914, *28*(548), 19–20.

47. "Señor Luis Colombo," *RRP,* Nov. 2, 1928, *66,* 26.

48. Ibid., 26.

49. Unión Industrial Argentina, "Defensa industrial," *REA,* Jan.–June 1922, *8,* 254.

50. Falcoff.

51. "Proyecto de ley," *Diario de sesiones,* June 18, 1920, *2,* 3–4; "Identificación de mercaderías," *Diario de sesiones, sesiones de prórroga,* Oct. 10, 1923, 7, 422.

52. Sharkey.

53. Law 11275, passed October 1923 regarding marking products of national origins.

54. UIA, "La ley de identificación de mercaderias de fabricación nacional," *BUIA,* Nov. 1926, *40*(695), 569–571.

55. Ministerio de Hacienda, *Tercer censo nacional,* 16; Luis Pascarella, *Los derechos aduaneros a los tejidos de algodón* (petición de los fabricantes a la H. Cámara de Diputados, 1918).

56. Luis Colombo, "La falta de protección a las industrias impide nuestra independencia económica," *BUIA,* Jan. 1928, *42*(721), 33–35 (reprinted from *La Nación,* 25 de Dic. de 1928).

57. UIA and Padilla, *Unión Industrial Argentina,* 14.

58. UIA, "Memorial Advocating Tariff Reform Addressed to President Irigoyen," *RRP,* Mar. 1, 1929, *67,* 13.

59. "Proyecto reproducido: Dumping," *Diario de sesiones, sesiones ordinarias,* Sept. 27, 1922, *4,* 649–651.

60. Colombo, "La falta de protección," 35.

61. Sharkey, 113.

62. Falcoff, 66.

63. "Mensaje del Presidente, 1917," in Hipólito Yrigoyen, *Pueblo y gobierno: Mensajes inaugurales del Congreso de la Nación.* Segunda edición (Buenos Aires: Editorial Raigal, 1957).

64. Solberg, *Oil and Nationalism,* 36.

65. Falcoff, 65.

66. Carl Solberg, *The Prairies and the Pampas: Agrarian Policy in Canada and Argentina, 1880–1930* (Palo Alto, Calif.: Stanford University Press, 1987), 191.

67. Section "Notes and News," *RRP* (1920).

68. "Conferencia económica nacional"; "Industrias fabriles, sección III"; "Combustibles, sección IV"; "Transportes, sección V"; etc., reprinted in *REA,* July–Dec. 1919, *3,* 455–464, 480–481, 486, 489–493, 511–513.

69. "Fomento industrial: Reproducción del anteproyecto de ley, presentado al Ministerio de Agricultura, por el Dr. Javier Padilla, Director General de Comercio e Industria," *BUIA,* Dec. 15, 1922, *36*(648), 3–4.

70. Ibid., 4–8.

71. "Informe de la Confederación Argentina," *REA,* Jan.–June 1922, *8,* 77.

72. Larry Sawers, "Income Distribution and Environmental Degradation in the Argentine Interior," *Latin American Research Review,* Spring 2000, *35,* 6.

73. Hora, "La política económica."

74. Sánchez Román, "Economic Elites."

75. Smith, "Argentine Chamber of Deputies."

76. "Proyecto de ley," *Diario de sesiones,* Aug. 19, 1920, 290–292.

77. "Industria del Tejido en Jujuy: Adquisición de maquinarias en Bélgica," *REA,* July–Dec. 1921, *7,* 244.

78. "Proyecto de ley," *Diario de sesiones, sesiones ordinarias,* Sept. 30, 1926, *6,* 592–593.

79. "Proyecto de ley: Comisión Nacional de Institutos de Mujeres del Campo," *Diario de sesiones de la Cámara de Senadores, sesiones ordinarias,* Sept. 18, 1928, 576–582.

80. Smith, "Argentine Chamber of Deputies."

81. Sánchez Román, "Shaping Taxation."

82. "Industria y agricultura: Su interdependencia y su equilibrio," *REA,* Oct. 1938, *37*(244), 310.

83. Ramm Doman, "Librecambio," 142.

84. "Industria y agricultura," 311.

85. Schvarzer, *Empresarios,* 51.

86. Ferrer, *The Argentine Economy*; Ortíz, *Historia económica*; and Dorfman, *Historia de la industria argentina*.

87. Lewis, "Immigrant Entrepreneurs," 100.

88. "El proteccionismo industrial: Los materiales de construcción y los impuestos aduaneros," *Vanguardia*, Apr. 14, 1924.

89. Schvarzer, *La industria que supimos conseguir*, 123.

90. Padilla did not define *ultraprotectionism,* but it likely referred to Brazil effectively keeping out all competition against rice. "Restricciones bancarias a los trusts," *Diario de sesiones*, June 30, 1921, *1*, 664.

91. Law number 11210, Aug. 28, 1923.

92. Any tampering with prices by lowering, increasing, or fixing them was illegal, including deliberately decreasing supply to manipulate price and demand. Violation of this law was punishable by a fine of up to one hundred thousand paper pesos or three years in prison. It was hard to prove, and the prosecuting party needed sufficient evidence to indict the defendant. There were no convictions before 1930. Argentine law 11210, Aug. 28, 1923.

93. "Represión de los trusts: Proyecto de resolución," *Diario de sesiones, sesiones ordinarias,* Sept. 9, 1925, *4*, 284.

94. Ibid., 280–284.

95. By 1929, the legal requirements to incorporate as a joint-stock company had grown cumbersome. The laws to incorporate (sociedades anónimas) called for following Articles 313 to 371 of the Commercial Code and hiring a lawyer to inform a company about the Articles' modifications and other relevant laws such as bankruptcy, patents, and trusts. Also, a corporation was mandated to have frequent stockholder meetings; its administration and accounting records were public and to be supervised by the government. "Proyecto de ley, Autorízase la formación de sociedades comerciales a responsabilidad limitada," *Diario de sesiones, sesiones ordinarias*, June 12, 1929, *1*, 219–220.

96. "Sociedades de responsabilidad limitada," ley número 11645, Oct. 8, 1932.

97. Ibid., artículo 9.

98. "Proyecto de ley: institúyanse dos premios . . . ," *Diario de sesiones,* May 27, 1925, *1*, pp. 189–190; "Proyecto de ley: institúyese cinco premios . . . ," *Diario de sesiones,* Sept. 2, 1926, *5*, 8–10.

99. "Explotación de petroleo," *Diario de sesiones, sesiones ordinarias,* Aug. 24, 1920, *4*, 452–463.

100. The glass manufacturers Rigolleau, Papini, and Compañía General de Envases focused on production of low-cost bottles, glassware, and small glass containers, particularly because the price of glass bottles was on a per-item scale and glassware at a per-kilogram scale. *Anuario del comercio exterior.*

101. "Invento de una máquina para fabricar vidrio," *BUIA,* Dec. 15, 1920, *24*(624), 9.

102. "El crédito industrial," *BUIA,* Aug. 15, 1920, *33*(620), 5.

Chapter 7

1. The 1895 census recorded that 81 percent (or 18,077) of all industrial establishments were located in the federal capital and three littoral provinces: Buenos Aires, Santa Fe, and Entre Ríos (8,439 establishments were located in the federal capital, 5,576 in Buenos Aires province, 2,678 in Santa Fé, and 1,378 in Entre Ríos). In 1914, the number of industrial establishments in these four areas was 33,334, or 68 percent; and 30,722, or 76 percent in 1935.

2. The industrial census of 1895 was the first complete census of industry. It recorded capital stock, labor, costs, power use, machines, and output. The censuses of 1914 and 1935 recorded additional information on labor including age, gender, seasonal migration, and ethnicity.

3. Alejandro Bunge, "Nueva orientación de la política económica argentina: Introducción al estudio de la industria nacional," *Revista de economía argentina,* 1921, *6,* 452.

4. Taylor, "Capital Accumulation," 194.

5. These cycles are based on the real rate of return of the stock exchange. Nakamura and Zarazaga, "Economic Growth in Argentina."

6. The economy picked up again in the 1920s because the government diversified and expanded the quality and quantity of agricultural and livestock products for export to European countries. Argentina began exporting diverse qualities and quantities of wheat, rye, barley, maize, linseed, beef, cooking oil, and cotton. Argentina's maize increased its share of world exports from 40 percent in 1913 to 70 percent in 1928. In the case of linseed, Argentina's production accounted for 80 percent of world exports by 1928. Bulmer-Thomas, *Economic History of Latin America,* 167.

7. Cortés Conde, *La economía argentina.*

8. Dorfman.

9. Korol and Sábato.

10. The Argentine government's practice of preferring compromise over conflict has been well articulated in the literature. Sánchez Román, 2008; Solberg, "Tariffs and Politics"; Horowitz.

11. Katz and Kosacoff, "Import-Substituting Industrialization," 303.

12. Ibid., 303.

13. Lewis, *Crisis of Argentine Capitalism.*

14. Cochran and Reina.

15. Solberg, "Tariffs and Politics," 260–261.

16. "Nuevas fuentes de riqueza," *La Nación,* Feb. 26, 1925, reprinted in *Revista de economía argentina,* 1925, *14,* 237.

Appendix A

1. Segundo censo nacional: Censo de las industrias de 1895,Vol. 3 (Buenos Aires, 1898).
2. "Censo social e industrial de 1895"; Segundo Censo Nacional (1898).

Appendix C

1. Regarding the fuel category, the main form of fuel was bituminous coal, which came largely from Britain and the United States. After 1914, Argentina shifted its fuel needs from coal to petroleum, which was also imported in smaller quantities from the United States and Britain. Imports of petroleum fuel, however, are incomplete because the bulk came from Colombia and Venezuela in the 1920s. Also, in that period Argentina began its own petroleum mining and refining industry. Solberg, *Oil and Nationalism.*
2. Keith Jonson, "Internal Combustion Engines," in *Economic Conditions in the Argentine Republic* (London: Department of Overseas Trade, HMSO, 1932), 48.
3. Ibid., 48.
4. Two journals, *Anales de la Unión Industrial Argentina* (after 1920) and *Monitor de sociedades anónimas y patentes de invención,* report new inventions and patents of new machinery and parts. They do not report quantities sold or domestic investment in these machine inventions.

Appendix D

1. The number of annual balances in my possession varies from three to twenty-seven years per company.The variation is in part due to some companies going bankrupt after only a few years in business. I have fewer than five years of financial statements for three companies: the cement manufacturer Cemento Argentina, the match firm Unión Fósforos Cooperativa, and the metallurgy company Unión Herradores. I included them because part of the goal of this book is to compare the performance of both failed and successful companies.
2. If written off as debt, it was reported on the liability side of the accounting balance sheet. If written off as a loss, it was reported on the cost side of the income statement.
3. Equity is calculated as the sum of paid-in capital and reserves. Debts are current liabilities, or short-term debt such as accounts payable, notes payable, salaries, income and taxes payable, and long-term liabilities (bonds, mortgages, bank loans).

4. In practice, all firms should have some short-term debt, in the form of accounts payable, wages payable, and the like.

5. The exception was the cement industry, whose return on physical capital was lower than equity. This is because the one cement firm under study, Cemento Pórtland Argentina, started purchasing capital equipment in 1913 but did not begin full operations until the 1920s.

Bibliography

Archives

Archivo del Banco de la Provincia de Buenos Aires, Argentina
Archivo General de la Nación, Buenos Aires, Argentina
Archivo Mitre, Buenos Aires, Argentina
Biblioteca Tornquist, Buenos Aires, Argentina

Primary Manuscript Documents

Archivo General de la Nación, Argentina. "Las resoluciones, memorias, disolución y retiro de personería jurídica de La Unión Sociedad Anónima Cooperativa de Fósforos, 1908–11." (Manuscript.) Buenos Aires: Archivo General de la Nación-Tribunales comerciales.

Archivo del Instituto Ravignani, Universidad de Buenos Aires. "Memoria y balance general, Cervecería Palermo, 30 de Junio de 1900." Box 17, Buenos Aires, Argentina.

"Baibiene y Antonini contra Morini." (Litigation, manuscript.) Letra B, legajo 70, año 1912. Buenos Aires: Departamento comerciales tribunales, Archivo General de la Nación [AGN], 1912.

Banco de la Provincia de Buenos Aires. *Libros de actas.* (Selected years 1905, 1910, 1915.) Transaction books available at Archivo y museo del Banco de la Provincia de Buenos Aires, Argentina.

"Censo social e industrial de 1895." Manuscript. Buenos Aires: Archivo General de la Nación Argentina, 1895.

"Chientelassa Hermanos." (Litigation, manuscript.) Letra C, legajo no. 2, 1891–1896. Buenos Aires: Departamento comerciales tribunales, AGN, 1898.

"Compañías de Ernesto Tornquist y Cía." Letter (6 pages), dated February 1930, available at BTQ, document no. Misc 130–20.

"Fosforera Argentina: Fósforos en gruesas de 4–40 hechos y vendidos." *Boletín Industrial*, 1910.

Honorio Pueyrredón, Ministry of Agriculture, "La industria cervecera." Letter dated May 15, 1917, Buenos Aires, available at BTQ.

"Las industrias nacionales: hilandería de lanas peinadas y fábrica de tejidos de Campomar y Soulas." *La Epoca*, Oct. 16, 1918, available at BTQ, file no. industria 332.

"Lockwood, Greene, y Co., Inc. a Carlos A. Tornquist." Letter dated Aug. 13, 1924, available at BTQ, file no. industrias 144–8271.

"Renovación de obligación hipotecaria otorgada por la sociedad anónima 'Cristalerías Rigolleau' y la fideicomisaria sociedad anónima 'Financiera, Comercial, e Industrial Ernesto Tornquist y Compañía, Ltda,'" company reorganization record and new mortgage terms, *BOB* (May 15, 1922), 807–816.

Smith, Peter. "Argentine Chamber of Deputies Roll Calls, Sessions 1904–1955." Deposited at the Data and Program Library Service, University of Wisconsin-Madison (Apr. 1974).

Silveyra, Carlos. *Sucesión Baenninger versus Cervecería Argentina Quilmes.* Printed civil suit case regarding inheritor's rights to a private company's shares and bonds. Document available at Biblioteca Nacional, Buenos Aires, 1925.

Talleres Metalúrgicos San Martín. *Revista Tamet.* Buenos Aires, Abril–Mayo 1944, available at Biblioteca Tornquist.

Tornquist, Ernesto y Compañía, Limitada. *Ernesto Tornquist y Cía, Ltda., 1874–1924. En ocasión del cincuentenario de la existencia de nuestra casa bajo el nombre Ernesto Tornquist y Cía., Ltda., y en homenaje a su ilustre fundador Don Ernesto Tornquist.* Buenos Aires: La Compañía, 1924.

Published Census Data

Argentina. *Segundo censo nacional: Censo de las industrias 1895, Vol. 3.* Buenos Aires: Ministerio de Hacienda, 1898.

Chueco, Manuel C. *Censo 1889. Estudio sobre los resultados del censo de las industrias.* Buenos Aires: Compañía Sud-Americana de Billetes de Banco, 1890. (Written for *Censo general de población, edificación, comercio e industrias de la ciudad de Buenos Aires, capital federal de la República Argentina, 1889.*)

Dirección de Comercio e Industria. *Censo industrial y comercial de la República Argentina, 1908–1914.* Buenos Aires: Talleres gráficos del Ministerio de Agricultura, 1915.

Dirección de Comercio e Industria. *Anuario de la República Argentina, nociones útiles.* Buenos Aires: Ministerio de Agricultura, 1922–23, 1926–27.

Dirección de Comercio e Industria. *Guía comercial e industrial de la República Argentina.* Buenos Aires: Ministerio de Agricultura, 1937.

Dirección General de Estadística de la Nación. *Censo industrial de 1935.* Buenos Aires: Ministerio de Hacienda, 1937.

Dirección General de Estadística de la Nación. *IV censo general de la nación, 1946,* Vol. 3. Buenos Aires: Ministerio de Hacienda, 1948.

Dirección General de Estadística Municipal, *Censo general de población, edificación, comercio é industrias de la Ciudad de Buenos Aires,* Levantado en los días 11 y 18 de septiembre de 1904 bajo la administración del Sr. Don Alberto Casares, por Alberto B. Martínez, director de la Dirección General de Estadística Municipal. Buenos Aires: Cía. Sud-Americana de billetes de Banco, 1906.

Dirección General de Estadística Municipal, Municipalidad de la Capital, República Argentina. *Anuario estadístico de la Ciudad de Buenos Aires.* Buenos Aires: Compañía Sud-Americana de Billetes de Banco, 1903–1915.

Dirección General de Estadística de la Provincia de Buenos Aires. *Anuario estadístico de la Provinicia de Buenos Aires, 1896, Vol. 3.* La Plata: Talleres de Publicaciones del Museo 1898. Available at Museo Mitre.

Ministerio de Hacienda. *Tercer censo nacional: Censo de las industrias, 1914,* Vol. 7. Buenos Aires: Talleres Gráficos de L. J. Rosso y Cía., 1917.

Municipalidad de Buenos Aires. *Censo general de población, edificación, comercio e industrias de la ciudad de Buenos Aires levantado en los días 17 de agosto, 15 y 30 de septiembre de 1887.* Buenos Aires: Compañía Sudamericana de Billetes de Banco, 1889.

Argentine Journals

These periodicals are available at the Biblioteca Tornquist and Biblioteca Nacional in Buenos Aires, Argentina. Many are also available in libraries in the United States, among them the Harvard Law Library, Harvard Lamont Library, Center for Research Libraries in Chicago, University of Massachusetts Amherst, and the New York Public Library.

Anuario argentino, 1921–22.

Anuario financiero-administrativo de la República Argentina, 1904–1912.

Boletín de la Unión Industrial Argentina [after 1914, also listed under title *Anales de la Unión Industrial Argentina*], monthly edition, surveyed years 1909, 1914, 1924–1931.

Boletín industrial, 1892–1910.

Boletín oficial de la bolsa de comercio de Buenos Aires, 1905–1931.

Boletín oficial de la República Argentina, 1910–1931.

Boletín quincenal de la bolsa de comercio de Buenos Aires, 1894–1902.

Cronista comercial, 1916–1930.

Diario de sesiones del honorable Cámara de Diputados, 1890–1930 [sesiones ordinarias y extraordinarias].

Dirección General de Estadística. *Informes sobre la industria de Argentina,* 1923–1940.

El avisador mercantíl, 1918–1920.

Guía de sociedades anónimas, 1923–1931.

Monitor de sociedades anónimas, 1904–1931.

Revista de economía argentina, 1918–1935.

Revista de economía y finanzas, 1911–12.

Foreign Reports, Journals, and Trade Statistics

Annual Statement of the Trade of the United Kingdom with Foreign Countries and British Colonies. London: Her Majesty's Stationary Office, 1893–1930.

Argentina. *Anuario de la Dirección General de Estadística.* Buenos Aires: Compañía Sud-americana de Billetes de Banco, 1892–1914.

Argentina. Dirección General de Estadística y Censos, *Anuario del comercio exterior de la República Argentina.* Buenos Aires: Dirección General de Estadística de la Nación, 1915–1935.

British Chamber of Commerce in the Argentine Republic (Incorporated). *Annual Report* for years 1920–1930.

Department of Overseas Trade. "The Market for Paper and Paper Products in the Argentine Republic." London: HMSO, 1920.

Direction Générale des Douanes. *Tableau Général du Commerce et de la Navigation: Commerce de la France Avec ses Colonies et les Puissances Etrangères.* Vol. 1. Paris: Imprimerie Nationale, 1897–1905, 1907–1914, 1921–22, 1926–1928.

Economist, 1890–1930.

Review of the River Plate, 1918–1925.

Deutschland, Kaiserliches Statistisches Amte (after 1919, Statistischen Reichs-amte), *Statistik des Deutschen Reichs, Auswartinger Handel des Deutschen.* Berlin: Verlag des Königlich Preussichen Statistischen Bureaus, 1890–1904, 1906–1913, 1923–1929.

Times Book on Argentina. London: Times Publishing, 1927.

U.S. Department of Commerce, Bureau of Foreign and Domestic Commerce. *The Foreign Commerce and Navigation of the United States.* Washington: U.S. GPO, 1890–1930.

Annuals and Commercial Guides

Album argentina de industrias. Buenos Aires, 1909 and 1910, available at Biblioteca Tornquist.

Anuario geográfico argentino. Buenos Aires, 1941.

Anuario Kraft, gran guía de la república Argentina: comercio, industria, agricultura, ganadería, profesionales, y elemento oficial. Buenos Aires: G. Kraft Ltda., 1915, 1920, 1942.

Argentine Yearbook, Commercial Guide. Buenos Aires: J. Grant, 1902, 1903, 1905–06, 1910, 1912, 1914–15, 1916.

Argentine Annual. Buenos Aires: Standard Directory, 1922–23, 1924–25, 1926–27 editions.

Finanzas, comercio e industria en la República Argentina de 1898. Buenos Aires: Imprenta "Roma" de Juan Carbone, 1899.

Finanzas, comercio e industria en la República Argentina de 1899. Buenos Aires: Imprenta "Roma" de Juan Carbone, 1900.

Guía descriptiva de las industrias argentinas. Buenos Aires, 1895, available at Biblioteca Tornquist.

Guía Kraft, 1885–1922. Available at Biblioteca Nacional.

Quien es quien en la Argentina: Biografías contemporáneas. Buenos Aires: Guillermo Kraft, 1939.

Pillado, Ricardo. *Anuario Pillado de la deuda pública y sociedades anónimas establecidas en la República Argentina para 1898.* Buenos Aires: Imprenta de La Nación, 1899.

Pillado, Ricardo. *Anuario Pillado de la deuda pública y sociedades anónimas establecidas en las repúblicas Argentina y del Uruguay para 1899–1900.* Buenos Aires: Imprenta de la Nación, 1900.

Official Government Publications, Primary Journal Articles, and Laws.

"Nuevas fuentes de riqueza," *La Nación,* Feb. 26, 1925, reprinted in *Revista de economía argentina,* 1925, *14,* 237.

Ainscough, T. R. "Growing Money in Argentina: A Concise Guide to Capital Investment for All Classes." *Review of the River Plate,* June 8, 1928, *65,* 26–27, 29.

Argentina del Cemento Pórtland. *Anuario.* Buenos Aires, 1946.

"Bolsa de Comercio de Buenos Aires: Historia de la jurisdicción y prácticas comerciales desde la época del Virreynato." Donated by Luis Colombo to Biblioteca Nacional, 1935.

Cervecería Argentina Quilmes. *Cebada cervecera: instrucciones para cultivar con éxito su semilla.* Buenos Aires: Casa Jacobo Peuser, Mar. 1918.

Código de comercio de 1889.

Compañía General de Fósforos. "Gastos de maquinaria para la fábrica en Uruguay" pamphlet, 1929.

"Constitución de la Nación Argentina," and "Código de comercio, ley no 2637: 9 de octubre 1889," en *Códigos de la República Argentina, edición oficial.* Buenos Aires: Compañia Sud-Americana de Billetes de Banco, 1901.

Datos estadísticos referentes a la industria cervecera. Buenos Aires, 1917.

Departamento nacional del trabajo, División de estadística. *Industria textil: capacidad normal de trabajo de los obreros, especialmente mujeres y menores.* Informe del Dr. José Figuerola. Buenos Aires: Dept. Nacional del Trabajo, 1939.

Dirección de comercio e industria. *La industria de papel,* 1932.

Honorable Cámara de Diputados de la Nación, Secretaria Parlamentaria. *Nómina de diputados de la nación por distrito electoral, período 1854–1991 (Hasta el 31–5–1991).* Buenos Aires: Dirección de Archivo, Publicaciones y Museo, Subdirección de publicaciones e investigaciones históricas, 1991.

Jonson, Keith. "Internal Combustion Engines." In *Economic Conditions in the Argentine Republic.* London: Department of Overseas Trade, HMSO, 1932.

Law numbers and titles (selected): law 3050, "Ley de tarifas," 1894; law 3551 (money conversion law), Nov. 1899; law number 4157 (allowed corporations to conduct business in gold or paper pesos), Dec. 23, 1902; law 4933, *Ley de tarifas,* Dec. 20, 1905; law 10362, *Ley de tarifas,* 1918; law 11210, *Contra los monopolies y trusts (Guía de sociedades anónimas),* 1923; law 11281, *Ley de tarifas,* Dec. 6, 1923; *Ley de sociedad de responsabilidad limitada,* 1932.

Laws of Argentina in English with Regulations and Recent Amendments to the Commercial Code and Copyright Law. Compiled and translated by J. A. and E. de Marval. Buenos Aires: J. A. and E. de Marval, 1933.

"Manuel Chueco versus Hilanderías Argentinas de Algodón, 1906," in *Monitor de sociedades anónimas, Vol.* 7 (1909), 126–129.

Massel, J. A. "Markets for Machinery and Machine Tools in Argentina." *Special Agent Series,* no. 116, Department of Commerce. Washington: U.S. GPO, 1916.

Mercado, Matilde Alejandra. *La primera ley de trabajo femenino, "La mujer obrera" (1890–1910).* Buenos Aires: Centro Editor de América Latina, 1988.

Ministerio de Justicia, Inspección General de Justicia. *Nueva fórmula obligatoria para balances de sociedades anónimas, nacionales y extranjeras.* Decreto aprobatorio del Ministerio de Justicia e Instrucción Pública. Edición especial del *Monitor de sociedades anónimas y patentes de invención.* Buenos Aires: Imprenta y casa editora "Coni," 1925.

Motz, Frank H. von. "Markets for Agricultural Implements and Machinery in Argentina." *Special Agent Series,* no. 125, Department of Commerce. Washington, DC: U.S. GPO, 1916.

Pascarella, Luis. *Los derechos aduaneros a los tejidos de algodón.* (Petición de los fabricantes a la H. Cámara de Diputados.) 1918.

"El proteccionismo industrial: Los materiales de construcción y los impuestos aduaneros." *Vanguardia,* Apr. 14, 1924.

Ramm Doman, R. A. "Política comercial y económica en el mundo después de la guerra." *Revista de economía argentina,* Jan. 1922, *8*(43), 43.

———. "Librecambio, proteccionismo, y prohibicionismo." *Revista de economía argentina,* July–Dec. 1918, *1,* 142.

Rutter, Frank R. *Tariff Systems of South American Countries.* (U.S. Department of Commerce, tariff series, no. 34.) Washington, DC: United States Government Printing Office, 1916.

U.S. Bureau of Statistics, Department of State, Special Consular Reports. *Cotton Textiles in Foreign Countries, Reports from the Consuls of the United States on the Cotton Textiles Imported into their Several Districts, etc.* Washington, DC: United States Government Printing Office, 1890.

Unión Industrial Argentina. "La industria argentina: lo que dicen las cifras." *Boletín de la Unión Industrial Argentina,* Jan. 15, 1909, *22*(481), 1–2.

———. "Dificultades que hay que vencer para explotar una invención." *Boletín oficial de la Unión Industrial Argentina,* July 15, 1909, *23*(487), 28–29.

———. *Fábricas de tejidos, número que existe en la república de Argentina.* Buenos Aires: Boletín de la Unión Industrial Argentina, 1917.

——— and Guillermo Padilla. *La Unión Industrial Argentina ante el Honorable Senado de la Nación.* Buenos Aires: Tipo-Litografía "La Buenos Aires," 1920.

———. *Texto del memorial con que la Unión Industrial Argentina respondió a la consulta que le formulara la Comisión de Presupuesto y Hacienda de la Honorable Cámara de Diputados sobre el actual estado económico del país.* Buenos Aires: L. J. Romo, 1922.

———. *La situación actual de la industria de cemento Pórtland en la República Argentina.* Buenos Aires: Unión Industrial Argentina, 1923.

———. *Origen y evolución de la industria de papel en la Argentina.* Buenos Aires: Unión Industrial Argentina, 1959.

Yrigoyen, Hipólito. *Pueblo y gobierno: Mensajes inaugurales del Congreso de la Nación. Segunda edición.* Buenos Aires: Editorial Raigal, 1957.

Secondary Sources

Adelman, Jeremy, editor. *Essays in Argentine Labour History, 1870–1930.* Oxford: St. Anthony's College, 1990.

———. *Frontier Development: Land, Labour, and Capital on the Wheat Lands of Argentina and Canada 1890–1914.* Oxford: Clarendon Press, 1994.

———. "The Politics of Money in Mid-Nineteenth Century Argentina." In John Harriss and others (eds.), *The New Institutional Economics and Third World Development.* New York: Routledge, 1995.

Arlt, Robert. *The Seven Madmen.* Translated by Nick Caistor. London: Serpent's Tail, 1998.

Arnold, A. J. "Innovation, Deskilling, and Profitability in the British Machine-Tools Industry: Alfred Herbert, 1887–1927." *Journal of Industrial History,* 1999, 2, 50–71.

Azzi, María Susana, and Ricardo de Titto. *Pioneros de la industria argentina.* Buenos Aires: Editorial El Ateneo, 2008.

Bain, H. Foster, C. E. Williams, and E. B. Swanson. *Las posibilidades de la manufactura de hierro y acero en la Argentina.* Buenos Aires: Talleres Gráficos del Instituto Geográfico Militar, 1925.

Banco de la Nación Argentina. *El Banco de la Nación Argentina en su cincuentenario, 1891–1941.* Buenos Aires: Impreso en la Argentina, 1941.

Barbero, María Inés. "Grupos empresarios, intercambio comercial e inversiones italianas en la Argentina: El caso de Pirelli (1910–1920)." *Estudios Migratorios Latinoamericanos,* 1990, 5, (15–16), 311–341.

———. "Treinta años de estudios sobre la historia de empresas en la Argentina," *Ciclos,* First semester 1995, 5, (8), 179–200.

———. "Argentina: Industrial Growth and Enterprise Organization, 1880s–1980s." In Alfred Chandler, Franco Amatori, and Takashi Hikino (eds.), *Big*

Business and the Wealth of Nations. Cambridge: Cambridge University Press, 1997, 368–393.

————. "Mercados, redes sociales y estrategias empresariales en los orígenes de los grupos económicos: De la Compañía de Fósforos al Grupo Fabril (1880–1929)." *Estudios Migratorios Latinoamericanos,* 2000, *15,* (44), 119–145.

———— and Fernando Rocchi, "Industry." In Gerardo Della Paolera and Alan Taylor (eds.), *A New Economic History of Argentina.* Cambridge: Cambridge University Press, 2003, 261–294.

Beatty, Edward. *Institutions and Investment: The Political Basis of Industrialization in Mexico Before 1911.* Palo Alto, Calif.: Stanford University Press, 2001.

————. "Patents and Technological Change in Late Industrialization: Nineteenth Century Mexico in Comparative Context." *History of Technology,* 2002, *24,* 121–150.

Belini, Claudio. "El grupo Bunge y la política económica del primer peronismo, 1943–1952." *Latin American Research Review,* Winter 2006, *41*(1), 27–51.

Bell, Martin, and Keith Pavitt. "Technological Accumulation and Industrial Growth: Contrasts Between Developed and Developing Countries." *Industrial and Corporate Change,* 1993, *2*(2), 157–210.

Berensztein, Sergio, and Horacio Spector. "Business, Government and Law." In Gerardo Della Paolera and Alan M. Taylor (eds.), *A New Economic History of Argentina.* Cambridge: Cambridge University Press, 2003, 324–368.

Berlinski, Julio. "International Trade and Commercial Policy." In Gerardo Della Paolera and Alan M. Taylor (eds.), *A New Economic History of Argentina.* Cambridge: Cambridge University Press, 2003, 197–232.

Bhagwati, Jagdish N. "Directly Unproductive, Profit-Seeking (DUP) Activities." *Journal of Political Economy,* Oct. 1982, *90*(5), 988–1002.

Bozzo, Rubén, and Horacio Mendoza. "Grupo Roberts." *Realidad económico,* 1974, *18,* 50–63.

Bulmer-Thomas, Victor. *The Economic History of Latin America Since Independence.* Cambridge: Cambridge University Press, 1994.

————. Second edition 2003.

Bunge, Alejandro. *Población total de la Argentina: Razón de su crecimiento.* Buenos Aires: Oceana, 1917.

————. "Nueva orientación de la política económica argentina: Introducción al estudio de la industria nacional," *Revista de economía argentina,* 1921, *6,* 452.

Campbell, Morfit. *A Treatise on Chemistry Applied to the Manufacture of Soap and Candles.* (Microfiche.) Philadelphia: Parry and McMillan, 1856.

Casson, Mark. "Entrepreneurship and Business Culture." In Jonathan Brown and Mary B. Rose (eds.), *Entrepreneurship, Networks, and Modern Business.* Manchester: Manchester University Press, 1993, 30–54.

Cervecería Quilmes. *Quilmes Cerveza: Quilmes Centenario.* Buenos Aires: Quilmes, 1990.

Chandler, Alfred D. *The Visible Hand: The Managerial Revolution in American Business.* Cambridge, Mass.: Harvard University Press, 1977.

————, and Herman Daems (eds.). *Managerial Hierarchies: Comparative Perspectives on the Rise of the Modern Industrial Enterprise.* Cambridge, Mass.: Harvard University Press, 1980.

Coase, Ronald H. "The Nature of the Firm." *Economica,* 1937, *4,* 386–405.

Coatsworth, John. "Obstacles to Economic Growth in Nineteenth-Century Mexico." *American Historical Review,* Feb. 1978, *83*(1), 80–100.

————, and Jeffrey G. Williamson. "Always Protectionist? Latin American Tariffs from Independence to Great Depression." *Journal of Latin American Studies,* May 2004, *36*(2), 205–232.

Cochran, Thomas C., and Ruben E. Reina. *Entrepreneurship in Argentine Culture; Torcuato Di Tella and S.I.A.M.* Philadelphia: University of Pennsylvania Press, 1962.

Cornblit, Oscar. "Inmigrantes y empresarios en la política argentina." *Desarrollo Económico,* Jan.–Mar. 1967, *6*(24), 641–691.

Cortés Conde, Roberto. "Problemas del crecimiento industrial (1870–1914)." In Torcuato Di Tella (ed.), *Argentina, sociedad de masas.* Buenos Aires: Editorial Universitaria de Buenos Aires, 1965, 59–83.

————. "Some Notes on the Industrial Development of Argentina and Canada in the 1920s." In Guido Di Tella and D.C.M. Platt (eds.), *Argentina and Canada: Studies in Comparative Development.* New York: St. Martin's Press, 1985, 149–160.

————. *La economía argentina en el largo plazo (Siglos XIX y XX).* Buenos Aires: Editorial Sudamericana, Universidad de San Andrés, 1997.

————, and Ezequiel Gallo. *La formación de la Argentina moderna.* Buenos Aires: Editorial Paidós, 1973.

Dávila, Carlos, and Rory Miller (eds.). *Business History in Latin America: The Experience of Seven Countries.* Liverpool: Liverpool University Press, 1999.

Della Paolera, Gerardo. "How the Argentine Economy Performed During the International Gold Standard: A Reexamination." Ph.D. dissertation, University of Chicago, 1988.

————, and Alan M. Taylor. "Finance and Development in an Emerging Market: Argentina in the Interwar Period." In John H. Coatsworth and Alan M. Taylor (eds.), *Latin America and the World Economy Since 1800.* Cambridge: Harvard University Press, 1998.

————, and Alan M. Taylor (eds.). *A New Economic History of Argentina.* Cambridge: Cambridge University Press, 2003.

Díaz Alejandro, Carlos. "The Argentine Tariff, 1906–1940." *Oxford Economic Papers,* Mar. 1967, *19*(1), 75–98.

————. *Essays on the Economic History of the Argentine Republic.* New Haven: Yale University Press, 1970.

————. *Ensayos sobre la historia económica argentina.* Buenos Aires: Amorrortu editores, 1976.

Di Tella, Guido, and Manuel Zymelman. *Las etapas del desarrollo económico argentino.* Buenos Aires: Editorial Universitaria de Buenos Aires, 1967.

————, and Alberto Petrecolla. *Los ciclos económicos argentinos.* Buenos Aires: Editorial Paidós, 1973.

Di Tella, Torcuato (ed.). *Argentina, sociedad de masas.* Buenos Aires: Editorial Universitaria de Buenos Aires, 1965.

Domenech, Roberto L. "Estadísticas de la evolución económica de Argentina, 1913–1984." *Estudios de IEERAL,* 1986, *9*(39), 103–185.

Dorfman, Adolfo. *Historia de la industria argentina.* Buenos Aires: Escuela de Estudios Argentinos, 1942.

Dutrénit, Gabriela. "Building Technological Capabilities in Latecomer Firms: A Review Essay." *Science, Technology, and Society,* Jul.–Dec. 2004, *9*(2), 209–241.

Falcoff, Mark. "Economic Dependency in a Conservative Mirror: Alejandro Bunge and the Argentine Frustration, 1919–1943." *Inter-American Economic Affairs,* 1982, *35*(4), 57–75.

Feinstein, C. H. *Statistical Tables of National Income, Expenditure, and Output of the U.K., 1855–1965.* Cambridge: Cambridge University Press, 1972.

Ferrer, Aldo. *The Argentine Economy.* Berkeley: University of California Press, 1967.

Fey, Ingrid. "First Tango in Paris." Ph.D. dissertation, University of California, Los Angeles, 1996.

Fleming, William J. "The Cultural Determinants of Entrepreneurship and Economic Development: A Case Study of Mendoza Province, Argentina, 1861–1914." *Journal of Economic History,* Mar. 1979, *39*(1), 211–224.

Floud, Roderick. *The British Machine-Tool Industry, 1850–1914.* Cambridge: Cambridge University Press, 1976.

Fodor, Jorge G., y Arturo O'Connell. "La Argentina y la economía atlántica en la primera mitad del siglo XX." *Desarrollo económico,* Apr. 1973, *13,* 3–65.

Ford, A. G. *The Gold Standard 1880–1914: Britain and Argentina.* New York: Garland, 1983.

Frank, André Gunder. *Capitalism and Underdevelopment in Latin America: Historical Studies of Chile and Brazil.* New York: Monthly Review Press, 1967.

Galiani, Sebastián, and Pablo Gerchunoff. "The Labor Market." In Gerardo Della Paolera and Alan M. Taylor (eds.), *A New Economic History of Argentina.* Cambridge: Cambridge University Press, 2003.

Gallo, Ezequiel. "Agrarian Expansion and Industrial Development in Argentina, 1880–1930." Buenos Aires: Instituto Torcuato Di Tella, Centro de Investigaciones Sociales, 1970.

García Heras, Raúl. "Historia empresarial e historia económica en Argentina: un balance a comienzos del siglo XXI." Historia del Desarrollo Empresarial, Monografías de Administración, Universidad de los Andes, April 2007.

Geller, Lucio. "Un teorema y un comentario sobre el efecto del crecimiento económico sobre el comercio internacional," *Desarrollo económico*, Jul.–Sep. 1970, *10*(38), 293–304.

Guerrero, Americo R. *La industria Argentina: su origen, organización y desarrollo.* Buenos Aires: Plantie, 1944.

Gerschenkron, Alexander. *Economic Backwardness in Historical Perspective: A Book of Essays.* Cambridge, Mass.: Harvard University Press, 1962.

Gilbert, Jorge. "El grupo Tornquist, 1906–30." (Unpublished manuscript.) XVI Jornadas de Historia Económica, Asociación Argentina de Historia Económica, Universidad Nacional de Quilmes, 1998.

————. "El grupo Tornquist entre la expansión y las crisis de la economía argentina en el siglo XX." *Ciclos en la historia, la economía, y la sociedad.* First and Second semester 2003, *13*(25–26), 65–92.

————. "Los negocios del holding Tornquist," in José Villarruel (ed), *Prosperidad y miseria. Contribuciones a la historia económica argentina*, Chapter 4. Buenos Aires: Editorial Al Margen, 2004.

Goldin, Claudia, and Kenneth Sokoloff. "Women, Children, and Industrialization in the Early Republic: Evidence from the Manufacturing Censuses." *Journal of Economic History,* Dec. 1982, *42*(4), 741–774.

Granovetter, Mark. "Coase Revisited: Business Groups in the Modern Economy." *Industrial and Corporate Change,* 1995, *4*(1), 93–130.

Gujarati, Damodar N. *Basic Econometrics*, Third Edition. New York: McGraw-Hill, 1995.

Guy, Donna. "Carlos Pellegrini and the Politics of Early Argentine Industrialization, 1873–1906." *Journal of Latin American Studies,* 1979, *2*(1), 123–144.

————. "La industria argentina 1870–1940: Legislación comercial, mercado de acciones y capitalización extranjera." *Desarrollo Económico,* Oct.–Dec. 1982, *22*(87), 351–374.

————. "Refinería Argentina, 1888–1930: límites de la tecnología azucarera en una economía periférica," *Desarrollo económico*, Oct.—Dec. 1988, *28*(111), 353–373.

Haber, Stephen. *Industry and Underdevelopment: The Industrialization of Mexico, 1890–1940.* Palo Alto, Calif.: Stanford University Press, 1989.

————. "Industrial Concentration and the Capital Markets: A Comparative Study of Brazil, Mexico, and the United States, 1830–1930." *Journal of Economic History,* Sept. 1991, *51*(3), 559–581.

————. "Assessing the Obstacles to Industrialisation: The Mexican Economy, 1830–1940." *Journal of Latin American Studies*, Feb. 1992, *24*(1), 2.

————. "The Political Economy of Industrialization." In Victor Bulmer-Thomas, John H. Coatsworth, and Roberto Cortés Conde (eds.), *The Cambridge Economic History of Latin America.* Cambridge: Cambridge University Press, 2006, 537–584.

————, Armando Razo, and Noel Maurer. "Political Instability and Economic

Performance in Revolutionary Mexico." In *Political Economy of Institutions and Decision.* Cambridge: Cambridge University Press, 2002.

―――, Armando Razo, and Noel Maurer. *The Politics of Property Rights: Political Instability, Credible Commitments, and Economic Growth in Mexico, 1876–1929.* Cambridge: Cambridge University Press, 2003.

Halperín, Isaac. *Manual de sociedades anónimas por Juez de la Cámara Nacional de Apelaciones en lo comercial.* Buenos Aires: Roque de Palma, 1961.

Hanley, Anne G. *Native Capital: Financial Institutions and Economic Development in São Paulo, Brazil, 1850–1920.* Palo Alto, Calif.: Stanford University Press, 2005.

Helguerra, Dimas. *La producción argentina en 1892, Descripción de la industria nacional—su desarrollo y progreso en toda la República.* Buenos Aires: Goyoaga y Cía., 1893.

Hirschman, Albert O. *The Strategy of Economic Development.* New Haven, Conn.: Yale University Press, 1958.

Hofman, André. *The Economic Development of Latin America in the Twentieth Century.* Northampton, Mass.: Edward Elgar Press, 2000,

Hora, Roy. "Terratenientes, empresarios industriales y crecimiento industrial en la Argentina: los estancieros y el debate sobre el proteccionismo (1890–1914)." *Desarrollo Económico,* Oct.–Dec. 2000, *40*(159), 465–491.

―――. *The Landowners of the Argentine Pampas: A Social and Political History, 1860–1945.* Oxford: Clarendon Press, 2001b.

―――. "Empresarios y política en la Argentina, 1880–1916." Unpublished work, presented at Internacional Economic History Association, Buenos Aires, July 2002.

―――. "Landowning Bourgeoisie or Business Bourgeoisie? On the Peculiarities of the Argentine Economic Elite, 1880–1945." *Journal of Latin American Studies,* 2001a, *34*(3), 587–623.

―――. "La política económica del proteccionismo en Argentina, 1870–1914." Paper presented at the XIV International Economic History Congress, Helsinki, Finland, Aug. 2006.

James, Dilmus. *Used Machinery and Economic Development.* East Lansing, MI: Michigan State University, 1974.

Jones, Charles. "The Transfer of Banking Techniques from Britain to Argentina, 1862–1914." *Revue Internationale d'histoire de la banque,* 1983, 252–264.

―――. "The State and Business Practice in Argentina, 1862–1914." In Christopher Abel and Colin M. Lewis (eds.), *Latin America, Economic Imperialism and the State: The Political Economy of the External Connection from Independence to the Present.* London: University of London, 1985, 184–197.

―――. "Institutional Forms of British Foreign Direct Investment in South America." *Business History,* 1997, *39*(2), 21–41.

Joslin, David. *A Century of Banking in Latin America to Commemorate the Centenary in 1962 of the Bank of London and South America, Limited.* London: Oxford University Press, 1963.

Katz, Jorge M. *Structural Reforms, Productivity and Technological Change in Latin America.* Santiago: UN Economic Commission for Latin America and the Caribbean, 2001.

———, and Bernardo Kosacoff. "Import-Substituting Industrialization in Argentina, 1940–1980: Its Achievements and Shortcomings." In Enrique Cárdenas, José Antonio Ocampo, and Rosemary Thorp (eds.), *An Economic History of Twentieth-Century Latin America. Vol. 3: Industrialization and the State in Latin America: The Postwar Years.* New York: Palgrave, 2000, 282–313.

Kim, Linsu. *Imitation to Innovation: The Dynamics of Korea's Technological Learning.* Boston: Harvard Business School Press, 1997.

———, and Richard R. Nelson (eds.). *Technology, Learning, and Innovation: Experiences of Newly Industrializing Economies.* Cambridge: Cambridge University Press, 2000.

Kirsch, Henry. *Industrial Development in a Traditional Society: The Conflict of Entrepreneurship and Modernization in Chile.* Gainesville: University Presses of Florida, 1977.

Kono, Clifford, Donald Palmer, Roger Friedland, and Matthew Zafonte. "Lost in Space: The Geography of Corporate Interlocking Directorates." *American Journal of Sociology,* Jan. 1998, *103*(4), 869–911.

Korol, Juan Carlos, and Hilda Sábato. "Incomplete Industrialization: An Argentine Obsession." *Latin American Research Review,* 1990, *25*(1), 7–30.

Lamoreaux, Naomi. "Banks, Kinship, and Economic Development: The New England Case." *Journal of Economic History,* Sept. 1986, *46*(3), 647–667.

Leff, Nathaniel H. *The Brazilian Capital Goods Industry, 1929–1964.* Cambridge, MA: Harvard University Press, 1968.

———. *Economic Policy-Making and Development in Brazil.* New York: Wiley, 1968.

———. "Industrial Organization and Entrepreneurship in the Developing Countries: The Economic Groups." *Economic Development and Cultural Change,* Jul. 1978, *26*(4), 661–675.

———. "'Monopoly Capitalism' and Public Policy in Developing Countries." Research Working Paper, Graduate School of Business, Columbia University, May 1979, 1–30.

Levenstein, Margaret. *Accounting for Growth: Information Systems and the Creation of the Large Corporation.* Palo Alto, Calif.: Stanford University Press, 1998.

Lewis, Colin M. "Immigrant Entrepreneurs, Manufacturing and Industrial Policy in the Argentine, 1922–28." *Journal of Imperial and Commonwealth History,* Oct. 1987, *16*(1), 77–108.

———. "Latin American Business History, 1870–1930: New Trends in Argentinian and Brazilian Literature." *América Latina en la historia económica: Boletín de Fuentes* July-Dec. 1995, 89–110.

Lewis, Paul H. *The Crisis of Argentine Capitalism*. Chapel Hill: University of North Carolina Press, 1990.

Lluch, Andrea. "La inversión extranjera directa norteamericana en Argentina (1900–1930)." Paper presented at the Fifth Colloquium on the History of the Firm, Universidad de San Andrés, Mar. 2007.

Maurer, Noel, and Tridib Sharma. "Enforcing Property Rights Through Reputation: Mexico's Early Industrialization, 1878–1913." *Journal of Economic History,* 2001, *61*(4), 950–973.

Miller, Rory. "Latin American Manufacturing and the First World War: An Explanatory Essay." *World Development,* 1981, *9*(8), 707–716.

Moya, José. *Cousins and Strangers: Spanish Immigrants in Buenos Aires, 1850–1930*. Berkeley: University of California Press, 1998.

Mueller, Gerhard G. *Accounting Practices in Argentina*. (International Business Series, Studies in Accounting.) Seattle: College of Business Administration, University of Washington, 1963.

Nakamura, Leonard I., and Carlos Zarazaga. "Economic Growth in Argentina in the Period 1900–1930: Some Evidence from Stock Returns." In John H. Coatsworth and Alan M. Taylor (eds.), *Latin America and the World Economy Since 1800*. Cambridge, Mass.: Harvard University Press, 1998.

Nari, Marcela. *Políticas de maternidad y maternalismo político, Buenos Aires, 1890–1940*. Buenos Aires: Editorial Biblos, 2004.

O'Connell, Arturo. "Argentina into the Depression: Problems of an Open Economy." In Rosemary Thorp (ed.), *An Economic History of Twentieth-Century Latin America, Vol. 2*. Oxford: Oxford University Press, 2000.

Ortíz, Ricardo. *Historia económica de la Argentina*. Buenos Aires: Ultra Plus, 1974.

Pavitt, Keith. "Technologies, Products, and Organisation in the Innovating Firms: What Adam Smith Tells Us and Joseph Schumpeter Doesn't." *Industrial and Corporate Change,* 1998, 7, 433–452.

Petrecolla, Alberto Oscar. "Prices, Import Substitution, and Investment in the Argentine Textile Industry (1920–1939)." Ph.D. dissertation, Columbia University, 1968.

Quiroz, Alfonso. "Financial Leadership and the Formation of Peruvian Elite Groups, 1884–1930." *Journal of Latin American Studies,* 1989, *20*, 49–81.

Rava, Americo E. "Historia y estado actual de la industria del papel en la Argentina." In Centro Argentino de Ingenieros (eds.). *Los ingenieros argentinos en la industria nacional*. Buenos Aires: El Centro, 1941, 123–138.

Regalsky, Andrés M. "La evolución de la banca privada nacional en Argentina (1880–1914): Una introducción a su estudio." In Pedro Tedde and Carlos Marichal (eds.), *La formación de los bancos centrales en España y América Latina. Vol. 2: Suramérica y el Caribe*. Madrid: Banco de España, 1994, 35–59.

———. "Banking, Trade, and the Rise of Capitalism in Argentina, 1850–1930." In Alice Teichova, Ginette Kurgan-van Hentenryk, and Dieter Ziegler (eds.), *Banking, Trade and Industry: Europe, America and Asia from the Thirteenth to the*

Twentieth Century. Cambridge: Cambridge University Press, 1997, 359–377.

————. "Financiamiento e inversión pública en la transición hacia el Estado empresario, Argentina 1900–1935." Paper presented at the XIV International Economic History Congress, Helsinki, Finland, Aug. 2006.

Rocchi, Fernando. *Chimneys in the Desert: Industrialization in Argentina During the Export Boom Years, 1870–1930.* Palo Alto, Calif.: Stanford University Press, 2006.

Rock, David. *Argentina 1516–1987: From Spanish Colonization to Alfonsín.* Berkeley: University of California Press, 1987.

Romero, Luis Alberto, and Hilda Sábato. "Between Rise and Fall: Self-Employed Workers in Buenos Aires, 1850–1880." In Jeremy Adelman (ed.), *Essays in Argentine Labour History, 1870–1930.* Oxford: St. Anthony's College, 1990, 52–72.

Sábato, Jorge. *La clase dominante en la Argentina moderna: Formación y características* (2nd ed.). Buenos Aires: Imago Mundi, 1991.

Sánchez-Alonso, Blanca. "Labor and Immigration." In Victor Bulmer-Thomas, John H. Coatsworth, and Roberto Cortés Conde (eds.), *The Cambridge Economic History of Latin America: The Long Twentieth Century.* Cambridge University Press, 2006, 377–426.

Sánchez Román, José Antonio. "Economic Elites, Regional Cleavages, and the Introduction of the Income Tax in Argentina," Paper presented at the XIV International Economic History Congress, Helsinki, Finland, Aug. 2006.

————. "Shaping Taxation: Economic Elites and Fiscal Decision-Making in Argentina, 1920–1945." *Journal of Latin American Studies*, Feb. 2008, *40*(1), 83–108.

Sanz-Villaroya, Isabel. "Economic Cycles in Argentina: 1875–1990." *Journal of Latin American Studies*, Aug. 2006, *38*(3), 549–570.

Sarlo, Beatriz. *La imaginación técnica: Sueños modernos de la cultura argentina.* Buenos Aires: Ediciones Nueva Visión, 1992.

Sawers, Larry. "Income Distribution and Environmental Degradation in the Argentine Interior." *Latin American Research Review*, Spring 2000, *35*(2).

Schumpeter, Joseph A. *The Theory of Economic Development.* New York: Oxford University Press, 1961.

Schvarzer, Jorge. *Empresarios del pasado: La Unión Industrial Argentina.* Buenos Aires: Imago Mundi, 1991.

————. *La industria que supimos conseguir: Una historia político-social de la industria argentina.* Buenos Aires: Grupo Planeta Editorial, 1996.

Scobie, James R. *Revolution on the Pampas: A Social History of Argentine Wheat, 1860–1910.* Austin: University of Texas Press, 1977.

Shapiro, Helen, and Lance Taylor. "The State and Industrial Strategy," *World Development*, 1990, *18*(6), 861–878.

Sharkey, Eugene. "Unión Industrial Argentina, 1887–1920: Problems of Industrial Development." Ph.D. dissertation, Rutgers University, 1977.

Smith, Peter H. *Argentina and the Failure of Democracy: Conflict Among Political Elites, 1904–1955.* Madison: University of Wisconsin Press, 1971.

———."Argentine Chamber of Deputies Roll Calls, Sessions 1904–1955." Deposited at Data and Program Library Service, University of Wisconsin-Madison, Apr. 1974.

Sokoloff, Kenneth L. "Productivity Growth in Manufacturing in Early Industrialization: Evidence from the American Northeast, 1820–1860." In Stanley L. Engerman and Robert E. Gallman (eds.), *Long-term Factors in American Economic Growth.* Chicago: University of Chicago Press, 1986, 679–736.

Solberg, Carl. "Tariffs and Politics in Argentina, 1916–30." *Hispanic American Historical Review,* May 1973, *53*(2), 260–284.

———. *Oil and Nationalism: A History.* Palo Alto, Calif.: Stanford University Press, 1979.

———. *The Prairies and the Pampas: Agrarian Policy in Canada and Argentina, 1880–1930.* Palo Alto, Calif.: Stanford University Press, 1987.

Sturzenegger, Adolfo, and Ramiro Moya. "Economic Cycles." In Gerardo Della Paolera and Alan M. Taylor (eds.), *A New Economic History of Argentina.* Cambridge: Cambridge University Press, 2003.

Suzigan, Wilson. *Indústria brasileira: Origem e desenvolvimento.* São Paulo: Brasiliense, 1986.

Taylor, Alan M. "External Dependence, Demographic Burdens, and Argentine Economic Decline After the Belle Epoque." *Journal of Economic History,* Dec. 1992, *52*(4), 907–936.

———. "Peopling the Pampa: On the Impact of Mass Migration to the River Plate, 1870–1914." *Explorations in Economic History,* Jan. 1997, *34*(1), 100–132.

———. "On the Costs of Inward-Looking Development: Price Distortions, Growth and Divergence in Latin America." *Journal of Economic History,* Mar. 1998, *58*(1), 1–28.

———. "Capital Accumulation." In Gerardo Della Paolera and Alan M. Taylor (eds.), *A New Economic History of Argentina.* Cambridge: Cambridge University Press, 2003.

Tedde, Pedro, and Carlos Marichal. *La formación de los bancos centrales en España y América Latina: Suramérica y el Caribe, Vol. 2.* Madrid: Banco de España, 1994.

Tirole, Jean. "A Theory of Collective Reputations." *Review of Economic Studies,* 1996, *63,* 1–22.

Wils, Frits. *Industrialization, Industrialists, and the Nation-State in Peru: A Comparative Sociological Analysis.* Berkeley, Calif.: Institute of International Studies, 1979.

Index